THREE PLAYS

IVAN TURGENEV
THREE PLAYS

A Month in the Country
A Provincial Lady
A Poor Gentleman

*Translated from the Russian
by* CONSTANCE GARNETT

faber and faber

This edition first published in 2008
by Faber and Faber Ltd
3 Queen Square, London WC1N 3AU

Printed by Books on Demand GmbH, Norderstedt

All rights reserved
Translation © Constance Garnett, 1934

The right of Constance Garnett to be identified as translator of this work
has been asserted in accordance with Section 77 of the
Copyright, Designs and Patents Act 1988

This book is sold subject to the condition that it shall not, by way of
trade or otherwise, be lent, resold, hired out or otherwise circulated
without the publisher's prior consent in any form of binding or cover other than
that in which it is published and without a similar condition including this
condition being imposed on the subsequent purchaser

A CIP record for this book is available from the British Library

ISBN 978–0–571–24554–3

A MONTH IN THE COUNTRY
(*A Comedy in Five Acts*)

Characters in the Play

ARKADY SERGEYITCH ISLAYEV, a wealthy landowner, aged 36.
NATALYA PETROVNA, his wife, aged 29.
KOLYA, their son, aged 10.
VERA, their ward, aged 17.
ANNA SEMYONOVNA ISLAYEV, mother of Islayev, aged 58.
LIZAVETA BOGDANOVNA, a companion, aged 37.
SCHAAF, a German tutor, aged 45.
MIHAIL ALEXANDROVITCH RAKITIN, a friend of the family, aged 30.
ALEXEY NIKOLAYEVITCH BELIAYEV, a student, Kolya's tutor, aged 21.
AFANASY IVANOVITCH BOLSHINTSOV, a neighbour, aged 48.
IGNATY ILYITCH SHPIGELSKY, a doctor, aged 40.
MATVEY, a manservant, aged 40.
KATYA, a maidservant, aged 20.

The action takes place on Islayev's estate.
There is an interval of one day between ACTS I and II, ACTS II and III, and ACTS IV and V.

A MONTH IN THE COUNTRY
(*A Comedy in Five Acts*)

ACT I

[*A drawing-room. On Right a card-table and a door into the study; in Centre a door into an outer room; on Left two windows and a round table. Sofas in the corners. At the card-table* ANNA SEMYONOVNA, LIZAVETA BOGDANOVNA *and* SCHAAF *are playing preference*; NATALYA PETROVNA *and* RAKITIN *are sitting at the round table; she is embroidering on canvas; he has a book in his hand. A clock on the wall points to three o'clock.*]

SCHAAF: Hearts.

ANNA SEMYONOVNA: Again? Why, if you go on like that, my good man, you will beat us every time.

SCHAAF (*Phlegmatically*): Eight hearts.

ANNA SEMYONOVNA (*To* LIZAVETA BOGDANOVNA): What a man! There's no playing with him. (LIZAVETA BOGDANOVNA *smiles*.)

NATALYA PETROVNA (*To* RAKITIN): Why have you left off? Go on.

RAKITIN (*Raising his head slowly*): 'Monte

Cristo se redressa haletant. . . .' Does it interest you Natalya Petrovna?

NATALYA PETROVNA: Not at all.

RAKITIN: Why are we reading it then?

NATALYA PETROVNA: Well, it's like this. The other day a woman said to me: 'You haven't read Monte Cristo? Oh, you must read it—it's charming.' I made her no answer at the time, but now I can say that I've been reading it and found nothing at all charming in it.

RAKITIN: Oh, well, since you have already made up your mind about it. . . .

NATALYA PETROVNA: You lazy creature!

RAKITIN: Oh, I don't mind. . . . (*Looking for the place at which he stopped.*) 'Se redressa haletant et. . . .'

NATALYA PETROVNA (*Interrupting him*): Have you seen Arkady to-day?

RAKITIN: I met him on the dam. . . . It is being repaired. He was explaining something to the workmen and to make things clearer waded up to his knees in the sand.

NATALYA PETROVNA: He gets too hot over things, he tries to do too much. It's a failing. Don't you think so?

RAKITIN: Yes, agree with you.

NATALYA PETROVNA: How dull that is! . . . You always agree with me. Go on reading.

RAKITIN: Oh, so you want me to quarrel with you. . . . By all means.

NATALYA PETROVNA: I want . . . I want . . . I want *you* to want. . . . Go on reading, I tell you.

RAKITIN: I obey, madam. (*Takes up the book again*.)

SCHAAF: Hearts.

ANNA SEMYONOVNA: What? Again? It's insufferable! (*To* NATALYA PETROVNA.) Natasha . . . Natasha! . . .

NATALYA PETROVNA: What is it?

ANNA SEMYONOVNA: Only fancy! Schaaf wins every point. He keeps on—if it's not seven, it's eight.

SCHAAF: And now it's seven.

ANNA SEMYONOVNA: Do you hear? It's awful.

NATALYA PETROVNA: Yes . . . it is.

ANNA SEMYONOVNA: Back me up then! (*To* NATALYA PETROVNA.) Where's Kolya?

NATALYA PETROVNA: He's gone out for a walk with the new tutor.

ANNA SEMYONOVNA: Oh! Lizaveta Bogdanovna, I call on you.

RAKITIN (*To* NATALYA PETROVNA): What tutor?

NATALYA PETROVNA: Ah! I forgot to tell you, while you've been away, we've engaged a new teacher.

RAKITIN: Instead of Dufour?

NATALYA PETROVNA: No . . . a Russian teacher. The princess is going to send us a Frenchman from Moscow.

Rakitin: What sort of man is he, the Russian? An old man?

Natalya Petrovna: No, he's young. . . . But we only have him for the summer.

Rakitin: Oh, a holiday engagement.

Natalya Petrovna: Yes, that's what they call it, I believe. And I tell you what, Rakitin, you're fond of studying people, analysing them, burrowing into them. . . .

Rakitin: Oh, come, what makes you . . .

Natalya Petrovna: Yes, yes. . . . You study him. I like him. Thin, well made, merry eyes, something spirited in his face. . . . You'll see. It's true he is rather awkward . . . and you think that dreadful.

Rakitin: You are terribly hard on me to-day, Natalya Petrovna.

Natalya Petrovna: Joking apart, do study him. I fancy he may make a very fine man. But there, you never can tell!

Rakitin: That sounds interesting.

Natalya Petrovna: Really? (*Dreamily.*) Go on reading.

Rakitin: 'Se redressa haletant et . . .'

Natalya Petrovna (*Suddenly looking round*): Where's Vera? I haven't seen her all day. (*With a smile, to* Rakitin.) Put away that book. . . . I see we shan't get any reading done to-day. . . . Better tell me something.

Rakitin: By all means. . . . What am I to tell you? . . . You know I stayed a few days at the Krinitsyns'. . . . Imagine, the happy pair are bored already.

NATALYA PETROVNA: How could you tell?

RAKITIN: Well, boredom can't be concealed. . . . Anything else may be, but not boredom. . . .

NATALYA PETROVNA (*Looking at him*): Anything else can then?

RAKITIN (*After a brief pause*): I think so.

NATALYA PETROVNA (*Dropping her eyes*): Well, what did you do at the Knnitsyns'?

RAKITIN: Nothing. Being bored with friends is an awful thing; you are at ease, you are not constrained, you like them, there's nothing to irritate you, and yet you are bored, and there's a silly ache, like hunger, in your heart.

NATALYA PETROVNA: You must often have been bored with friends.

RAKITIN: As though you don't know what it is to be with a person whom one loves and who bores one!

NATALYA PETROVNA (*Slowly*): Whom one loves, that's saying a great deal. . . . You are too subtle to-day. . . .

RAKITIN: Subtle. . . . Why subtle?

NATALYA PETROVNA: Yes, that's a weakness of yours. Do you know, Rakitin, you are very clever, of course, but . . . (*Pausing*) sometimes we talk as though we were making lace. . . . Have you seen people making lace? In stuffy rooms, never moving from their seats. . . . Lace is a fine thing, but a drink of fresh water on a hot day is much better.

RAKITIN: NATALYA Petrovna, you are . . .

NATALYA PETROVNA: What?

RAKITIN: You are cross with me about something.

NATALYA PETROVNA: Oh, you clever people, how blind you are, though you are so subtle! No, I'm not cross with you.

ANNA SEMYONOVNA: Ah! at last, he has lost the trick! (*To* NATALYA PETROVNA.) Natasha, our enemy has lost the trick!

SCHAAF (*Sourly*): It's Lizaveta Bogdanovna's fault.

Lizaveta Bogdanovna (*Angrily*): I beg your pardon—how could I tell Anna Semyonovna had no hearts?

Schaaf: In future I call not on Lizaveta Bogdanovna.

ANNA SEMYONOVNA (*To* SCHAAF): Why, how is she, Lizaveta Bogdanovna, to blame?

SCHAAF (*Repeats in exactly the same tone of voice*): In future I call not on Lizaveta Bogdanovna.

LIZAVETA BOGDANOVNA: As though I care! What next! . . .

RAKITIN: You look somehow different, I see that more and more.

NATALYA PETROVNA (*With a shade of curiosity*): Do you mean it?

RAKITIN; Yes, really. I find a change in you,

NATALYA PETROVNA: Yes? . . . If that's so, please. . . . You know me so well—guess what the change is, what has happened to me . . . will you?

RAKITIN: Well. . . . Give me time. . . .
> [*Suddenly* KOLYA *runs in noisily from the outer room and straight up to* ANNA SEMYONOVNA.]

KOLYA: Granny, Granny! Do look what I've got! (*Shows her a bow and arrows.*) Look!

ANNA SEMYONOVNA: Show me, darling. . . . Oh what a splendid bow! Who made it for you?

KOLYA: He did . . . he. . . . (*Points to* Beliayev, *who has remained at the door.*)

ANNA SEMYONOVNA: Oh! but how well it's made. . . .

KOLYA: I shot at a tree with it, Granny, and hit it twice. . . . (*Skips about.*)

NATALYA PETROVNA: Show me, Kolya.

KOLYA (*Runs to her and while* NATALYA PETROVNA *is examining the bow*): Oh, maman, you should see how Alexey Nikolaitch climbs trees! He wants to teach me and he's going to teach me to swim too. He's going to teach me all sorts of things. (*Skips about.*)

NATALYA PETROVNA: It is very good of you to do so much for Kolya.

KOLYA (*Interrupting her, warmly*): I do like him, maman, I love him.

NATALYA PETROVNA (*Stroking* KOLYA'S

head): He has been too softly brought up. . . . Make him a sturdy, active boy.

[BELIAYEV *bows*.]

KOLYA: Alexey Nikolaitch, let's go to the stable and take Favourite some bread.

BELIAYEV: Very well.

ANNA SEMYONOVNA (*To* KOLYA): Come here and give me a kiss first. . . .

KOLYA (*Running off*): Afterwards, Granny, afterwards! (*Runs into the outer room;* BELIAYEV *goes out after him*.)

ANNA SEMYONOVNA (*Looking after* KOLYA): What a darling boy! (*To* SCHAAF *and* LIZAVETA BOGDANOVNA.) Isn't he?

LIZAVETA BOGDANOVNA: To be sure he is.

SCHAAF (*After a brief pause*): Pass.

NATALYA PETROVNA (*With some eagerness to* RAKITIN): Well, how does he strike you?

RAKITIN: Who?

NATALYA PETROVNA (*Pausing*): That . . . Russian tutor.

RAKITIN: Oh, I beg your pardon—I'd forgotten him. . . . I was so absorbed by the question you asked me. . . .

[NATALYA PETROVNA *looks at him with a faintly perceptible smile of irony.*]

But his face . . . certainly. . . . Yes, he has a good face. I like him. Only he seems very shy.

NATALYA PETROVNA: Yes.

RAKITIN (*Looking at her*): But anyway I can't quite make out . . .

Natalya Petrovna: How if we were to look after him a bit, Rakitin? Will you? Let us finish his education. Here is a splendid opportunity for discreet sensible people like you and me! We are very sensible, aren't we?

Rakitin: This young man interests you. If he knew it . . . he'd be flattered.

Natalya Petrovna: Oh, not a bit, believe me! You can't judge him by what . . . anyone like us would feel in his place. You see he's not at all like us, Rakitin. That's where we go wrong, my dear, we study ourselves very carefully and then imagine we understand human nature.

Rakitin: The heart of another is a dark forest. But what are you hinting at? . . . Why do you keep on sticking pins into me?

Natalya Petrovna: Whom is one to stick pins into if not one's friends? . . . And you are my friend. . . . You know that. (*Presses his hand.* Rakitin *smiles and beams.*) You are my old friend.

Rakitin: I'm only afraid. . . you may get sick of the old friend.

Natalya Petrovna (*Laughing*): It's only very nice things one takes enough of for that.

Rakitin: Perhaps. But that doesn't make it any better for them.

Natalya Petrovna: Nonsense. . . . (*Dropping her voice.*) As though you don't know ce que vous êtes pour moi.

Rakitin: Natalya Petrovna, you play with me like a cat with a mouse. . . . But the mouse does not complain.

Natalya Petrovna: Oh! poor little mouse!

Anna Semyonovna: That's twenty from you, Adam Ivanitch. . . . Aha!

Schaaf: In future I call not on Lizaveta Bogdanovna.

Matvey (*Enters and announces*): Ignaty Ilyitch.

Shpigelsky (*Following him in*): Doctors don't need showing in. (*Exit* Matvey.) My humblest respects to all the family. (*Kisses* Anna Semyonovna's *hand*.) How do you do, gracious lady. Winning, I expect?

Anna Semyonovna: Winning indeed! I've hardly got my own back and I'm thankful for that. It's all this villain. (*Indicates* Schaaf.)

Shpigelsky (*To* Schaaf): Adam Ivanitch, when you're playing with ladies, it's too bad. . . . I should never have thought it of you.

Schaaf (*Muttering through his teeth*): Blaying wif ladies. . . .

Shpigelsky (*Going up to the round table on the left*): Good afternoon, Natalya Petrovna! Good afternoon, Mihail Alexandritch!

Natalya Petrovna: Good afternoon, Doctor. How are you?

Shpigelsky: I like that inquiry. . . . It shows that you are quite well. What can ail me? A respectable doctor is never ill; at the most he just goes and dies. . . . Ha! ha!

Natalya Petrovna: Sit down. I'm quite well, certainly. . . . But I'm in a bad humour . . . and that's a sort of illness too, you know.

Shpigelsky (*Sitting down beside* Natalya Petrovna): Let me feel your pulse. (*Feels her pulse.*) Oh, nerves, nerves. . . . You don't walk enough, Natalya Petrovna, you don't laugh enough . . . that's what it is. . . . Why don't you see to it, Mihail Alexandritch? But of course I can prescribe some drops.

Natalya Petrovna: I'm ready enough to laugh. . . . (*Eagerly.*) Now, Doctor, . . . you have a spiteful tongue, I like it so much in you, I respect you for it, really . . . do tell me something amusing. Mihail Alexandritch is so solemn to-day.

Shpigelsky (*With a sly glance at* Rakitin): Ah, it seems, it's not only the nerves that are upset, there's just a touch of spleen too. . . .

Natalya Petrovna: There you are, at it, too! Be as critical as you like, Doctor, but not aloud. We all know how sharp-sighted you are. You are both so sharp-sighted.

Shpigelsky: I obey, madam.

Natalya Petrovna: Tell us something funny.

Shpigelsky: I obey, madam. Tell us a story straight away, it's a bit sudden. . . . Allow me a pinch of snuff. (*Takes snuff.*)

Natalya Petrovna: What preparations!

Shpigelsky: Well, you see, my dear lady, you must graciously consider there are all sorts of funny stories. One for one person, and one for another. . . . Your neighbour, Mr. Hlopushkin, for instance, roars and laughs till he cries, if I simply hold up my finger . . . while you. . . . But, there, here goes, you know Verenitsyn?

Natalya Petrovna: I fancy I've met him. I've heard of him anyway.

Shpigelsky: He has a sister who's mad. To my thinking, they are either both mad, or both sane; for really there's nothing to choose between them, but that's neither here nor there. It's the finger of destiny, dear lady, everywhere, and in everything. Verenitsyn has a daughter, a greenish little thing, you know, with little pale eyes, and a little red nose, and little yellow teeth, a charming girl in fact; plays the piano, and talks with a lisp, so everything's as it should be. She has two hundred serfs of her own besides her aunt's hundred and fifty. The aunt's still alive to be sure, and will go on living for years; mad people always live to be old, but one need never despair. She has made a will in her niece's favour anyway, and, the day before she did it, with my own hand I poured cold water on her head—it was a complete waste of time for there's no chance of curing her. Well, so Verenitsyn's daughter is a bit of a catch, you see. He has begun bringing her out, suitors are turning up, and among others Perekuzov, an anæmic young man, timid but of excellent principles. Well, the father liked our Perekuzov; and the daughter liked him, too. . . . There seemed to be no hitch, simply bless them and haste to the wedding! And, as a matter of fact, all was going swimmingly; Mr. Verenitsyn was already beginning to poke the young man in the ribs and slap him on the back, when all of a sudden, a bolt from the blue, an officer, Ardalion Protobekasov! He saw Verenitsyn's daughter at the Marshal's ball, danced three polkas with her, said to her, I suppose, rolling his eyes like this, 'Oh, how unhappy I am!' and our young lady was bowled over at once. Tears, sighs, moans. . . . Not a look, not a word for Perekuzov, hysterics at the mere mention of the wedding. . . . Oh, Lord, there was the deuce of a fuss. Oh well, thinks Verenitsyn, if Protobekasov it is to be, Protobekasov let it be! Luckily he was a man of property too. Protobekasov is invited to give them the honour of his company. He does them the honour, arrives, flirts, falls in love, and finally offers his hand and heart. Verenitsyn's daughter accepts him joyfully on the spot, you'd suppose. Not a bit of it! Mercy on us, no! Tears again, sighs, hysterics! Her father is at his wits' end. What's the meaning of it? What does she want? And what do you suppose she answers? 'I don't know,' she says, 'which of them I love.' 'What!?' 'I really don't know which I love, and so I'd better not marry either, but I am in love!' Verenitsyn, of course, had an attack of cholera at once;

the suitors can't make head or tail of it either. But she sticks to it. So you see what queer things happen in these parts.

NATALYA PETROVNA: I don't see anything wonderful in that. . . . Surely it's possible to love two people at once?

RAKITIN: Ah! you think so. . . .

NATALYA PETROVNA (*Slowly*): I think so. . . . I don't know, though . . . perhaps it only shows one doesn't love either.

SHPIGELSKY (*Taking snuff and looking now at* NATALYA PETROVNA, *now at* RAKITIN): So that's how it is.

NATALYA PETROVNA (*Eagerly to* SHPIGELSKY): Your story is very good, but you haven't made me laugh.

SHPIGELSKY: Oh, my dear lady, who'll make you laugh just now? That's not what you want at the moment.

NATALYA PETROVNA: What is it I want then?

SHPIGELSKY (*With an affectedly meek air*): The Lord only knows!

NATALYA PETROVNA: Oh, how tiresome you are, as bad as Rakitin.

SHPIGELSKY: You do me too much honour upon my word. . . .

[NATALYA PETROVNA *makes an impatient gesture.*]

ANNA SEMYONOVNA (*Getting up*): Well, well, at last. . . . (*Sighs.*) My legs are quite stiff from sitting so long. (LIZAVETA BOGDANOVNA *and* SCHAAF *stand up also.*) O-ooh!

Natalya Petrovna (*Stands up and goes to them*): Why do you sit still so long? (Rakitin *and* Shpigelsky *stand up*.)

Anna Semyonovna: You owe me seventy kopecks, my good sir. (Schaaf *bows frigidly*.) You can't punish us all the time. (*To* Natalya Petrovna.) You look pale, Natasha? Are you quite well? Shpigelsky, is she quite well?

Shpigelsky (*Who has been whispering something to* Rakitin): Oh, perfectly!

Anna Semyonovna: That's right. . . . I'll go and have a little rest before dinner. . . . I'm dreadfully tired! Liza, come along. . . . Oh, my legs, my legs. . . .

> [*Goes into the outer room with* Lizaveta Bogdanovna. Natalya Petrovna *walks with her to the door.* Shpigelsky, Rakitin *and* Schaaf *are left in the front of the stage.*]

Shpigelsky (*Offering* Schaaf *his snuff-box*): Well, Adam Ivanitch, wie befinden sie sich?

Schaaf (*Taking a pinch with dignity*): Quite vell. And you?

Shpigelsky: Thank you kindly, pretty middling. (*Aside to* Rakitin.) So you don't know what's the matter with Natalya Petrovna to-day?

Rakitin: I don't, really.

Shpigelsky: Well, if *you* don't. . . . (*Turns round and goes to meet* Natalya Petrovna *who is coming back from the door*.) I have a little matter to talk to you about, Natalya Petrovna.

NATALYA PETROVNA (*Going to the window*): Really! What is it?

SHPIGELSKY: I must speak to you alone. . . .

NATALYA PETROVNA: Oh dear! . . . You alarm me. . . .

> [RAKITIN *meanwhile has taken* SCHAAF'S *arm and walks to and fro with him, murmuring something to him in German.* SCHAAF *laughs and says in an undertone*, 'Ja, ja, ja! ja wohl, ja wohl, sehr gut!']

SHPIGELSKY (*Dropping his voice*): This business, strictly speaking, does not concern you only. . . .

NATALYA PETROVNA (*Looking out into the garden*): What do you mean?

SHPIGELSKY: Well, it's like this. A good friend of mine has asked me to find out . . . that is . . . your intentions in regard to your ward . . . Vera Alexandrovna.

NATALYA PETROVNA: My intentions?

SHPIGELSKY: That is . . . to speak plainly . . . my friend. . . .

NATALYA PETROVNA: You don't mean to say he wants to marry her?

SHPIGELSKY: Just so.

NATALYA PETROVNA: Are you joking?

SHPIGELSKY: Certainly not.

NATALYA PETROVNA (*Laughing*): Good gracious! She's a child; what a strange commission!

SHPIGELSKY: Strange, Natalya Petrovna? How so? My friend . . .

NATALYA PETROVNA: You're a great schemer, Shpigelsky. And who is your friend?

SHPIGELSKY (*Smiling*): One minute. You haven't said anything definite yet in reply. . . .

NATALYA PETROVNA: Nonsense, Doctor. Vera is a child. You know that yourself, Monsieur le diplomate. (*Turning round*). Why, here she is. (VERA *and* KOLYA *run in from the outer room.*)

KOLYA (*Runs up to* RAKITIN): Rakitin, some glue, tell them to give us some glue. . . .

NATALYA PETROVNA (*To* VERA): Where have you been? (*Strokes her cheek.*) How flushed you are!

VERA: In the garden. . . . (SHPIGELSKY *bows to her.*) Good afternoon, Ignaty Ilyitch.

RAKITIN (To KOLYA): What do you want with glue?

KOLYA: We must have it. . . . Alexey Nikolaitch is making us a kite. . . . Ask for it. . . .

RAKITIN (*Is about to ring*): Very well. In a minute.

SCHAAF: Erlauben Sie. . . . Master Kolya has not learned his lesson to-day. . . . (*Takes* KOLYA'*s hand.*) Kommen Sie.

KOLYA (*Gloomily*): Morgen, Herr Schaaf, morgen. . . .

SCHAAF (*Sharply*): Morgen, morgen, nur nicht heute, sagen alle faule leute. . . . Kommen Sie. (KOLYA *resists.*)

Natalya Petrovna (*To* Vera): Whom have you been out with all this time? I've seen nothing of you all day.

Vera: With Alexey Nikolaitch . . . with Kolya. . . .

Natalya Petrovna: Ah! (Turning round.) Kolya, what's the meaning of this?

Kolya (*Dropping his voice*): Mr. Schaaf. . . . Maman. . . .

Rakitin (*To* Natalya Petrovna): They are making a kite, and you see, it's time for a lesson.

Schaaf (*With a sense of dignity*): Gnädige Frau. . . .

Natalya Petrovna (*Severely, to* Kolya): You have been playing about enough to-day, do you hear. Go along with Mr. Schaaf.

Schaaf (*Leading* Kolya *towards the outer room*): Es ist unerhört!

Kolya (To Rakitin *in a whisper as he goes out*): Ask for the glue, all the same. . . . (Rakitin *nods*.)

Schaaf (*Pulling* Kolya): Kommen sie, mein Herr. . . . (*Goes out with him.* Rakitin *follows them out.*)

Natalya Petrovna (*To* Vera): Sit down . . . you must be tired. . . . (*Sits down herself*)

Vera (*Sitting down*): Not at all, Natalya Petrovna.

Natalya Petrovna (To Shpigelsky, *with a smile*): Shpigelsky, look at her, she is tired, isn't she?

SHPIGELSKY: But that's good for Vera Alexandrovna, you know.

NATALYA PETROVNA: I don't say it's not. . . . (*To* VERA.) Well, what have you been doing in the garden?

VERA: Playing, running about. First we looked at the men digging the dam, then Alexey Nikolaitch climbed up a tree after a squirrel, ever so high, and began shaking the tree-top. . . . It really frightened us. . . . The squirrel dropped at last, and Trésor nearly caught it. . . . But it got away.

NATALYA PETROVNA (*glancing with a smile at* SHPIGELSKY): And then?

VERA: Then Alexey Nikolaitch made Kolya a bow . . . and so quickly . . . and then he stole up to our cow in the meadow and all at once leapt on her back . . . and the cow was scared and set off running and kicking . . . and he laughed (*Laughs herself*) and then Alexey Nikolaitch wanted to make us a kite and so we came in.

NATALYA PETROVNA (*Pats her cheek*): Child, child, you are a perfect child. . . . What do you think, Shpigelsky?

SHPIGELSKY (*Slowly, looking at* NATALYA PETROVNA): I agree with you.

NATALYA PETROVNA: I should think so.

SHPIGELSKY: But that's no hindrance. . . . On the contrary . . .

NATALYA PETROVNA: You think so? (*To* VERA.) And you've been enjoying yourself?

VERA: Yes. . . . Alexey Nikolaitch is so amusing.

Natalya Petrovna: Oh, he is, is he? (*After a brief pause.*) And, Vera, how old are you? (Vera *looks at her with some surprise.*) You're a child . . . a child.

[Rakitin *comes in from the outer room.*]

Shpigelsky (*Fussily*): Ah, I was forgetting . . . your coachman is ill . . . and I haven't had a look at him yet. . . .

Natalya Petrovna: What's the matter with him?

Shpigelsky: He's feverish, but it's nothing serious.

Natalya Petrovna (*Calling after him*): You are dining with us, Doctor?

Shpigelsky: With your kind permission. (*Goes out by centre door.*)

Natalya Petrovna: Mon enfant, vous feriez bien de mettre une autre robe pour le diner. . . . (Vera *gets up.*) Come to me. . . . (*Kisses her on the forehead.*) Child. . . . Child. (Vera *kisses her hand and goes towards door on right.*)

Rakitin (*Aside to* Vera *with a wink*): I've sent Alexey Nikolaitch all you need.

Vera (*Aside*): Thank you, Mihail Alexandritch. (*Goes out.*)

Rakitin (*Goes up to* Natalya Petrovna, *she holds out her hand to him. He at once presses it*): At last, we are alone. Natalya Petrovna, tell me, what's the matter?

Natalya Petrovna: Nothing, Michel, nothing. And if there were, it's all over now.

Sit down. (RAKITIN *sits down beside her.*) That happens to everybody. Clouds pass over the sky. Why do you look at me like that?

RAKITIN: I'm looking at you. . . . I am happy.

NATALYA PETROVNA (*Smiles in answer to him*): Open the window, Michel. How lovely it is in the garden! (RAKITIN *gets up and opens the window.*) How I welcome the wind! (*Laughs.*) It seems to have been waiting for a chance to burst in. . . . (*Looks round.*) How completely it's taken possession of the room. . . . There's no turning it out now. . . .

RAKITIN: You are as soft and sweet yourself now as an evening after a storm.

NATALYA PETROVNA (*Dreamily repeating the last words*): After a storm? . . . But has there been a storm?

RAKITIN (*Shaking his head*): It was gathering.

NATALYA PETROVNA: Really? (*Gazing at him, after a short silence.*) Do you know, Michel, I can't imagine a kinder man than you? (RAKITIN *tries to stop her.*) No, don't prevent my speaking out. You are sympathetic, affectionate, constant. You never change. I owe you so much.

RAKITIN: Natalya Petrovna, why are you telling me this just now?

NATALYA PETROVNA: I don't know; I feel light-hearted, I'm at rest; don't stop me from chattering. . . .

RAKITIN (*Pressing her hand*): You are kind as an angel, . . .

Natalya Petrovna (*Laughing*): You wouldn't have said so this morning. But listen, Michel, you know me, you must make allowances for me. Our relations are so pure, so genuine, . . . and at the same time, not quite natural. . . . You and I have the right to look everybody in the face, not only Arkady. . . . Yes, but . . . (*Sinking into thought.*) That's what makes me sometimes depressed and ill at ease. I feel spiteful like a child, I'm ready to vent my spite on others, especially on you. . . . You don't resent that privilege?

Rakitin (*Earnestly*): Quite the contrary.

Natalya Petrovna: Yes, at times it gives one pleasure to torture the man whom one loves . . . whom one loves. . . . Like Tatyana, I too can say, why not be frank?

Rakitin: Natalya Petrovna, you . . .

Natalya Petrovna (*Interrupting him*): Yes, I love you; but do you know, Rakitin? Do you know what sometimes seems strange to me? I love you . . . and the feeling is so clear, so peaceful. . . . It does not agitate me. . . . I am warmed by it. . . . (*Earnestly.*) You have never made me cry . . . and it seems as though I ought to have. . . . (*Breaking off.*) What does that show?

Rakitin (*Rather mournfully*): That's a question that needs no answer.

Natalya Petrovna (*Dreamily*): And we have known each other a long while.

Rakitin: Four years. Yes, we are old friends.

NATALYA PETROVNA: Friends. . . . No, you are more to me than a friend.

RAKITIN: Natalya Petrovna, don't touch on that. . . . I'm afraid for my happiness, I'm afraid it may vanish at your touch.

NATALYA PETROVNA: No . . . no . . . no. The whole point is that you are too good. . . . You give way to me too much. . . . You have spoilt me. . . . You are too good, do you hear?

RAKITIN (*With a smile*): I hear, madam.

NATALYA PETROVNA (*Looking at him*): I don't know what you feel but I desire no other happiness. Many women might envy me. (*Holds out both hands to him.*) Mightn't they?

RAKITIN: I'm in your hands. . . . Do with me what you will. . . . (*The voice of* ISLAYEV *from the outer room*: 'So you've sent for him, have you?')

NATALYA PETROVNA (*Getting up quickly*): Arkady! I can't see him just now. . . . Good-bye! (*Goes out by door on Right.*)

RAKITIN (*Looking after her*): What does it mean? The beginning of the end, or the end? (*A brief pause.*) Or the beginning?

[*Enter* ISLAYEV *looking worried.*]

ISLAYEV (*Taking off his hat*): Good afternoon, Michel.

RAKITIN: We've seen each other already to-day.

ISLAYEV: Oh! I beg your pardon. . . . I've had so much to see to. . . . (*Walks up and down the room.*) It's a queer thing! The Russian peasant is very intelligent, very quick of understanding, I've a respect for the Russian peasant . . . and yet sometimes, you may talk to him, and explain away. . . . It's clear enough you'd think, but it's all no use at all. The Russian peasant hasn't that . . . that . . .

RAKITIN: You're still busy with the dam, are you?

ISLAYEV: That . . . so to speak . . . love for work . . . that's just it, he has no love for it. He won't let you tell him what you think properly. 'Yes, Sir. ' . .. Yes, indeed, when he hasn't taken in a word. Look at a German now, it's quite a different thing! The Russian has no patience. For all that, I have a respect for him. . . . Where's Natasha? Do you know?

RAKITIN: She was here just now.

ISLAYEV: What time is it? Surely, dinner-time. I've been on my feet all day—such a lot to do. . . . And I haven't been to the building yet. . . . The time goes so fast. It's dreadful! One's simply behindhand with everything—— (RAKITIN *smiles*.) You're laughing at me, I see. . . . But I can't help it, old man. People are different. I'm a practical man, born to look after my land—and nothing else. There was a time when I dreamed of other things; but I burnt my fingers—I can tell you—came to grief, you know. Why isn't Beliayev here?

RAKITIN: Who's Beliayev?

ISLAYEV: Our new teacher. He's a shy bird, but he'll get used to us. He has a head on his shoulders. I asked him to see how the building was going on to-day. . . . (*Enter* BELIAYEV.) Oh, here he is! Well, How are they getting one Doing nothing, I expect?

BELIAYEV: No, Sir, they are working.

ISLAYEV: Have they finished the framing of the second barn?

BELIAYEV: They have begun the third.

ISLAYEV: And did you speak to them about the beams?

BELIAYEV: Yes.

ISLAYEV: Well, what did they say?

BELIAYEV: They say that's how they always do it.

ISLAYEV: Hm. . . . Is Yermil the carpenter there?

BELIAYEV: Yes.

ISLAYEV: Ah! well, thanks! (*Enter* NATALYA.) Ah! Natasha! Good afternoon.

RAKITIN: Why twenty greetings to each of us to-day?

ISLAYEV: I tell you, I'm tired out with all I've had to see to. Oh! by the way. I haven't shown you my new winnowing machine, have I? Do come along, it's worth seeing. It's marvellous, a whirlwind, a regular whirlwind. We've time before dinner. . . . What do you say?

RAKITIN: Oh, by all means·

ISLAYEV: Won't you come with us, Natasha?

NATALYA PETROVNA: As though I know anything about your machines! You go by yourselves—and mind you're not late.

ISLAYEV (*Going out with* RAKITIN): We'll be back immediately.

[BELIAYEV *is about to follow them.*]

NATALYA PETROVNA (*To* BELIAYEV): Where are you going, Alexey Nikolaitch?

BELIAYEV: I . . . I. . . .

NATALYA PETROVNA: Of course go, if you want a walk. . . .

BELIAYEV: Why no, I've been out of doors all the morning.

NATALYA PETROVNA: Well, then, sit down. . . . Sit here. (*Motions him to a chair.*) We have not had a proper talk, Alexey Nikolaitch. We have not made friends yet. (BELIAYEV *bows and sits down.*) I want to get to know you.

BELIAYEV: I'm . . . it's very kind of you.

NATALYA PETROVNA (*With a smile*): You are afraid of me, I see. . . but wait a little, you won't be afraid of me, when you know me. Tell me . . . tell me now how old are you?

BELIAYEV: Twenty-one.

NATALYA PETROVNA: Are your parents living?

BELIAYEV: My mother is dead, my father is living.

NATALYA PETROVNA: Has your mother been dead long?

BELIAYEV: Yes, a long time.

NATALYA PETROVNA: But you remember her?

BELIAYEV: Oh yes . . . I remember her.

NATALYA PETROVNA: And does your father live in Moscow?

BELIAYEV: Oh no, in the country.

NATALYA PETROVNA: And have you any brothers and sisters?

BELIAYEV: One sister.

NATALYA PETROVNA: Are you fond of her?

BELIAYEV: Yes. She's much younger than I am.

NATALYA PETROVNA: And what's her name?

BELIAYEV: Natalya.

NATALYA PETROVNA (*Eagerly*): Natalya! How odd! I'm Natalya too! . . . (*Pauses.*) And you are very fond of her?

BELIAYEV: Yes.

NATALYA PETROVNA: Tell me what do you think of my Kolya?

BELIAYEV: He is a dear boy.

NATALYA PETROVNA: He is, isn't he? And so affectionate. He's devoted to you already.

BELIAYEV: I'll do my best. . . . I'm glad·

NATALYA PETROVNA: You see, Alexey Nikolaitch, of course I should like to make him a thoroughly able man—I don't know whether I shall succeed in that, but anyway I want him to look back on his childhood with pleasure. Let him grow up in freedom, that's the great thing. I was brought up very differently, Alexey Nikolaitch; my father was not an unkind man, but he was stern and irritable; everyone in the house, including my mother, was afraid of him. My brother and I used to cross ourselves in terror whenever we were summoned to his room. Sometimes my father would pet me, but even in his arms I was in a panic. My brother grew up, and you may perhaps have heard of his rupture with my father. . . . I shall never forget that awful day. . . . I remained an obedient daughter up to my father's death. . . . He used to call me his consolation, his Antigone (he was blind for some years before his death) . . . but however tender he was he could never make me forget those early impressions. . . . I was afraid of him, a blind old man, and never felt at ease in his presence. The traces of timidity, of those years of repression, haven't perhaps quite disappeared even now. . . . I know that at first sight I seem. . . . how shall I say? . . . frigid, perhaps. . . . But I notice I'm talking to you about myself, instead of talking about Kolya. I only meant to say that I know from my own experience how good it is for a child to grow up in freedom. You now, I imagine, have never been repressed as a child, have you?

BELIAYEV: I don't know really. . . . Of course nobody repressed me, nobody bothered about me.

NATALYA PETROVNA (*Shyly*): Why, didn't your father. . . .

BELIAYEV: He'd no time to spare. He was always going round among the neighbours . . . on business . . . or if not business exactly. . . . He got his living through them, in a way. . . . By his services. . . .

NATALYA PETROVNA: Oh! So then nobody troubled about bringing you up?

BELIAYEV: As a matter of fact, nobody did.

I dare say that's evident though, I'm only too aware of my defects.

NATALYA PETROVNA: Perhaps . . . but on the other hand. . . . (*Checks herself and adds in some embarrassment.*) Oh, by the way, Alexey Nikolaitch, was that you singing in the garden yesterday?

BELIAYEV: When?

NATALYA PETROVNA: In the evening . . . by the pond . . . was it you?

BELIAYEV: Yes. (*Hurriedly.*) I didn't think . . . the pond is such a long way off. . . . I didn't think it could be heard from here.

NATALYA PETROVNA: Are you apologizing? You have a very pleasant musical voice and you sing so well. You have studied music?

BELIAYEV: No, not at all. I only sing by ear . . . only simple songs.

NATALYA PETROVNA: You sing them capitally. . . . I'll ask you some time . . . not just now, but when we know each other better, when we are friends. . . . We are going to be friends, Alexey Nikolaitch, aren't we? feel confidence in you; the way I've been chattering is a proof of it. . . .

> [*She holds out her hand for him to shake hands.* BELIAYEV *takes it irresolutely and after some hesitation, not knowing what to do with the hand, kisses it.* NATALYA PETROVNA *flushes and draws away her hand. At that moment* SHPIGELSKY *comes in from the outer room, stops short, then takes a step*

forward, NATALYA PETROVNA *gets up quickly,* BELIAYEV *does the same.*]

NATALYA PETROVNA (*Embarrassed*): Oh, it's you, Doctor . . . here Alexey Nikolaitch and I have been having . . . (*Stops.*)

SHPIGELSKY (*In a loud, free and easy voice*): Really, Natalya Petrovna, the goings on in your house! I walk into the servants' hall and ask for the sick coachman, and my patient is sitting at the table gobbling up pancake and onion. Much good it is being a doctor and relying on illness for getting a living.

NATALYA PETROVNA (*With a constrained smile*): Really. . . . (BELIAYEV is about to go away.) Alexey Nikolaitch I forgot to tell you . . .

VERA (*Running in from the outer room*): Alexey Nikolaitch! Alexey Nikolaitch! (*She stops abruptly at the sight of* NATALYA PETROVNA.)

NATALYA PETROVNA (*With some surprise*): What is it? What do you want?

VERA (*Blushing and dropping her eyes, indicates* BELIAYEV): He is wanted.

NATALYA PETROVNA: By whom?

VERA: Kolya . . . that is Kolya asked me . . . about the kite. . . .

NATALYA PETROVNA: Oh! (*Aside to* VERA.) On n'entre pas comme cela dans une chambre. . . . Cela ne convient pas. (*Turning to* SHPIGELSKY.) What time is it, Doctor? Your watch is always right. . . . It's time for dinner.

SHPIGELSKY: Allow me. (*Takes out his watch.*) It is just . . . I beg to inform you . . . just exacly twenty minutes past four.

NATALYA PETROVNA: There, you see, it's dinner-time. (*Goes to the looking-glass and tidies her hair. Meanwhile* VERA *whispers something to* BELIAYEV. *Both laugh.* NATALYA PETROVNA *sees them reflected in the looking-glass.* SHPIGELSKY *gives her a sidelong look.*)

BELIAYEV (*Laughing, in a low voice*): Really?

VERA (*Nodding and speaking in a low voice too*): Yes, yes, she just went flop.

NATALYA PETROVNA (*Turning with assumed indifference to* VERA): What? Who went flop?

VERA (*In confusion*): Oh no . . . Alexey Nikolaitch made us a swing, and so nurse took it into her head . . .

NATALYA PETROVNA (*Without waiting for her to finish, turns to* SHPIGELSKY): Oh, by the way, Shpigelsky, come here. . . . (She draws him aside and speaks again to VERA.) She wasn't hurt, I hope?

VERA: Oh, no!

NATALYA PETROVNA: But . . . all the same Alexey Nikolaitch, you shouldn't have done it.

MATVEY (*Enters from the outer room and announces*): Dinner is served.

NATALYA PETROVNA: Ah! But where is Arkady Sergeyitch? They'll be late again, he and Mihail Alexandritch.

MATVEY: The gentlemen are in the dining-room.

NATALYA PETROVNA: And mother?

MATVEY: Madam is in the dining-room too.

Natalya Petrovna: Well, then, come along. (*Motioning to* Beliayev.) Vera, allez en avant avec monsieur.

> [Matvey *goes out, followed by* Vera *and* Beliayev.)

Shpigelsky (*To* Natalya Petrovna): You had something to say to me.

Natalya Petrovna: Oh yes! To be sure . . . you see . . . we'll have another talk about . . . about your proposal.

Shpigelsky: Concerning . . . Vera Alexandrovna??

Natalya Petrovna: Yes . . . I will think about it. I'll think about it.

> [*Both go out.*]

ACT II

[*The garden. Seats to Right and to Left under trees; in the foreground raspberry bushes.* KATYA *and* MATVEY *come in on Right.* KATYA *has a basket in her hand.*]

MATVEY: So how is it to be, Katerina Vassilyevna? Kindly explain yourself, I beg you earnestly.

KATYA: Matvey Yegoritch, I really can't.

MATVEY: You are very well aware, Katerina Vassilyevna, what my feelings, I may say, are for you. To be sure, I'm older than you in years, there's no denying that, certainly; but I can still hold my own, I'm still in my prime. I'm of mild disposition, as you are aware; I should like to know what more you want?

KATYA: Matvey Yegoritch, believe me, I feel it very much, I'm very grateful, Matvey Yegoritch. . . . But you see . . . Better wait a bit, I think.

MATVEY: But, dear me, what is there to wait for, Katerina Vassilyevna? You used not to say that, allow me to tell you. And as for consideration, I can answer for that, I believe I may say—— You couldn't ask for more consideration than you will get from me,

Katerina Vassilyevna. And I'm not given to drink, and I never hear a word of blame from the master and mistress either.

Katya: Really, Matvey Yegoritch, I don't know what to say. . . .

Matvey: Ah, Katerina Vassilyevna, something's come over you lately. . . .

Katya: (*Blushing a little*): Lately? Why lately?

Matvey: I don't know . . . but there was a time when you didn't treat me like this.

Katya (*Glancing hurriedly behind the scene*): Mind. . . . The German's coming.

Matvey (*With annoyance*): Bother him, the long-nosed crane! . . . I must talk to you again. (*He goes out to Right.* Katya *is moving towards the raspberries. Enter* Schaaf *from the Left with a fishing-rod on his shoulder*.)

Schaaf (*Calling after* Katya): Vere you go, vere you go, Katerin?

Katya (*Stopping*): We've been told to pick raspberries, Adam Ivanitch.

Schaaf: Raspberries? . . . The raspberry is a pleasant fruit. You love raspberries?

Katya: Yes, I like them.

Schaaf: He. . . he! And I do too! I love all that you love. (*Seeing that she is going*.) Oh, Katerin, vait a leetle.

Katya: I've no time to spare. The house-keeper will scold me.

Schaaf: Oh! That's nothing. You see I'm going . . . (*Points to the rod*) how do you say . . . to feesh, you understand, to feesh, that is, to catch feesh. You love feesh?

Katya: Yes.

Schaaf: He, he, I do too, I do too. Do you know what I vill tell you, Katerin. There's a song in German: (*Sings*) Katrinchen, Katrinchen, wie lieb ich dich so sehr! that is, in Russian O Katrinushka, Katrinushka, you are so pretty I love you! (*Tries to put one arm round her.*)

Katya: Give over, give over, for shame. . . . Here's the mistress coming! (*Escapes into the raspberry patch.*)

Schaaf (*Assuming a glum expression, aside*): Das ist dumm. . . .

> [*Enter on Right* Natalya Petrovna, *arm in arm with* Rakitin.)

Natalya Petrovna (*To* Schaaf): Ah! Adam Ivanitch! Are you going fishing?

Schaaf: Yes, madam.

Natalya Petrovna: Where's Kolya?

Schaaf: With Lizaveta Bogdanovna . . . the music lesson.

Natalya Petrovna: Ah! (*Looking round.*) You are alone here?

Schaaf: Yes.

Natalya Petrovna: You haven't seen Alexey Nikolaitch?

Schaaf: No, madam.

Natalya Petrovna (*After a pause*): We'll go with you, Adam Ivanitch, shall we? We'll look on while you fish.

Schaaf: I am very glad.

Rakitin (*Aside to* Natalya Petrovna): What possesses you?

NATALYA PETROVNA: Come along, come along, beau ténébreux.

[*All three go out on Right.*]

KATYA (*Cautiously raising her head above the raspberries*): They've gone. . . . (*Comes out, stops for a little and ponders.*) That German! . . . (*Sighs and begins picking raspberries again, singing in a low voice*):

> 'No fire is burning, no ember is glowing,
> But the wild heart is glowing, is burning.'

Yes, Matvey Yegoritch is right! (*Goes on singing*):

> 'But the wild heart is glowing, is burning,
> Not for father dear, not for mother dear. . . .'

What big raspberries! . . . (*Goes on singing*):

> 'Not for father dear, not for mother dear.'

How hot it is! Stifling. . . . (*Goes on singing*):

> 'Not for father dear, not for mother dear,
> It glows and it burns for. . . .'

[*Suddenly turns round; is quiet and half hides behind the bushes. From Left* BELIAYEV *and* VERA *come in;* BELIAYEV *has a kite in his hand.*]

BELIAYEV (*As he passes the raspberries, to* KATYA): Why have you stopped, Katya? (*Sings*):

> 'It glows and it burns for a maiden so fair.'

KATYA (*Blushing*): That's not how we sing it.

BELIAYEV: How then? (KATYA *laughs and does not answer*.) What are you doing? Picking raspberries? Let us taste them.

KATYA (*Giving him the basket*): Take them all.

BELIAYEV: Why all? . . . Vera Alexandrovna, won't you have some? (VERA *takes some from the basket, and he does so too*.) Well, that's enough. (*Is giving back the basket to* KATYA.)

KATYA (*Putting back his hand*): Take them, take them all.

BELIAYEV: No, thanks, Katya. (*Gives her the basket*.) Thank you. (*To* VERA.) Vera Alexandrovna, let's sit down on this seat. You see (*Showing the kite*) we must fasten the tail on. You'll help me. (*They go and sit down on the seat.* BELIAYEV *puts the kite in her hands*.) That's it. Mind now, hold it straight. (*Begins to tie on the tail*.) What's the matter?

VERA: I can't see you.

BELIAYEV: Why must you see me?

VERA: I mean I want to see how you fix the tail on.

BELIAYEV: Oh—wait a minute. (*Arranges the kite so that she can see him*.) Katya, why aren't you singing? Sing.

> [*After a brief interval* KATYA *begins singing in a low voice*.]

VERA: Tell me, Alexey Nikolaitch, do you sometimes fly kites in Moscow too?

BELIAYEV: I've no time for kites in Moscow! Hold the string, that's right. Do you suppose we've nothing else to do in Moscow?

VERA: What do you do in Moscow?

BELIAYEV: What do we do? We study, listen to the professors.

VERA: What do they teach you?

BELIAYEV: Everything.

VERA: I expect you're a very good student. Better than all the rest.

BELIAYEV: No, I'm not very good. Better than all the rest, indeed! I'm lazy.

VERA: Why are you lazy?

BELIAYEV: Goodness knows! I was born so, apparently.

VERA (*After a pause*): Have you any friends in Moscow?

BELIAYEV: Of course. . . . I say, this string isn't strong enough.

VERA: And are you fond of them?

BELIAYEV: I should think so. Aren't you fond of your friends?

VERA: I haven't any.

BELIAYEV: I meant the girls you know.

VERA (*Slowly*): Yes.

BELIAYEV: I suppose you have some girl-friends?

VERA: Yes . . . only I don't know why . . . for some time past I've not thought much about them. . . . I haven't even answered Lisa Moshnin, though she begged me to in her letter.

BELIAYEV: How can you say you have no friends . . . what am I?

VERA (*With a smile*): Oh, you . . . that's a different thing (*After a pause*), Alexey Nikolaitch.

BELIAYEV: Well?

VERA: Do you write poetry?

BELIAYEV: No. . . . Why?

VERA: Oh, nothing. (*After a pause.*) A girl in our school used to write poetry.

BELIAYEV (*Pulling the knot with his teeth*): Did she? Was it good?

VERA: I don't know. She used to read it to us, and we cried.

BELIAYEV: What did you cry for?

VERA: Pity. We were all so sorry for her.

BELIAYEV: Were you educated in Moscow?

VERA: Yes, at Madame Beauluce's school in Moscow. Natalya Petrovna took me away last year.

BELIAYEV: Are you fond of Natalya Petrovna?

VERA: Yes, she's so kind. I'm very fond of her.

BELIAYEV (*With a smile*): And you're afraid of her, I bet.

VERA (*Also with a smile*): A little.

BELIAYEV (*After a pause*): And who sent you to school?

VERA: Natalya Petrovna's mother. I grew up in her house. I'm an orphan.

BELIAYEV (*Letting his hands fall*): You're an orphan? And you don't remember your father or your mother?

VERA: No.

BELIAYEV: My mother is dead too. We are both motherless. Well we must put up with it! We mustn't be down-hearted for all that.

Vera: They say orphans quickly make friends with one another.

Beliayev: (*Looking into her eyes*): Do they? And do you think so?

Vera (*Looks into his eyes with a smile*): I think they do.

Beliayev (*Laughs and sets to work on the kite again*): I should like to know how long I've been in these parts.

Vera: This is the twenty-eighth day.

Beliayev: What a memory you have! Well, here's the kite finished. Look what a tail! We must go and fetch Kolya.

Katya (*Coming up to him with the basket*): Won't you have some more raspberries?

Beliayev: No, thanks, Katya. (Katya *goes off without speaking.*)

Vera: Kolya's with Lizaveta Bogdanovna.

Beliayev: How absurd to keep a child indoors in this weather!

Vera: Lizaveta Bogdanovna would only be in our way....

Beliayev: But I'm not talking about her....

Vera (*Hurriedly*): Kolya couldn't come with us without her. . . . She was praising you ever so yesterday, though.

Beliayev: Really?

Vera: Don't you like her?

Beliayev: Oh, I don't mind her. Let her enjoy her snuff, bless the woman. Why do you sigh?

Vera (*After a pause*): I don't know. How clear the sky is!

Beliayev: Does that make you sigh? (*A silence.*) Perhaps you are depressed?

Vera: Depressed? No! I never know myself why I sigh. . . . I'm not depressed at all. On the contrary . . . (*A pause.*) I don't know. . . . I think I can't be quite well. Yesterday I went upstairs to fetch a book—and all at once, fancy, on the staircase, I sat down and began to cry. Goodness knows why, and my tears kept on coming into my eyes for a long while afterwards. . . . What's the meaning of it? And yet I am quite happy.

Beliayev: It's because you're growing. It's growing up. It does happen so. . . . Of course, I noticed your eyes looked swollen yesterday evening.

Vera: You noticed it?

Beliayev: Yes.

Vera: You notice everything.

Beliayev: Oh no, not everything.

Vera (*Dreamily*): Alexey Nikolaitch . . .

Beliayev: What is it?

Vera (*After a pause*): What was it I was going to ask you? I've forgotten what I was going to say.

Beliayev: You are absent-minded!

Vera: No . . . but . . . oh yes! This is what I meant to ask. I think you told me—you have a sister?

Beliayev: Yes.

Vera: Tell me, am I like her?

Beliayev: Oh no. You're much better looking.

VERA: How can that be? Your sister. . . I should like to be in her place.

BELIAYEV: What? You'd like to be in our poor little house at this moment?

VERA: I didn't mean that. . . . Is your home so small?

BELIAYEV: Tiny. Very different from this house.

VERA: Well, what's the use of so many rooms?

BELIAYEV: What's the use? You'll find out one day how useful rooms are.

VERA: One day. . . . When?

BELIAYEV: When you're the mistress of a house yourself. . . .

VERA (*Dreamily*): Do you think so?

BELIAYEV: Yes, you will see. (*A pause.*) Hadn't we better go and fetch Kolya, Vera Alexandrovna?

VERA: Why don't you call me Verotchka?

BELIAYEV: You can't call me Alexey, can you?

VERA: Why not? . . . (*Suddenly starting.*) Oh!

BELIAYEV: What's the matter?

VERA (*In a low voice*): There's Natalya Petrovna coming this way.

BELIAYEV (*Also in a low voice*): Where?

VERA (*Nodding towards the Right*): Over there . . . along the path, with Mihail Alexandritch.

BELIAYEV (*Getting up*): Let's go to Kolya. . . . He must have finished his lesson by now.

VERA: Let's go . . . or I'm afraid she'll scold me. . . .

> [*They get up and walk away quickly to the Left.* KATYA *hides again in the raspberry bushes.* NATALYA PETROVNA *and* RAKITIN *come in on Right.*]

NATALYA PETROVNA (*Standing still*): I believe that's Mr. Beliayev with Vera.

RAKITIN: Yes, it is. . . .

NATALYA PETROVNA: It looks as though they were running away from us.

RAKITIN: Perhaps they are.

NATALYA PETROVNA (*After a pause*): But I don't think Verotchka ought . . . to be alone like this with a young man in the garden. . . . Of course, she's only a child, still, it's not the proper thing. . . . I'll tell her.

RAKITIN: How old is she?

NATALYA PETROVNA: Seventeen! She's actually seventeen. . . . It is hot to-day. I'm tired. Let's sit down. (*They sit down on the seat on which* VERA *and* BELIAYEV *have been sitting*.) Has Shpigelsky gone home?

RAKITIN: Yes, he's gone.

NATALYA PETROVNA: It's a pity you didn't keep him. I can't imagine what induced that man to become a district doctor. . . . He's very amusing. He makes me laugh.

RAKITIN: Well, I thought you were not in a very laughing humour to-day.

NATALYA PETROVNA: What made you think that?

Rakitin: Oh, I don't know.

Natalya Petrovna: Because nothing sentimental appeals to me to-day? Oh, certainly, I must warn you there's absolutely nothing that could touch me to-day. . . . But that doesn't prevent me from laughing; on the contrary. Besides, there's something I had to discuss with Shpigelsky to-day.

Rakitin: May I ask what?

Natalya Petrovna: No, you mayn't. As it is, you know everything I think, everything I do. That's boring.

Rakitin: I beg your pardon. . . . I had no idea. . . .

Natalya Petrovna: I want to have some secrets from you.

Rakitin: What next! From what you say, one might suppose I know everything. . . .

Natalya Petrovna (*Interrupting*): And don't you?

Rakitin: You are pleased to make fun of me.

Natalya Petrovna: Why don't you know everything that goes on in me? If you don't I can't congratulate you on your insight. When a man watches me from morning to night. . . .

Rakitin: What do you mean? Is that a reproach?

Natalya Petrovna: A reproach? (*A pause.*) No, I see; you certainly have not much insight.

Rakitin: Perhaps not . . . but since I watch you from morning to night, allow me to tell you one thing I have noticed. . . .

Natalya Petrovna: About me? Please do.

Rakitin: You won't be angry with me?

Natalya Petrovna: Oh no! I should like to be, but I shan't.

Rakitin: For some time past, Natalya Petrovna, you have been in a state of permanent irritability, and that irritability is something unconscious, involuntary: you seem to be in a state of inward conflict, as though you were perplexed. I had never observed anything of the sort in you before my visit to the Krinitsyns'; it has only come on lately. (Natalya Petrovna *draws lines in the sand before her with her parasol*) At times you sigh—such deep, deep sighs—like a man who's very tired, so tired that he can't find rest.

Natalya Petrovna: And what do you deduce from that, you observant person?

Rakitin: I deduce? Nothing. . . . But it worries me.

Natalya Petrovna: Humbly grateful for your sympathy.

Rakitin: And besides . . .

Natalya Petrovna (*With some impatience*): Please, change the subject.

[*A pause.*]

Rakitin: You have no plans for going out anywhere to-day?

Natalya Petrovna: No.

Rakitin: Why not? It's so fine.

Natalya Petrovna: Too lazy. (*A pause.*) Tell me . . . you know Bolshintsov, of course?

Rakitin: Our neighbour, Afanasy Ivanitch?

Natalya Petrovna: Yes.

Rakitin: What a question! Only the day before yesterday we were playing preference with him in your house.

Natalya Petrovna: I want to know what sort of man he is.

Rakitin: Bolshintsov?

Natalya Petrovna: Yes, yes, Bolshintsov.

Rakitin: Well, I must say, that I never expected that!

Natalya Petrovna (*Impatiently*): What didn't you expect?

Rakitin: That you would ever be making inquiries about Bolshintsov! A foolish, fat, tedious man—though of course there's no harm in the man.

Natalya Petrovna: He's by no means so foolish or tedious as you think.

Rakitin: Perhaps not. I must own, I haven't studied the gentleman very carefully.

Natalya Petrovna (*Ironically*): You haven't been watching him.

Rakitin (*With a constrained smile*): And what has induced you?. . .

Natalya Petrovna: Oh, nothing!
[*Again a pause.*]

Rakitin: Look, Natalya Petrovna, how lovely that dark green oak is against the dark blue sky. It's all bathed in the sunlight and what rich colours. . . . What inexhaustible life and strength in it especially when you compare it with that young birch tree. . . . She looks as though she might pass away in radiance, her tiny leaves gleam with a liquid brilliance, as though melting, yet she is lovely too. . . .

Natalya Petrovna: Do you know, Rakitin, I noticed it ages ago. You have a very delicate feeling for the so–called beauties of nature, and talk very elegantly, and cleverly about them . . . so elegantly and cleverly that I imagine nature ought to be unutterably grateful for your choice and happy phrases; you dance attendance on her like a perfumed marquis on high red heels dallying with a pretty peasant girl. . . . Only I'll tell you what's wrong, it sometimes seems to me that she could never understand or appreciate your subtle observations, just as the peasant girl wouldn't understand the courtly compliments of the marquis; nature is far simpler, even coarser, than you suppose, because, thank God, she's healthy. . . . Birch trees don't melt or fall into swoons like nervous ladies.

Rakitin: Quelle tirade! Nature is healthy . . . that is, in other words, I'm a sickly creature.

Natalya Petrovna: You're not the only sickly creature, we are neither of us too healthy.

Rakitin: Oh, I know that way of telling a person the most unpleasant things in the most inoffensive way. . . . Instead of telling him to his face, for instance, you're a fool, my friend, you need only tell him with a good-natured smile, we are both fools, you know.

Natalya Petrovna: You're offended? What nonsense! I only meant to say that we are both . . . since you don't like the word sickly . . . we are both old, very old.

Rakitin: In what way are we old? I don't think so of myself.

Natalya Petrovna: Well, listen; here we are sitting . . . on this very seat a quarter of an hour ago two really young creatures have been sitting, perhaps.

Rakitin: Beliayev and Verotchka? Of course they are younger than we are. . . there's a few years' difference between us, that's all. . . . But that doesn't make us old yet.

Natalya Petrovna: The difference between us is not only in years.

Rakitin: Ah! I understand. . . . You envy them . . . their naivete; their freshness and innocence . . . their foolishness, in fact.

Natalya Petrovna: You think so? Oh, you think that they are foolish? You think everybody foolish to-day, I see. No, you don't understand me. And besides . . . foolish? What does that matter? What's the good of being clever, if you're not amusing. Nothing is more depressing than that sort of gloomy cleverness.

Rakitin: Hm. . . . Why don't you say it straight out, without these hints? I don't amuse you . . . that's what you mean. Why find fault with cleverness in general on account of one miserable sinner like me?

Natalya Petrovna: No, that's not what I mean. . . . (Katya *comes out from among the bushes*.) Have you been picking raspberries, Katya?

Katya: Yes, madam.

Natalya Petrovna: Show me. (Katya *goes up to her*.) What splendid raspberries! What a colour . . . though your cheeks are redder still. (Katya *smiles and looks down*.) Well, run along——

[Katya *goes out*]

Rakitin: There's a young creature after your taste.

Natalya Petrovna: Of course. (*Gets up*.)

Rakitin: Where are you going?

Natalya Petrovna: First, I want to see what Verotchka's doing . . . it's time she was indoors . . . and secondly I must own I don't like our conversation. We had better drop our discussions of nature and youth for a time.

Rakitin: Perhaps you would rather walk alone?

Natalya Petrovna: To tell the truth, I should. We shall see each other again soon. . . . But we are parting friends? (*Holds out her hand to him*.)

Rakitin (*Getting up*): Yes indeed! (*Presses her hand.*)

Natalya Petrovna: Good-bye for the present. (*She opens her parasol and goes off at Left.*)

Rakitin: (*Walks up and down for some time*): What is the matter with her? (*A pause.*) Simply caprice. But is it? I have never seen that in her before. On the contrary, I know no woman less moody. What is the reason? (*Walks to and fro again and suddenly stands still.*) Ah, how absurd a man is who has only one idea in his head, one object, one interest in life. . . . Like me, for instance. It was true what she said: one keeps watching trifling things from morning to night, and one grows trivial oneself. . . . That's so; but without her I can't live, in her presence I am more than happy; the feeling can't be called happiness, I belong to her entirely, parting from her would . . . without exaggeration . . . be exactly like parting with life. What is wrong with her? What's the meaning of her agitation, the involuntary bitterness of her words? Is she beginning to be weary of me? Hm? (*Sits down.*) I have never deceived myself, I know very well how she loves me; but I hoped that with time that quiet feeling . . . I hoped? Have I the right to hope, dare I hope? I confess my position is pretty absurd . . . almost contemptible. . . . (*A pause.*) What's the use of talking like that? She's an honest woman, and I'm not a Lovelace. (*With a bitter smile.*) More's the pity! (*Get-*

ting up quickly.) Well, that's enough! I must put this nonsense out of my head! (*Walking up and down.*) What a glorious day! (*A pause.*) How skilfully she stung me! . . . My choice and happy expressions. . . . She's very clever, especially when she's in a bad humour. And what's this sudden adoration of youth and innocence? . . . This tutor. . . . She often talks about him. I must say I see nothing very striking in him. He's simply a student, like all students. Can she . . . impossible! She's out of humour . . . she doesn't know what she wants and so she snaps at me, as children beat their nurse. . . . A flattering comparison! But she must go her own way. When this fit of depression and uneasiness is over, she will be the first to laugh at that lanky boy, that raw youth. . . . Your explanation is not bad, Mihail Alexandritch, but is it true? God knows! Well, we shall see. It's not the first time, my dear fellow, that after endless fretting and pondering you have had suddenly to give up all your subtle conjectures, fold your hands and wait meekly for what is to come. And meanwhile you must recognize it's pretty awkward and bitter for you. . . . But that's what I'm for, it seems. . . . (*Looking round.*) Ah, here he is, our unsophisticated young man!. . . Just when he's wanted. . . . I haven't once had a real talk with him. Let's see what he's like. (BELIAYEV *comes in on Left.*) Ah! Alexey Nikolaitch! So you have come out for a turn in the fresh air too?

BELIAYEV: Yes.

RAKITIN: Though I must say the air is not so very fresh to-day: the heat's terrific, but in the shade here under these lime trees it's endurable. (*A pause*.) Did you see Natalya Petrovna?

BELIAYEV: I met her just now. . . . She's gone indoors with Vera Alexandrovna.

RAKITIN: Wasn't it you I saw here half an hour ago with Vera Alexandrovna?

BELIAYEV: Yes. . . . We were having a walk.

RAKITIN: Ah! (*Takes his arm*.) Well, how do you like living in the country?

BELIAYEV: I like the country. The only thing is, the shooting is not good here.

RAKITIN: You're fond of shooting then?

BELIAYEV: Yes. . . . Aren't you?

RAKITIN: I? No; I'm a poor shot. I'm too lazy.

BELIAYEV: I'm lazy too . . . but not in that way.

RAKITIN: Oh! Are you lazy about reading then?

BELIAYEV: No, I love reading. But I'm too lazy to work long at a time, especially too lazy to go on doing the same thing.

RAKITIN (*Smiling*): Talking to ladies, for instance?

BELIAYEV: Ah, you're laughing at me. . . . I'm frightened of ladies.

RAKITIN (*Slightly embarrassed*): What an idea! Why should I laugh at you?

Beliayev: Oh, that's all right. . . . I don't mind! (*A pause.*) Tell me where can I get gunpowder about here?

Rakitin: You can get it no doubt in the town; it is sold there. But do you want good powder?

Beliayev: No, it's not for shooting, it's for making fireworks.

Rakitin: Oh, can you make them?

Beliayev: Yes; I've picked out the right place already, the other side of the pond. I heard it's Natalya Petrovna's name-day next week, so they will come in for that.

Rakitin: Natalya Petrovna will be pleased at such an attention from you. She likes you, Alexey Nikolaitch, I may tell you.

Beliayev: I'm very much flattered. . . . Ah, by the way, Mihail Alexandritch, I believe you take a magazine. Could you let me have it to read?

Rakitin: Certainly, with pleasure. . . . There's good poetry in it.

Beliayev: I'm not fond of poetry.

Rakitin: How's that?

Beliayev: I don't know. Comic verses strike me as far-fetched, besides there aren't many; and sentimental ones. . . . I don't know. There's something unreal in them somehow.

Rakitin: You prefer novels?

Beliayev: Yes. I like good novels; but critical art icles—they appeal to me——

Rakitin: Oh, why?

Beliayev: It's a fine man that writes them.

Rakitin: And you don't go in for authorship yourself?

Beliayev: Oh no! It's silly to write if you've no talent. It only makes people laugh at you. Besides, it's a queer thing, I wish you would explain it to me, sometimes a man seems sensible enough, but when he takes up a pen, he's perfectly hopeless. No, writing's not for us, we must thank God if we understand what's written.

Rakitin: Do you know, Alexey Nikolaitch, not many young men have as much common sense as you have.

Beliayev: Thank you for the compliment. (*A pause.*) I'm going to let off the fireworks the other side of the pond, because I can make Roman candles, and they will be reflected in the water. . . .

Rakitin: That will be beautiful. . . . Excuse me, Alexey Nikolaitch, by the way, do you know French?

Beliayev: No, I translated a novel of Paul de Kock's, 'La Laitière de Montfermeil,' perhaps you've heard of it, for fifty roubles; but I didn't know a word of French. For instance: quatre-vingt-dix I translated four-twenty-ten. . . . Being hard-up drove me to it, you know. But it's a pity. I should like to know French. It's my cursed laziness. I should like to read Georges Sand in French. But the accent . . . how is one to get over the accent? An, on, en, in, isn't it awful?

Rakitin: Well, that's a difficulty that can be got over. . . .

Beliayev: Please tell me, what's the time?

Rakitin (*Looking at his watch*): Half-past one.

Beliayev: Lizaveta Bogdanovna is keeping Kolya a long time at the piano. . . . I bet he's dying to be running about.

Rakitin (*Cordially*): But one has to study too, you know, Alexey Nikolaitch. . . .

Beliayev (*With a sigh*): You oughtn't to have to say that, Mihail Alexandritch, and I oughtn't to have to hear it. . . . Of course, it would never do for everyone to be a loafer like me.

Rakitin: Oh, nonsense. . . .

Beliayev: But I know that only too well.

Rakitin: Well, I know too, on the contrary, that just what you regard as a defect, your impulsiveness, your freedom from constraint is what's attractive.

Beliayev: To whom, for instance?

Rakitin: Well, to Natalya Petrovna, for example.

Beliayev: Natalya Petrovna? With her I don't feel that I am free, as you call it.

Rakitin: Ah! Is that really so?

Beliayev: And after all, Mihail Alexandritch, isn't education the thing that matters most in a man? It's easy for you to talk. . . . I can't make you out, really. (*Suddenly looking round.*) What's that? I thought I heard a corncrake calling in the garden, (*Is about to go.*)

Rakitin: Perhaps. . . . But where are you off to?

Beliayev: To fetch my gun. . . . (*Goes to Left*; Natalya Petrovna *comes in, meeting him.*)

Natalya Petrovna (*Seeing him, suddenly smiles*): Where are you going, Alexey Nikolaitch?

Beliayev: I was . . .

Rakitin: To fetch his gun. . . . He heard a corncrake in the garden. . . .

Natalya Petrovna: No, please don't shoot in the garden. . . . Let the poor bird live. . . . Besides, you may startle Granny.

Beliayev: I obey, madam.

Natalya Petrovna (*Laughing*): Oh, Alexey Nikolaitch, aren't you ashamed? 'I obey, madam,' what a way to speak! How can you . . . talk like that? But wait, you see Mihail Alexandritch and I will see to your education. . . . Yes, yes . . . we have talked together about you more than once already. . . . There's a plot against you, I warn you. . . . You will let me have a hand in your education, won't you?

Beliayev: Why, of course. . . . I shall be only too . . .

Natalya Petrovna: To begin with, don't be shy, it doesn't suit you at all. Yes, we will look after you. (*Indicating* Rakitin.) We are old people, you know, he and I, while you are young. You are, aren't you? You will see how good it will be. You will look after Kolya and I . . . we . . . will look after you.

BELIAYEV: I shall be very grateful.

NATALYA PETROVNA: That's right. What have Mihail Alexandritch and you been talking about?

RAKITIN (*Smiling*): He has been telling me how he translated a French book without knowing a word of French.

NATALYA PETROVNA: Ah! Now there, we will teach you French. What have you done with your kite, by the way?

BELIAYEV: I've taken it indoors. I thought you didn't like it.

NATALYA PETROVNA (*With some embarrassment*): What made you think that? Was it because of Vera . . . because I took Vera indoors? No, that . . . No, you were mistaken. (*Eagerly.*) I tell you what . . . Kolya must have finished his lesson by now. Let us take him and Vera and the kite, shall we? . . . and all of us together fly it in the meadow? Yes?

BELIAYEV: With pleasure, Natalya Petrovna.

NATALYA PETROVNA: That's right then. Come, let us go, let us go. (*Holding out her arm to him.*) But take my arm, how awkward you are! Come along . . . make haste. (*They go off quickly to Left.*)

RAKITIN (*Looking after them*): What eagerness . . . what gaiety. . . . I have never seen a look like that on her face. And what a sudden transformation! (*A pause.*) Souvent femme varie. . . . But . . . I am certainly not in her good books to-day. That's clear.

(*A pause.*) Well, we shall see what will come later. (*Slowly.*) Is it possible? . . . (*With a gesture of dismissal*) It can't be! . . . But that smile, that warm, soft, bright look in her eyes. . . . Oh, God spare me from knowing the tortures of jealousy, especially a senseless jealousy! (*Suddenly looking round.*) Hullo, what do I see? (SHPIGELSKY *and* BOLSHINTSOV *enter from Left.* RAKITIN *goes to meet them.*) Good day, gentlemen. . . . I confess I didn't expect to see you to-day, Shpigelsky. . . . (*Shakes hands.*)

SHPIGELSKY: Well, I didn't expect it myself. . . . I never imagined . . . But you see I called in on him (*Indicating* BOLSHINTSOV) and he was already sitting in his carriage, coming here. So I turned round and came back with him.

RAKITIN: Well, you are very welcome.

BOLSHINTSOV: I certainly was intending. . .

SHPIGELSKY (*Cutting him short*): The servants told us you were all in the garden. . . . Anyway there was nobody in the drawing-room. . . .

RAKITIN: But didn't you meet Natalya Petrovna?

SHPIGELSKY: When?

RAKITIN: Why, just now.

SHPIGELSKY: No. We didn't come here straight from the house. Afanasy Ivanovitch wanted to see whether there were any mushrooms in the copse.

BOLSHINTSOV (*Surprised*): I really . . .

Shpigelsky: Oh, there, we know how fond you are of mushrooms. So Natalya Petrovna has gone in? Well then, we can go back again.

Bolshintsov: Of course.

Rakitin: Yes, she has gone in to fetch them all out for a walk. . . . They are going to fly a kite, I believe.

Shpigelsky: Ah! That's capital. It's just the weather for a walk.

Rakitin: You can stay here. . . . I'll go in and tell her you have come.

Shpigelsky: Why should you trouble. . . . Really, Mihail Alexandritch . . .

Rakitin: No trouble. . . . I'm going in anyway. . . .

Shpigelsky: Oh, well, in that case we won't keep you. . . . No ceremony, you know. . . .

Rakitin: Good-bye for the present. . . . (*Goes out to Left*.)

Shpigelsky: Good-bye. (To Bolshintsov.) Well, Afanasy Ivanovitch. . . .

Bolshintsov (*Interrupting him*): What did you mean about mushrooms, Ignaty Ilyitch? . . . I'm amazed, what mushrooms?

Shpigelsky: Upon my soul, would you have had me say my Afanasy Ivanovitch was overcome with shyness; he wouldn't go straight in, and insisted on taking another turn?

Bolshintsov: That's so . . . but all the same, mushrooms. . . . I don't know, may be, I'm mistaken. . . .

Shpigelsky: You certainly are, my dear fellow. I'll tell you what you'd better be thinking about. You see we've come here . . . done as you wished. Look out now and don't make a mess of it.

Bolshintsov: But, Ignaty Ilyitch, you know you . . . You told me, I mean . . . I should like to know for certain what answer . . .

Shpigelsky: My honoured friend! It's reckoned over fifteen miles from your place here; at least three times every mile you put that very question to me. . . . Isn't that enough for you? Now listen; but this is the last time I give way to you. This is what Natalya Petrovna said to me: 'I . . .'

Bolshintsov (*Nodding*): Yes.

Shpigelsky (*With annoyance*): Yes! Why, what do you mean by 'yes'? I've told you nothing yet. . . . 'I don't know,' says she, 'Mr. Bolshintsov very well, but he seems to me a good man; on the other hand, I don't intend to force Vera's inclinations; and so, let him visit us, and if he wins. . . '

Bolshintsov: Wins? She said 'wins'?

Shpigelsky: 'If he wins her affections, Anna Semyonovna and I will not oppose. . . '

Bolshintsov: Will not oppose? Is that what she said? Will not oppose?

Shpigelsky: Yes, yes, yes. What a queer fellow you are! 'We will not oppose their happiness.'

Bolshintsov: Hm.

Shpigelsky: 'Their happiness.' . . . Yes, but observe, Afanasy Ivanitch, what your task is now. . . . You have now to persuade Vera Alexandravna herself that marrying you really will be happiness for her; you have to win her affection.

Bolshintsov (*Blinking*): Yes, yes, win . . . exactly so. I agree with you.

Shpigelsky: You insisted on my bringing you here. . . . Well, let's see how you will act.

Bolshintsov: Act? Yes, yes, we must act, we must win . . . exactly so. Only you see, Ignaty Ilyitch . . . May I confess, admit to you, as to my best friend, one of my weaknesses: I did, as you truly say, wish you to bring me here to-day. . . .

Shpigelsky: You didn't wish it, you insisted, absolutely insisted on it. . . .

Bolshintsov: Oh, well, we'll grant that, . . . I agree with you. But you see . . . at home . . . I certainly . . . at home I felt I was ready for anything; but now you know I feel overcome with fears.

Shpigelsky: But what are you afraid of?

Bolshintsov (*Glancing at him from under his brows*): The risk, sir.

Shpigelsky: Wha-at?

Bolshintsov: The risk. There's a great risk. I must, Ignaty Ilyitch, I must confess to you that . . .

Shpigelsky (*Interrupting him*): As to 'your best friend.' We know all about it. . . . Get on. . . .

BOLSHINTSOV: Exactly so. . . . I agree with you. I must confess to you, Ignaty Ilyitch, that I have had very little to do with ladies, with the female sex, in general, if I may say so; I will confess frankly, Ignaty Ilyitch, that I simply can't imagine what one can talk about to a person of the female sex—and alone with her too . . . and especially a young lady.

SHPIGELSKY: You surprise me. I really don't know what one can't talk about to a person of the female sex, especially a young lady, and particularly alone with her.

BOLSHINTSOV: Oh . . . you . . . Good gracious, but I'm not you. So you see it's just in this case I want to appeal to you, Ignaty Ilyitch. They say that in these affairs it's the first step that counts, so couldn't you just . . . to give me a start in the conversation . . . tell me of something to say, something agreeable in the way, for instance, of an observation . . . and then I can get along. After that I could manage somehow by myself.

SHPIGELSKY: I won't tell you anything to say, Afanasy Ivanovitch, because nothing I could tell you would be of any use to you . . . but I will give you some advice if you like.

BOLSHINTSOV: My dear sir, pray do. . . . And as to my gratitude . . . you know . . .

SHPIGELSKY: Oh, come, come, I'm not bargaining with you, am I?

BOLSHINTSOV (*Dropping his voice*): You can reckon on the three horses.

Shpigelsky: Oh, that will do. . . . You see, Afanasy Ivanovitch . . . You are unquestionably a capital fellow in every respect . . . (Bolshintsov *makes a slight bow*) a man of excellent qualities. . . .

Bolshintsov: Oh dear!

Shpigelsky: You are, besides, the owner, I believe, of three hundred serfs.

Bolshintsov: Three hundred and twenty, sir.

Shpigelsky: Not mortgaged?

Bolshintsov: I owe nobody a farthing.

Shpigelsky: There you are. I've been telling you, you're an excellent man and the most eligible of suitors. But you say yourself you've had very little to do with ladies. . . .

Bolshintsov (*With a sigh*): That's just so. I may say, Ignaty Ilyitch, I've avoided the female sex from a child.

Shpigelsky (*With a sigh*): Quite so. That's not a vice in a husband; quite the contrary; but still in certain circumstances, at the first declaration of love, for instance, it is essential to be able to say *something* . . . isn't it?

Bolshintsov: I quite agree with you.

Shpigelsky: Or else, you know, Vera Alexandrovna may simply suppose that you feel unwell—and nothing more. Besides, though your exterior figure is also perfectly presentable in all respects, it does not offer any feature very striking at first sight . . . not at first sight, you know, and that's what's wanted in this case.

BOLSHINTSOV (*With a sigh*): That's what's wanted in this case.

SHPIGELSKY: Young ladies are attracted by it, anyway. And then, your age too . . . in fact, it's not for you and me to try to please. And so it's no good for you to think of agreeable remarks. That's a poor thing to depend on. But you have something else to count upon, far firmer and more reliable, and that's virtues, my dear Afanasy Ivanovitch, and your three hundred and twenty serfs. In your place I should simply say to Vera Alexandrovna . . .

BOLSHINTSOV: Alone with her?

SHPIGELSKY: Oh, of course, alone with her! 'Vera Alexandrovna!' (*From the movement of* BOLSHINTSOV'S *lips it is evident that he is repeating in a whisper every word after* SHPIGELSKY.) 'I love you and ask your hand in marriage. I'm a kind-hearted, good-natured, harmless man and I'm not poor. You will be perfectly free with me; I will do my best to please you in every way. And I beg you to find out about me, to take a little more notice of me than you have done hitherto, and to give me an answer as you please and when you please. I am ready to wait and shall consider it a pleasure to do so.'

BOLSHINTSOV (*Uttering the last words aloud*): To do so! Yes, yes, yes. . . . I quite agree with you. Only I tell you what, Ignaty Ilyitch; I believe you used the word 'harmless.' . . . You said a harmless man. . . .

Shpigelsky: Well, aren't you a harmless man?

Bolshintsov: Ye-e-es. . . but still I fancy. . . . Will it be the right thing, Ignaty Ilyitch? Wouldn't it be better to say, for instance? . . .

Shpigelsky: For instance?

Bolshintsov: For instance . . . for instance. . . . (*A pause.*) But maybe 'harmless' will do.

Shpigelsky: Now, Afanasy Ivanovitch, you listen to me; the more simply you express yourself, the plainer your words, the better it will go, trust me. And above all, don't be too pressing, Afanasy Ivanovitch. Vera Alexandrovna is very young; you may scare her. . . . Give her time to think over your offer. Avoid fine words and I guarantee your success. (*Looking round.*) Why, here they are all coming too—— (Bolshintsov *wants to make off.*) Where are you going? To pick mushrooms again? (Bolshintsov *smiles, turns red and remains.*) The great thing is not to be scared!

Bolshintsov (*Hurriedly*): Vera Alexandrovna knows nothing about it yet, does she?

Shpigelsky: I should think not!

Bolshintsov: Well, I rely on you. . . . (*Blows his nose. Enter from Left* Natalya Petrovna, Vera, Beliayev *with the kite, and* Kolya, *followed by* Rakitin *and* Lizaveta Bogdanovna. Natalya Petrovna *is in a very good humour.*)

NATALYA PETROVNA (*To* BOLSHINTSOV *and* SHPIGELSKY): How do you do; how are you, Shpigelsky; I didn't expect you to-day, but I am very glad to see you. How are you, Afanasy Ivanitch. (*He bows with some embarrassment.*)

SHPIGELSKY (*To* NATALYA PETROVNA, *indicating* BOLSHINTSOV): This gentleman here insisted on bringing me....

NATALYA PETROVNA (*Laughing*): I'm very much obliged to him. . . . But do you need forcing to come to see us?

SHPIGELSKY: Oh, good heavens! but . . . I was only here . . . this morning . . . dear me....

NATALYA PETROVNA: Ah! our diplomat's caught!

SHPIGELSKY: I'm delighted, Natalya Petrovna, to see that you are in a very good humour.

NATALYA PETROVNA: You think it necessary to remark it—is it so rare then with me?

SHPIGELSKY: Oh, good gracious—no . . . but . . .

NATALYA PETROVNA: Monsieur le Diplomate, you're getting more and more in a tangle.

KOLYA (*Who has been all this time impatiently fidgeting about* VERA *and* BELIAYEV): But, Maman, when are we going to fly the kite?

NATALYA PETROVNA: When you like. . . . Alexey Nikolaitch, and you Vera, let us go to the meadow. (*Turning to the others.*) You won't care about it, I expect. Lizaveta Bogdanovna, and you, Rakitin, I leave our good friend Afanasy Ivanovitch with you.

RAKITIN: But what makes you think we shan't care about it, Natalya Petrovna?

NATALYA PETROVNA: You are sensible people . . . it must seem childish to you. . . . But as you like. We don't want to prevent your following us. (*To* BELIAYEV *and* VERA.) Come along. (NATALYA PETROVNA, VERA, BELIAYEV *and* KOLYA *go off to Right*.)

SHPIGELSKY (*Glancing with some surprise at* RAKITIN, *says to* BOLSHINTSOV): Our good friend Afanasy Ivanovitch, give your arm to Lizaveta Bogdanovna.

BOLSHINTSOV (*Nervously*): With the greatest pleasure.

[*Gives* LIZAVETA BOGDANOVNA *his arm*.]

SHPIGELSKY: And we'll go along together, if you'll allow me, Mihail Alexandritch. (*Takes his arm*.) My word! How they're racing along the avenue. Let's go and see them fly the kite, though we are sensible people. . . . Afanasy Ivanovitch, will you lead the way?

BOLSHINTSOV (*As they walk, to* LIZAVETA BOGDANOVNA): The weather is certainly very agreeable to-day, one may say.

LIZAVETA BOGDANOVNA (*Mincing*): Yes, indeed, very agreeable!

SHPIGELSKY (*To* RAKITIN): I've something I want to talk to you about, Mihail Alexandritch. . . . (RAKITIN *suddenly laughs*.) What is it?

Rakitin: Oh . . . nothing. . . . I was amused at our following in the rear like this.

Shpigelsky: The front rank easily turns into the rear-guard, you know. . . . It all depends which way you are going.

[*All go out to Right.*]

ACT III

[*The scene is the same as in Act I.* Rakitin *and* Shpigelsky *come in from the outer room.*]

Shpigelsky: Well, how about it, Mihail Alexandritch? For goodness sake do help me.

Rakitin: In what way can I help you, Ignaty Ilyitch?

Shpigelsky: In what way? Why, put yourself in my place, Mihail Alexandritch. This is no concern of mine, really. Indeed, I've been acting chiefly from a wish to serve others. . . . My kind heart will be my ruin!

Rakitin (*Laughing*): Well, ruin's a good way off still.

Shpigelsky (*Laughing too*): About that there's no knowing, but my position is certainly awkward. I brought Bolshintsov here at Natalya Petrovna's wish, and have given him her answer with her permission, and now on one side I get sulky looks as though I'd done something foolish, and on the other, Bolshintsov gives me no peace. They avoid him and won't say a word to me. . . .

Rakitin: What possessed you to take up this business, Ignaty Ilyitch? Why, Bolshintsov, between ourselves . . . he's simply a fool.

Shpigelsky: Well, I declare! Between ourselves! That's a piece of news! And since when have sensible men been the only ones to marry? We must leave the fools free to get married, if nothing else. You say I've taken up this business. . . . Not at all, I'll tell you how it came about: a friend asks me to put in a word for him. Well, was I to refuse? I'm a good-natured man, I don't know how to refuse. I carry out my friend's commission: the answer I get is: 'Very much obliged; pray, don't trouble yourself further.' I understand and don't trouble myself further. Then they take it up themselves and encourage me, so to speak. I obey; and now they're indignant with me. And in what way am I to blame?

Rakitin: Why, who says you are to blame? . . . The only thing that puzzles me is what induces you to take so much trouble.

Shpigelsky: What induces . . . what induces. . . . The man gives me no peace.

Rakitin: Come, nonsense. . . .

Shpigelsky: Besides, he's an old friend.

Rakitin (*With an incredulous smile*): Is he? Oh, well, that's another matter.

Shpigelsky (*Smiling too*): I'll be open with you, though. . . . There's no deceiving you. . . . Oh well—he has promised me . . . one of my horses has gone lame, so you see he has promised me . . .

RAKITIN: A horse to replace it?

SHPIGELSKY: Well, since I must own up, three new ones.

RAKITIN: You should have said that before!

SHPIGELSKY (*Eagerly*): But please don't you imagine . . . I would never have consented to be a go-between in this affair, it would have been utterly unlike me (Rakitin *smiles*), if I had not known Bolshintsov to be a thoroughly honest man. . . . Besides, all I want even now is a definite answer—yes or no.

RAKITIN: Surely, things haven't reached that stage yet?

Shpigelsky: But what are you imagining? . . . It's not a question of marriage, but of permission to come, to visit. . . .

RAKITIN: But whoever forbids it?

SHPIGELSKY: Forbids . . . what a thing to say! Of course, if it were anybody else . . . but Bolshintsov's a shy man, a blessed innocent, straight out of the Golden Age, scarcely weaned from the feeding bottle. . . . He has so little self-confidence, he needs some encouragement. While his intentions are most honourable.

RAKITIN: Yes, and his horses good.

SHPIGELSKY: And his horses are good. (*Takes a pinch of snuff and offers the box to* RAKITIN.) Won't you have some?

RAKITIN: No, thanks.

SHPIGELSKY: So that's how it is, Mihail Alexandritch. As you see, I don't want to deceive you. Indeed, why should I? The thing's perfectly clear and straightforward. A man of excellent principles, with property, quite harmless. . . . If he suits—good. If he doesn't—well, they should say so.

RAKITIN: That's all very well, no doubt, but how do I come in? I really don't see what I can do about it.

SHPIGELSKY: Oh, Mihail Alexandritch! As though we don't know that Natalya Petrovna has a very great respect for you and even sometimes follows your advice. . . . Now do, Mihail Alexandritch (*Puts his arm round him*), be a friend, put in a word. . . .

RAKITIN: And you think this is a good husband for little Vera?

SHPIGELSKY (*Assuming a serious air*): I'm convinced of it. You don't believe it. . . . Well, you'll see. As you know, the great thing in marriage is solid character. And Bolshintsov is solidity itself. (*Looking round.*) And here I do believe is Natalya Petrovna herself coming in. . . . My dear good friend, my benefactor! The two chestnuts as tracehorses, and the bay in the shafts! You will do your best?

RAKITIN (*Smiling*): Oh, very well, very well. . . .

SHPIGELSKY: Mind now, I rely on you. . . . (*Escapes into the outer room.*)

RAKITIN (*Looking after him*): What a sly rogue that doctor is! Vera . . . and Bolshintsov! But there you are! There are marriages worse than that. I'll do as he asks me, and then—it's not my business! (*Turns round*. Natalya Petrovna, *coming out of the study and seeing him, stops*.)

NATALYA PETROVNA (*Irresolutely*): It's . . . you. . . . I thought you were in the garden.

RAKITIN: You seem sorry I'm not. . . .

NATALYA PETROVNA (*Interrupting*): Oh! nonsense. (*Advancing to front of stage*.) Are you alone here?

RAKITIN: Shpigelsky has just gone.

NATALYA PETROVNA (*With a slight frown*): Oh! that local Talleyrand. . . . What has he been saying to you? Is he still hanging about?

RAKITIN: The local Talleyrand, as you call him, is evidently in disfavour to-day . . . but yesterday, I fancy . . .

NATALYA PETROVNA: He's funny; he's amusing, certainly, but . . . he meddles in what's not his business. . . . It's disagreeable. . . . Besides, for all his obsequiousness, he is very impudent and persistent. . . . He's a great cynic.

RAKITIN (*Going up to her*): You didn't speak of him like that yesterday. . . .

NATALYA PETROVNA: Perhaps not. (*Eagerly*.) So what was he talking about?

RAKITIN: He talked to me . . . about Bolshintsov.

NATALYA PETROVNA: Oh? About that stupid creature?

RAKITIN: Of him, too, you spoke very differently yesterday.

NATALYA PETROVNA (*With a constrained smile*): Yesterday is not to-day.

Rakitin: True, for others . . . but it seems not for me.

Natalya Petrovna (*Dropping her eyes*): How's that?

Rakitin: For me to-day is the same as yesterday.

Natalya Petrovna (*Holding out her hand to him*): I understand your reproach, but you are mistaken. Yesterday I wouldn't admit that I was behaving badly to you. . . . (Rakitin *attempts to stop her.*) Don't contradict me. . . . I know and you know what I mean . . . but to-day I admit it. I have been thinking things over to-day. . . . But believe me, Michel, whatever silly thoughts take hold of me, whatever I say, whatever I do, there is no one I depend upon as I do on you. (*Dropping her voice.*) There is no one . . . I love as I do you. . . . (*A brief silence.*) You don't believe me?

Rakitin: I believe you . . . but you seem depressed to-day, what's the matter?

Natalya Petrovna (*Goes on speaking without hearing him*): But I am convinced of one thing, Rakitin; one can never answer for oneself, one can never be sure of oneself. We often don't understand our past, how can we expect to answer for the future! There's no putting the future in fetters!

Rakitin: That's true.

Natalya Petrovna (*After a long silence*): Do you know, I want to tell you the truth. Perhaps I shall wound you a little, but I know you will be more hurt by my keeping things from you. I confess, Michel, this young student . . . this Beliayev, has made rather an impression on me. . . .

RAKITIN (*In a low voice*): I know that.

NATALYA PETROVNA: Oh? You have noticed it? For some time?

RAKITIN: Only yesterday.

NATALYA PETROVNA: Ah!

RAKITIN: The day before yesterday, you remember, I spoke of the change in you. . . . I did not know then what to put it down to. But yesterday after our talk . . . and in the meadow . . . if you could have seen yourself! I didn't know you; you were like another woman. You laughed, you skipped and played about like a little girl; your eyes were shining, your cheeks were flushed, and with what confiding interest, with what joyful attention you gazed at him, how you smiled. (*Glancing at her.*) Why, even now your face glows at the memory of it! (*Turns away.*)

NATALYA PETROVNA: No, Rakitin, for God's sake, don't turn away from me. . . . Listen, why exaggerate? This man has infected me with his youth—that's all. I have never been young myself, Michel, from childhood up to now. . . . You know what my life has been. . . . The novelty of it has gone to my head like wine, but I know it will pass as quickly as it has come. . . . It's not worth talking about. . . . (*A pause.*) Only don't turn away from me, don't take your hand away. . . . Help me. . . .

Rakitin (*In a low voice*): Help you—a cruel saying! (*Aloud.*) You don't know what is happening to you, Natalya Petrovna. You are sure it's not worth talking about, and you ask for help. . . . Evidently you feel you are in need of it!

Natalya Petrovna: That is . . . yes. . . . I appeal to you as a friend.

Rakitin (*Bitterly*): Quite so. . . . I hope to justify your confidence . . . but let me have a moment to try and face it.

Natalya Petrovna: Face it? Why, are you dreading . . . anything unpleasant? Is anything changed?

Rakitin (*Bitterly*): Oh no! everything's the same.

Natalya Petrovna: What are you imagining, Michel? Surely you can't suppose. . . .

Rakitin: I suppose nothing.

Natalya Petrovna: Surely you can't have such a contempt for me as . . .

Rakitin: For God's sake, stop. We'd better talk about Bolshintsov. The doctor's expecting an answer from you about Vera, you know.

Natalya Petrovna (*Sadly*): You're angry with me.

Rakitin: Me? Oh no! But I'm sorry for you.

Natalya Petrovna: Really, it's positively annoying, Michel, aren't you ashamed? . . . (Rakitin *is silent. She shrugs her shoulders, and goes on in a tone of vexation*.) You say the doctor is expecting an answer? But who asked him to interfere? . . .

RAKITIN: He assured me that you yourself . . .

NATALYA PETROVNA (*Interrupting*): Perhaps, perhaps. . . . Though I believe I said nothing definite. . . . Besides, I may have changed my mind. And, good gracious, what does it matter? Shpigelsky has a hand in all sorts of affairs; he can't expect to have everything his own way.

RAKITIN: He only wants to know what answer. . .

NATALYA PETROVNA: What answer. . . . (*A pause.*) Michel, don't! Give me your hand. . . . Why this indifferent expression, this cold politeness? . . . What have I done? Think a little, is it my fault? I came to you hoping for good advice, I didn't hesitate for one instant, I never thought of concealing things from you, and you . . . I see I was wrong to be open with you. . . . It would never have entered your head. You suspected nothing, you deceived me. And now, goodness knows what you're imagining.

RAKITIN: Imagining? Not at all.

NATALYA PETROVNA: Give me your hand. . . . (*He does not move; she goes on, somewhat offended.*) You turn away from me? So much the worse for you, then. But I don't blame you. . . . (*Bitterly.*) You are jealous!

RAKITIN: I have no right to be jealous, Natalya Petrovna. . . . How could I be?

Natalya Petrovna (*After a pause*): As you please. About Bolshintsov, I haven't yet spoken to Verotchka.

Rakitin: I can send her to you at once.

Natalya Petrovna: Why at once? . . . But as you please.

Rakitin (*Moving towards the study-door*): So you want me to fetch her?

Natalya Petrovna: Michel, for the last time. . . . You said just now that you were sorry for me. . . . Is this how you show it? Can you really . . .

Rakitin (*Coldly*): Am I to send her?

Natalya Petrovna (*With annoyance*): Yes. (Rakitin *goes into the study.* Natalya Petrovna *stands for some time motionless, sits down, takes a book from the table, opens it, lets it fall on her lap.*) He too! It's awful. He . . . he too! And I relied upon him. And Arkady? Good heavens! I have never even thought of him! (*Drawing herself up.*) I see it's high time to put a stop to all this. . . . (Vera *comes in from the study.*) Yes . . . high time.

Vera (*Timidly*): You sent for me, Natalya Petrovna?

Natalya Petrovna (*Looking round quickly*): Ah! Verotchka! Yes, I wanted you.

Vera (*Going up to her*): Are you unwell?

Natalya Petrovna: Me? Oh no, why?

Vera: I fancied . . .

Natalya Petrovna: No, it's nothing. I'm feeling the heat a little. . . . That's all. Sit down. (Vera *sits down*.) Tell me, Vera, are you doing anything particular just now?

Vera: No.

Natalya Petrovna: I ask you because I want to have a talk with you . . . a serious talk. You see, my dear, I've always looked on you as a child; but you are seventeen; you are a sensible girl. . . . It's time for you to think about your future. You know I love you as a daughter; my house will always be your home. . . but all the same, in other people's eyes, you are an orphan; you have no fortune. You may in time grow tired of always living with strangers; tell me would you like to be mistress in your own house, absolute mistress in it?

Vera (*Slowly*): I don't understand you, Natalya Petrovna.

Natalya Petrovna (*After a pause*): I have received an offer of marriage for you. (Vera *stares at her in amazement*.) You didn't expect that; I must own it seems strange to me too. You are so young. . . . I need not tell you that I do not mean to put pressure on you. . . . In my opinion you're too young to be married; but I thought it my duty to tell you. . . . (Vera *suddenly hides her face in her hands*.) Vera . . . what is it? You're crying? (*Takes her hand*.) You're trembling all over? . . . Surely you're not afraid of me, Vera?

Vera (*In a toneless voice*): I'm in your power, Natalya Petrovna.

NATALYA PETROVNA (*Taking* VERA's *hands from her face*): Vera, aren't you ashamed to cry? Aren't you ashamed to say that you're in my power? What do you take me for? I am speaking to you as I would to a daughter, and you . . . (VERA *kisses her hands*.) What? You are in my power? Then please laugh at once! . . . I tell you to. . . . (VERA *smiles through her tears*.) That's right. (NATALYA PETROVNA *puts one arm round her and draws her closer*.) Vera, my child, treat me as though I were your mother, or no, imagine that I'm an elder sister and let us have a little talk together about all these wonderful things. . . . Will you?

VERA: Oh, yes.

NATALYA PETROVNA: Well, listen then. . . . Come a little nearer. That's right. To begin with, as you're my sister, we suppose there's no need for me to assure you that this is your home; a girl with eyes like yours is at home everywhere. So it ought never to enter your head that you are a burden to anybody in the world or that anybody wants to get rid of you. . . . You hear? But now one fine day your sister comes to you and says: Just think, Vera, you have a suitor. . . . Well? What answer would you make? That you are too young, that you are not thinking of marriage?

VERA: Yes, Natalya Petrovna.

NATALYA PETROVNA: But you wouldn't speak like that to your sister.

VERA (*Smiling*): Oh . . . yes, then.

NATALYA PETROVNA: Your sister agrees with you, the suitor is refused and there's the end of it. But suppose the suitor is a good man, and well-to-do, and if he is willing to wait, if he only asks permission to see you occasionally in the hope of gaining your affections in time?

VERA: Who is this suitor?

NATALYA PETROVNA: Ah! you would like to know? You don't guess?

VERA: No.

NATALYA PETROVNA: You have seen him to-day. (VERA *flushes crimson.*) It is true he is not very handsome, and not very young. . . . Bolshintsov.

VERA: Afanasy Ivanitch?

NATALYA PETROVNA: Yes. . . . Afanasy Ivanitch.

VERA (*Gazes for some time at* NATALYA PETROVNA, *suddenly begins laughing, then stops*): You're not joking?

NATALYA PETROVNA (*Smiling*): No . . . but I see there's no hope for Bolshintsov. If you had cried at his name, he might have hoped, but you laugh; there's nothing for him but to go his way, bless him!

VERA: I'm sorry . . . but really I didn't expect. . . Surely people don't get married at his age?

NATALYA PETROVNA: What an idea! How old is he? He's not fifty. The very age to marry.

VERA: Perhaps . . . but he has such a queer face. . . .

NATALYA PETROVNA: Well, don't let us say any more about him. He's dead and buried . . . bless him! But it's only natural a child of your age cannot care for a man like Bolshintsov. . . . You all want to marry for love, not from prudence, don't you?

VERA: Yes, Natalya Petrovna, and you . . . didn't you marry Arkady Sergeyitch for love too?

NATALYA PETROVNA (*After a pause*): Of course. (*Another pause, squeezing* VERA'S *hands.*) Yes, Vera. . . . I called you a child just now. . . but children are right. (VERA *drops her eyes.*) And so that business is settled. Bolshintsov is dismissed. I must own it wouldn't have been quite pleasant to me to see his puffy old countenance beside your fresh young face, though he is a very good man. Do you see now how little reason you had to be afraid of me? How quickly it's all settled! . . . (*Reproachfully.*) Really, you behaved to me as though I were your patroness! You know how I hate that word. . . .

VERA (*Embracing her*): Forgive me, Natalya Petrovna.

NATALYA PETROVNA: I should hope so. Really? You're not afraid of me?

VERA: No, I love you. I'm not afraid of you.

NATALYA PETROVNA: Thank you. So now we are great friends, and will have no secrets from each other. Well, suppose I were to ask you, Verotchka, whisper in my ear; is it only because Bolshintsov is much older than you, and not a beauty, that you don't want to marry him?

VERA: Surely that's reason enough, Natalya Petravan?

NATALYA PETROVNA: I don't deny it. . . but is there no other reason?

VERA: I don't know him at all.

NATALYA PETROVNA: Quite so; but you don't answer my question.

VERA: There's no other reason.

NATALYA PETROVNA: Really? In that case, I should advise you to think it over. It wouldn't be easy to be in love with Bolshintsov, I know . . . but I say again, he's a good man. Of course, if you cared for anyone else . . . that would be a different matter. But your heart has told you nothing so far, has it?

VERA (*Timidly*): What do you mean?

NATALYA PETROVNA: You love no one else?

VERA: I love you . . . Kolya; I love Anna Semyonovna too.

NATALYA PETROVNA: I'm not speaking of that sort of love; you don't understand me. . . . Among the young men you may have seen here, for instance, or at parties, is there no one who attracts you?

VERA: No. . . . I like some of them, but. . .

NATALYA PETROVNA: I noticed, for instance, that at the Krinitsyns' you danced three times with that tall officer, what's his name?

VERA: An officer?

Natalya Petrovna: Yes, that man with a big moustache.

Vera: Oh! that man! . . . No; I don't like him.

Natalya Petrovna: Well, and Shalansky?

Vera: Shalansky is a nice man, but he. . . I don't think he cares about me.

Natalya Petrovna: Oh! why?

Vera: He . . . I fancy he thinks more of Liza Velsky.

Natalya Petrovna (*Glancing at her*): Ah! . . . you noticed that? (*A pause.*) Well . . . Rakitin?

Vera: I love Mihail Alexandritch very much indeed.

Natalya Petrovna: Yes, like a brother. And, by the way, there's Beliayev?

Vera (*Flushing*): Alexey Nikolaitch? I like Alexey Nikolaitch.

Natalya Petrovna (*Watching her*): Yes, he's a nice fellow. But he's so shy with everybody. . . .

Vera (*Innocently*): No. . . . He's not shy with me.

Natalya Petrovna: Ah!

Vera: He talks to me. Perhaps you fancy that because he . . . he's afraid of you. He has not got to know you yet.

Natalya Petrovna: How do you know he's afraid of me?

Vera: He told me so.

Natalya Petrovna: Oh! he has told you. . . . So he is more unreserved with you than with other people?

Vera: I don't know how he is with other people, but with me . . . perhaps it's because we are both orphans. Besides . . . he looks on me . . . as a child.

Natalya Petrovna: Do you think so? But I like him very much too. He must have a very kind heart.

Vera: Oh! the kindest! If only you knew . . . everyone in the house likes him. He's so friendly. He talks to everybody, he's ready to help anyone. The day before yesterday he carried a poor old beggar-woman in his arms from the high road to the hospital. He gathered a flower for me one day from such a high crag that I shut my eyes in terror, I kept thinking he would fall and be hurt, but he's so clever! You saw yesterday in the meadow how clever he is at that sort of thing.

Natalya Petrovna: Yes, that's true.

Vera: Do you remember the great ditch he jumped over when he was running after the kite? It was nothing to him.

Natalya Petrovna: And did he really pick a flower for you from a dangerous place? He must be fond of you.

Vera (*After a pause*): And he's always good-humoured . . . always in good spirits. . . .

Natalya Petrovna: It's strange, though. Why isn't he like that with me? . . .

Vera (*Interrupting her*): But I tell you he doesn't know you. Wait a little, I'll tell him. . . . I'll tell him there's no need to be afraid of you, shall I? That you're so kind. . . .

NATALYA PETROVNA (*With a constrained laugh*): Thanks so much.

VERA: You'll see. . . . He does what I tell him though I am younger than he is.

NATALYA PETROVNA: I didn't know you were such friends. . . . But mind, Vera, be careful. Of course, he's an excellent young man. . . but you know, at your age. . . . It's not suitable, people may imagine things. . . . I mentioned that, you remember?. . . in the garden yesterday. (VERA *looks down.*) On the other hand, I don't want to check your inclinations either. I have too much confidence in you and in him. . . but still . . . you mustn't be angry with me for my scruples, my dear . . . it's the duty of us old folks to worry young people with our lectures. Though I really need not say all this, you simply like him, don't you—and nothing more?

VERA (*Timidly raising her eyes*): He. . . .

NATALYA PETROVNA: Now there you are looking at me like that again! Is that the way to look at a sister? Vera, listen, and lean down to me. . . . (*Caressing her.*) What if a sister, a real sister whispered now in your ear: 'Verotchka, is it true, you don't love anyone, do you?' What would you answer? (VERA *looks uncertainly at* NATALYA PETROVNA.) Those eyes want to tell me something. . . . (VERA *suddenly presses her face to* NATALYA PETROVNA'S *bosom.* NATALYA PETROVNA *turns pale—and after a pause goes on.*) You do love him? Tell me, do you?

VERA (*Not raising her head*): Oh! I don't know what I feel. . . .

NATALYA PETROVNA: Poor child! You're in love. . . . (VERA *huddles still more closely to* NATALYA PETROVNA.) You're in love . . . and he? Vera, he?

VERA (*Still not raising her head*): Why do you ask me questions? . . . I don't know. . . . Perhaps . . . I don't know, I don't know. . . . (NATALYA PETROVNA *shudders and sits motionless.* VERA *lifts her head and at once notices the change in her face.*) Nnatalya Petrovna, what's the matter?

NATALYA PETROVNA (*Recovering herself*): The matter. . . nothing. Why? Nothing.

VERA: You're so pale, Natalya Petrovna. . . . What's wrong? Let me ring. . . . (*Gets up.*)

NATALYA PETROVNA: No, no . . . don't ring. It's nothing. . . . It will pass. There, it's over now.

VERA: Let me fetch somebody, anyway.

NATALYA PETROVNA: No, don't, I. . . I want to be alone. Leave me alone, do you hear? We will finish our talk later. Run along.

VERA: You are not angry with me, Natalya Petrovna?

NATALYA PETROVNA: Angry? What for? Not at all. No, I'm grateful to you for your confidence. . . . Only leave me, please, just now.

> [VERA *is about to take her hand, but* NATALYA PETROVNA *turns away as though not noticing her movement.*]

VERA (*With tears in her eyes*): Natalya Petrovna. . . .

NATALYA PETROVNA: I ask you to leave me alone. (VERA *slowly goes out of the study*.)

NATALYA PETROVNA (*Alone, remains for some time motionless*): Now it's all clear to me. . . . These children love each other. . . . (*Stops and passes her hand over her face*.) Well? So much the better. . . . God give them happiness! (*Laughing*.) And I . . . I could imagine. . . . (*Stops again*.) She was not long blurting it out. . . . I must own I did not suspect it, I must own the news has startled me. . . . But wait a bit, it's not all settled yet. My God. . . what am I saying? What's wrong with me? I don't know myself. What am I coming to? (*A pause*.) What am I about? Trying to marry the poor girl to an old man! . . . I used the doctor as a go-between. . . he suspects, he drops hints. . . Arkady Rakitin. . . while I. . . (*Shudders and suddenly raises her head*.) But what does this mean? Me jealous of Vera! Me in love with him! (*A pause*.) And you still doubt it, do you? You're in love to your misery! How it has come about. . . I don't know. It's as though I'd been poisoned. . . . All at once everything's destroyed, scattered, swept away. . . . He's afraid of me. They're all afraid of me! What could he see in me?. . . What use is a creature like me to him? He is young and she is young. While I! (*Bitterly*.) How could he think much of me? They are both foolish, as Rakitin says. . . . Oh! I hate that clever friend! And Arkady, my good trusting Arkady! My God! my God! It's killing me! (*Gets up.*) But I believe I'm going out of my mind! Why exaggerate? Yes . . . of course . . . I'm overwhelmed. . . . It's so strange to me . . . it's the first time. . . I. . . yes, the first time! I'm in love for the first time now! (*She sits down again.*) He must go away. Yes. And Rakitin too. It's time to come to my senses. I've allowed myself to take one step. . . and see! See what I've come to! And what is it in him attracts me? (*Ponders.*) So this is it, this dreadful feeling. . . . Arkady! Yes, I will fall into his arms, I will beg him to forgive me, to protect me, to save me. . . . He. . . and no one else! All the others are strangers to me and must remain strangers. . . . But can there be. . . can there be no other way out? That girl—she's a child. She may be mistaken. That's all childishness really. . . . Why should I. . . . I will talk to him myself, I will ask him. . . . (*Reproachfully.*) What? What? You are hoping? You still want to hope? And what am I hoping for? My God! don't make me despise myself! (*Drops her head on her arms.* RAKITIN *comes in from the study, pale and agitated.*)

RAKITIN (*Going up to* NATALYA PETROVNA): Natalya Petrovna. . . . (*She does not stir.*) (*To himself.*) What can have happened with Vera? (*Aloud.*) Natalya Petrovna. . . .

NATALYA PETROVNA (*Raising her head*): Who is it? Ah! you.

Rakitin: Vera Alexandrovna told me you were unwell. . . . I. . .

Natalya Petrovna (*Turning away*): I am quite well. . . . What made her?. . .

Rakitin: No, Natlya Petrovna, you are not well, you should see yourself.

Natalya Petrovna: Well, perhaps not . . . but what's that to you? What do you want? What have you come for?

Rakitin (*In a voice of deep feeling*): I'll tell you what I have come for. I have come to ask your forgiveness. Half an hour ago I was unspeakably stupid and rude. . . . Forgive me. . . . You see, Natalya Petrovna, however modest a man's desires and. . . and hopes, it is hard, for a moment anyway, for him to keep his head, when they are suddenly snatched away from him; but I have come to my senses. I understand my position and my fault, and I want only one thing. . . your forgiveness. (*He gently sits down beside her.*) Look at me . . . don't you too turn away from me. Beside you is your old Rakitin, your friend, a man who asks nothing but to be allowed to serve you, as you said . . . to help you. . . . Don't deprive me of your confidence, rely on me and forget that I ever. . . . Forget everything that may have wounded you. . . .

Natalya Petrovna (*Who has been all the while staring fixedly at the floor*): Yes, yes. . . . (*Stopping.*) Oh! I'm sorry, Rakitin, I haven't heard a word of what you've been saying.

Rakitin (*Mournfully*): I said . . . I begged you to forgive me, Natalya Petrovna, I asked you whether you would let me be your friend still.

Natalya Petrovna (*Slowly turning to him and laying her hands on his shoulders*): Rakitin, tell me, what's the matter with me?

Rakitin (*After a pause*): You're in love.

Natalya Petrovna (*Slowly repeating it after him*): I'm in love. . . . But it's madness, Rakitin, it's impossible. Can such things happen all of a sudden. . . . You say I'm in love. . . . (*Breaks off.*)

Rakitin: Yes, you're in love, poor dear woman. . . . Don't deceive yourself.

Natalya Petrovna (*Not looking at him*): What am I to do?

Rakitin: I can tell you, Natalya Petrovna, if you promise. . .

Natalya Petrovna (*Interrupting, still without looking at him*): You know that girl, Vera, loves him. . . . They are in love with each other. . . .

Rakitin: If so, a reason the more. . .

Natalya Petrovna (*Interrupting again*): I've long suspected it, but she acknowledged it herself. . . just now.

Rakitin (*In a low voice, as though to himself*): Poor woman!

Natalya Petrovna (*Passing her hand over her face*): Come.. . . I must pull myself together. I believe you were going to say something. . . . For God's sake, Rakitin, advise me what to do. . . .

Rakitin: I'm willing to advise you, Natalya Petrovna, only on one condition.

Natalya Petrovna: Tell me.

Rakitin: Promise that you won't suspect my motives. Tell me that you believe in my disinterested desire to help you; do you help me too. Let your confidence give me strength, or else let me keep silence.

Natalya Petrovna: Speak, speak.

Rakitin: You have no doubt of me?

Natalya Petrovna: Speak!

Rakitin: Well then, listen, he must go away. (Natalya Petrovna *looks at him in silence.*) Yes, he must go. I'm not going to speak to you of. . . your husband, your duty. On my lips, such words are. . . out of place. . . . But those children love each other. You told me so yourself just now, imagine yourself now between them. . . . Why, your position will be awful!

Natalya Petrovna: He must go. . . . (*A pause.*) And you? You remain?

Rakitin (*Confused*): I?. . . I?. . . (*A pause.*) I must go too. For the sake of your peace, your happiness, Verotchka's happiness, both he. . . and I. . . we must both go away for ever.

Natalya Petrovna: Rakitin. . . I have sunk so low that I. . . was almost ready to sacrifice that poor girl, an orphan entrusted to me by my mother, to marry her to a stupid, absurd old man! I couldn't bring myself to it, Rakitin, the words died away on my lips when she burst out laughing at the suggestion

. . . but I have been plotting with the doctor; I have put up with his meaning smiles, I have borne with his grins, his compliments, his hints. . . . Oh, I feel I am on the brink of a precipice; save me!

RAKITIN: Natalya Petrovna, you see that I am right. . . . (*She is silent; he goes on hurriedly.*) He ought to go . . . we ought both to go. . . . There is no other way to save you.

NATALYA PETROVNA (*Dejectedly*): But what to live for afterwards?

RAKITIN: Good God, is it as bad as that? . . . Natalya Petrovna, you will get over it, believe me. . . . This will pass. What, nothing to live for!

NATALYA PETROVNA: Yes, yes, what have I to live for when all abandon me?

RAKITIN: But. . . . your family. . . . (NATALYA PETROVNA *looks down*.) If you like, after he is gone, I might stay a few days just to. . .

NATALYA PETROVNA (*Gloomily*): Ah! I understand. You are reckoning on habit, on our old friendship. . . . You hope I shall come to myself, and turn to you again, don't you? I understand you.

RAKITIN (*Flushing*): Natalya Petrovna! Why do you insult me?

NATALYA PETROVNA (*Bitterly*): I understand you. . . but you are mistaken.

RAKITIN: What? After your promise, when simply for your sake, your sake only, for your happiness, for your position in society, in fact...

NATALYA PETROVNA: Oh! how long have you been concerned about that? Why is it you have never spoken of it before?

RAKITIN (*Getting up*): Natalya Petrovna, I will leave this place to-day, at once, and you shall never see me again.... (*Is going.*)

NATALYA PETROVNA (*Stretching out her hands to him*): Michel, forgive me; I don't know what I'm saying.... You see the state I'm in. Forgive me.

RAKITIN (*Turning rapidly to her and taking her by the hands*): Natalya Petrovan...

NATALYA PETROVNA: Oh, Michel, I'm unutterably miserable.... (*Leans on his shoulder and presses her handkerchief to her eyes.*) Help me, I am lost without you. (*At that instant the door of the outer room is flung open, and* ISLAYEV *and* ANNA SEMYONOVNA *walk in.*)

ISLAYEV (*Loudly*): I was always of that opinion. (*Stops in amazement at the sight of* RAKITIN *and* NATALYA PETROVNA. NATALYA PETROVNA *looks round and goes out quickly.* Rakitin *remains where he is, overwhelmed with confusion.*)

Islayev (*To* RAKITIN): What's the meaning of this? What's this scene?

RAKITIN: Oh... nothing... it's..

ISLAYEV: Is Natalya Petrovan unwell?

RAKITIN: No... but...

ISLAYEV: And why has she run away so suddenly? What were you talking about?

She seemed to be crying. . . . You were consoling her. . . . What's the matter?

RAKITIN: Nothing really.

ANNA SEMYONOVNA: How can there be nothing the matter, Mihail Alexandritch? (*After a pause.*) I'll go and see. . . . (*Is about to go into the study.*)

RAKITIN (*Stopping her*): No, you had better leave her in peace, please.

ISLAYEV: But what does it all mean? Tell us.

RAKITIN: Nothing, I assure you. . . . I promise to explain it to you both to-day. I give you my word. But now, please, if you have any trust in me, don't ask me. . . and don't worry Natalya Petrovna.

ISLAYEV: Very well. . . but it is strange. This sort of thing has never happened with Natasha before. It's something quite out of the way.

ANNA SEMYONOVNA: What I want to know is what could make Natasha cry? And why has she gone away?. . . Are we strangers?

RAKITIN: Of course not. What an idea! But as a matter of fact, we had not finished our conversation. . . . I must ask you. . . both —to leave us alone for a little while.

ISLAYEV: Indeed? There's some secret between you, then?

RAKITIN: Yes. . . but you shall know it.

ISLAYEV (*After a moment's thought*): Come along, Mamma. . . . Let us leave them. Let them finish their mysterious conversation.

ANNA SEMYONOVNA: But . . .

ISLAYEV: Come, let us go. You hear he promises to explain.

RAKITIN: You needn't worry. . . .

ISLAYEV (*Coldly*): I'm not worrying. (*To* ANNA SEMYNOVNA.) Let us go. (*They go out.*)

RAKITIN (*Looks after them and goes quickly to the study door*): Natalya Petrovna, Natalya Petrovna, please come back.

NATALYA PETROVNA (*Comes out of the study. She is very pale*): What did they say?

RAKITIN: Nothing, don't worry yourself. . . . They were rather surprised, certainly. Arkady thought you were ill. . . . He noticed how upset you were. . . . Sit down, you can hardly stand. . . . (NATALYA PETROVNA *sits down*.) I said. . . I begged him not to worry you. . . to leave us alone.

NATALYA PETROVNA: And he agreed?

RAKITIN: Yes. I had, I must say, to promise I'd explain it all to-morrow. Why did you go away?

NATALYA PETROVNA (*Bitterly*): Why indeed! What are you going to say?

RAKITIN: I'll. . . I'll think of something to say. But that's no matter just now. We must take advantage of this reprieve. You see that this can't go on. . . . These violent emotions are too much for you. . . . They are unworthy of you. . . . I myself . . . But that's not the point. Only be firm and I'll manage. You agreed with me, you know.

NATALYA PETROVNA: About what?

Rakitin: The necessity of . . . our going. You do agree? If that's so, it's no good to delay. If you'll let me, I'll talk to Beliayev at once. . . . He's a decent fellow, he'll understand.

Natalya Petrovna: You want to talk to him? You? But what can you say to him?

Rakitin (*In embarrassment*): I'll . . .

Natalya Petrovna (*After a brief pause*): Rakitin, listen, don't you think that we're both behaving like lunatics? . . . I was in a panic, I frightened you, and perhaps it's all about nothing that matters.

Rakitin: What?

Natalya Petrovna: Really? What's the matter with us? It seems only a little while ago everything was so quiet and peaceful in this house. . . and all at once . . . goodness knows how! Really we've all gone out of our minds. Come, it's time to stop, we've been silly enough. . . . Let us go on as before. . . . And there'll be no need to explain anything to Arkady; I'll tell him about our antics myself and we'll laugh over them together. I need no one to intercede between my husband and me!

Rakitin: Natalya Petrovna, you are frightening me now. You are smiling and you're as pale as death. . . . Do remember what you said to me only a quarter of an hour ago. . . .

Natalya Petrovna: I dare say! But I see what it is. . . . You're raising this storm . . . that you may not sink alone.

Rakitin: Again, again suspicion, again reproaches, Natalya Petrovna. . . . God forgive you . . . but you torture me. Or do you regret having spoken so freely?

Natalya Petrovna: I regret nothing.

Rakitin: Then how am I to understand you?

Natalya Patalya *(Eagerly)*: Rakitin, if you say a single word from me or about me to Beliayev, I will never forgive you.

Rakitin: Oh! so that's it! . . . Don't worry, Natalya Petrovna. So far from telling Mr. Beliayev anything, I won't even say good-bye to him, when I take my departure. I don't mean to pester you with my services.

Natalya Petrovna (*With some embarrassment*): You imagine perhaps that I have changed my mind about . . . his going?

Rakitin: I imagine nothing.

Natalya Petrovna: That's not so. I'm so convinced of the necessity, as you say, of his leaving that I mean to dismiss him myself (*A pause.*) Yes, I will dismiss him myself.

Rakitin: You?

Natalya Petrovna: Yes. And at once. I beg you to send him to me.

Rakitin: What? This minute?

Natalya Patalya: This very minute. I ask you to do so, Rakitin. You see I am composed now. Besides, I shan't be interrupted just now. I must seize the opportunity. . . . I shall be very much obliged to you. I'll question him.

Rakitin: But he won't tell you anything. I can assure you. He admitted to me that he felt awkward with you.

Natalya Petrovna (*Suspiciously*): Ah! You've been talking to him about me. (Rakitin *shrugs his shoulders*.) Oh, forgive me, forgive me, Michel, and send him to me. You'll see, I will dismiss him and all will be over. It will all pass and be forgotten, like a bad dream. Please fetch him. I absolutely must have a final conversation with him. You will be pleased with me. Pray do.

Rakitin (*Who has not taken his eyes off her all this time, coldly and mournfully*): Certainly. Your wishes shall be obeyed. (*Goes towards door of outer room.*)

Natalya Petrovna (*After him*): Thank you, Michel.

Rakitin (*Turning*): Oh, spare me your thanks, at least. . . . (*Goes out quickly.*)

Natalya Petrovna (*Alone, after a pause*): He's a good man. . . . But is it possible I ever loved him? (*Stands up.*) *He* is right. He must go. But how can I dismiss him? I only want to know whether he really cares for that girl. Perhaps it's all nonsense. . . . How could I be worked up into such a state? What was the object of all that outburst? Well, it can't be helped now. I want to know what he is going to say. But he must go. . . . He must . . . he must. . . . He may not be willing to answer. . . . He's afraid of me, of course. . . . Well? So much the better. There's no need for me to say much to him.

. . . (*Lays her hand on her forehead*.) My head aches. Shall I put it off till to-morrow? Yes. I keep fancying they are all watching me to-day. . . . What am I coming to! No, better make an end of it at once. . . . Just one last effort and I am free. . . . Oh yes! I yearn for freedom and peace.

[BELIAYEV *comes in from the outer room.*]
Here he is. . . .

BELIAYEV (*Going up to her*): Natalya Petrovna, Mihail Alexandritch tells me you want to see me.

NATALYA PETROVNA (*With some effort*): Yes, certainly . . . I have to . . . speak to you. . . .

BELIAYEV: Speak to me?

NATALYA PETROVNA (*Without looking at him*): Yes . . . speak to you. (*A pause.*) I must tell you, Alexey Nikolaitch, I'm . . . I'm displeased with you.

BELIAYEV: May I ask on what ground?

NATALYA PETROVNA: Listen . . . . I . . . I really don't know how to begin. However, I must tell you first that my dissatisfaction is not due to any remissness in your work. On the contrary, I am pleased with your methods with Kolya.

BELIAYEV: Then what can it be?

NATALYA PETROVNA (*Glancing at him*): You need not be alarmed. . . . Your fault is not so serious. You are young, you have probably never before stayed with strangers, you could not foresee . . .

BELIAYEV: But, Natalya Petrovna . . . .

Natalya Petrovna: You want to know what is wrong? I understand your impatience. So I must tell you that Verotchka . . . (*Glancing at him*) Verotchka has confessed everything.

Beliayev (*In amazement*): Vera Alexandrovna? What can Vera Alexandrovna have confessed? And what have I to do with it?

Natalya Petrovna: So you really don't know what she can have confessed? You can't guess?

Beliayev: I? No, I can't.

Natalya Petrovna: If so, I beg your pardon. If you really can't guess, I must apologize. I supposed . . . I was mistaken. But allow me to say, I don't believe you. I understand what makes you say so. . . . I respect your discretion.

Beliayev: I haven't the least idea what you mean, Natalya Petrovna.

Natalya Petrovna: Really? Do you expect to persuade me that you haven't noticed that child's feeling for you?

Beliayev: Vera Alexandrovna's feeling for me? I really don't know what to say to that. . . . Good gracious! I believe I have always behaved with Vera Alexandrovna as a——

Natalya Petrovna: As with everybody else, haven't you? (*After a brief silence.*) However that may be, whether you are really unaware of it, or are pretending to be, the fact is the girl loves you. She admitted it to meherself. Well, now I am asking you, what do you mean to do?

BELIAEV (*With embarrassment*): What do I mean to do?

NATALYA PETROVNA (*Folding her arms*): Yes.

BELIAYEV: All this is so unexpected, Natalya Petrovna. . . .

NATALYA PETROVNA (*After a pause*): Alexey Nikolaitch, I see . . . I have not put the matter properly. You don't understand me. You think I'm angry with you . . . but I'm. . . . only . . . a little upset. And that's very natural. Calm yourself. Let us sit down. (*They sit down.*) I will be frank with you. Alexey Nikolaitch, and you too be a little less reserved with me. You have really no need to be on your guard with me. Vera loves you. . . . Of course, that's not your fault, I am willing to assume that you are in no way responsible for it. . . . But you see, Alexey Nikolaitch, she is an orphan, she is my ward. I am responsible for her, for her future, for her happiness. She is very young, and I feel sure that the feeling you have inspired in her may soon pass off. . . . At her age, love does not last long. But you understand, it was my duty to warn you. It's always dangerous to play with fire. . . and I do not doubt that, knowing her feeling for you, you will adopt a different behaviour with her, will avoid seeing her alone, walking in the garden. . . . Won't you? I can rely on you. With another man I should be afraid to speak so plainly.

Beliayev: Natalya Petrovna, I assure you I appreciate....

Natalya Petrovna: I tell you that I do not distrust.... Besides, all this will remain a secret between us.

Beliayev: I must own, Natalya Petrovna, all you have told me seems to me so strange... of course, I can't venture to disbelieve you, but...

Natalya Petrovna: Listen, Alexey Nikolaitch. All I said to you just now... I said it on the supposition that on your side there is nothing... (*Breaks off*) because if that's not so... of course I don't know you well, but I do know you well enough to see no reason to make serious objections. You have no fortune... but you are young, you have your future before you, and when two people love each other... I tell you again, I thought it my duty to warn you, as a man of honour, of the consequences of your friendship with Vera, but if you...

Beliayev (*In perplexity*): I really don't know what you mean, Natalya Petrovna.

Natalya Petrovna (*Hurriedly*): Oh! believe me, I'm not trying to wring out a confession, there's no need.... I shall see from your manner how it is.... (*Glancing at him.*) But I ought to tell you that Vera fancied that you were not quite indifferent to her.

Beliayev (*After a brief silence, stands up*): Natalya Petrovna, I see that I can't go on living in your house.

NATALYA PETROVNA (*Firing up*): You might have waited for me to decide that. . . . (*Stands up.*)

BELIAYEV: You have been frank with me. Let me be frank with you. I don't love Vera Alexandrovna, at least, I don't love her in the way you suppose.

NATALYA PETROVNA: But I didn't. . . . (*Stops short.*)

BELIAYEV: And if Vera Alexandrovna cares for me, if she fancied, as you say, that I care for her, I don't want to deceive her; I will tell her the whole truth myself. But after such plain speaking, you must see, Natlya Petrovna, that it would be difficult for me to stay here, my position would be too awkward. I can't tell you how sorry I. shall be to leave . . . but there's nothing else for me to do. I shall always think of you with gratitude. . . . May I go now? . . . I shall come to say good-bye properly later on.

NATALYA PETROVNA (*With affected indifference*): As you please . . . but I own I did not expect this. That was not my object in wishing to speak to you. . . . I only wanted to warn you . . . Vera is still a child . . . I have perhaps taken it all too seriously. I don't see the necessity of your leaving us. However, as you please.

BELIAYEV: Natalya Petrovna . . . it's really impossible for me to go on staying here.

NATALYA PETROVNA: I see you are very ready to leave us!

BELIAYEV: No, Natalya Petrovna, I'm not.

Natalya Petrovna: I'm not in the habit of keeping people against their will, but I must own I don't like it at all.

Beliayev (*After some indecision*): Natalya Petrovna, I shouldn't like to cause you the slightest annoyance. . . . I'll stay.

Natalya Petrovna (*Suspiciously*): Ah! (*After a pause.*) I didn't expect you would change your mind so quickly. . . . I am grateful, but . . . Let me think it over. Perhaps you are right, perhaps you ought to go. I'll think it over. I'll let you know. . . . May I leave you in uncertainty till this evening?

Beliayev: I am willing to wait as long as you like. (*Bows and is about to go.*)

Natalya Petrovna: You promise me. . . .

Beliayev (*Stopping*): What?

Natalya Petrovna: I believe you meant to speak to Vera. . . . I'm not sure that it's the right thing. But I'll let you know what I decide. I begin to think that you really ought to go away. Good-bye for now. (Beliayev *bows again and goes off into the outer room.* Natalya Petrovna *looks after him.*) My mind's at rest! He does not love her. . . . (*Walks up and down the room.*) And so instead of sending him away, I've myself prevented his going. . . . He'll stay. . . . But what shall I say to Rakitin? What have I done? (*A pause.*) And what right had I to publish abroad the poor girl's love? I trapped her into confessing it . . . a half-confession, and then I go . . . so ruthlessly, so brutally. . . . (*Hides her face in her hands.*) Perhaps he was beginning to care for her. . . . What right had I to trample on that flower in the bud? . . . But have I trampled on it? He may have deceived me. . . . I tried to deceive him! Oh! no! He's too good for that. . . . He's not like me! And why was I in such haste? Blurting it all out at once? (*Sighing.*) I needn't have done it! If I could have foreseen. . . . How sly I was, how I lied to him! And he! How boldly and independently he spoke! . . . I felt humbled by him. . . . He is a man! I didn't know him before. . . . He must go away. If he stays . . . I feel that I shall end by losing all self-respect. . . . He must go, or I am lost! I will write to him before he has had time to see Vera. . . . He must go! (*Goes quickly into the study.*)

ACT IV

[*A large unfurnished outer room. The walls are bare, the stone floor is uneven; the ceiling is supported by six brick columns, three each side, covered with whitewash which is peeling off. On Left two open windows and a door into the garden. On Right a door into the corridor leading to the main building; in Centre an iron door opening into the store-room. Near first column on Right a green garden seat; in a corner spades, watering-cans and flower-pots. Evening. The red rays of the sun fall through the windows on the floor.*]

KATYA (*Comes in from door on Right, goes briskly to the window and stands for some time looking into the garden*): No, he's not to be seen. They told me he'd gone into the conservatory. I suppose he hasn't come out yet. Well, I'll wait till he comes by. There's no other way he can go. . . . (*Sighs and leans against the window.*) They say he's going away. (*Sighs again.*) However shall we get on without him. . . . Poor young lady! How she did beseech me. . . . And why shouldn't I oblige her? Let him have a last talk with her. How warm it is to-day. And I do believe it's beginning to spot with rain. . . . (*Again glances out of window and at once draws back.*) Surely they're not coming in here? They are. My gracious. . . . (*Tries to run off, but has not time to reach the door before* SHPIGELSKY *and* LIZAVETA BOGDANOVNA *come in from the garden.* KATYA *hides behind a column.*)

SHPIGELSKY (*Shaking his hat*): We can shelter here from the rain. . . . It will soon be over.

LIZAVETA BOGDANOVNA: If you like.

SHPIGELSKY (*looking round*): What is this building? A storehouse or what?

LIZAVETA BOGDANOVNA (*Pointing to the iron door*): No, the storeroom's there. This room, I'm told, Arkady Sergeyitch's father built when he came back from abroad.

SHPIGELSKY: Oh, I see the idea, Venice, if you please. (*Sits down on the seat.*) Let's sit down. (LIZAVETA BOGDANOVNA *sits down.*) You must confess, Lizaveta Bogdanovna, the rain has come in an unlucky moment. It has interrupted our talk at the most touching point.

LIZAVETA BOGDANOVNA (*Casting down her eyes*): Ignaty Ilyitch. . . .

SHPIGELSKY: But there's nobody to hinder our beginning again. . . . You say, by the way, that Anna Semyonovna is out of humour to-day?

LIZAVETA BOGDANOVNA: Yes, she's put out. She actually did not come down to dinner, but had it in her room.

Shpigelsky: You don't say so! What a calamity, upon my word!

Lizaveta Bogdanovna: She came upon Natalya Petrovna in tears this morning . . . with Mihail Alexandritch. . . . Of course he's almost like one of the family, but still. . . . However, Mihail Alexandritch has promised to explain it.

Shpigelsky: Ah! well, she need not worry herself. Mihail Alexandritch has never, to my thinking, been a dangerous person, and now he's less so than ever.

Lizaveta Bogdanovna: Why?

Shpigelsky: Oh, he talks a bit too cleverly. Where other people would come out in a rash, they work it all off in talk. Don't be afraid of chatterers in future, Lizaveta Bogdanovna; they're not dangerous; it's these silent men, slow in the uptake, with no end of temperament and thick necks, who are dangerous.

Lizaveta Bogdanovna (*After a pause*): Tell me is Natalya Petrovna really ill?

Shpigelsky: She's no more ill than you or I.

Lizaveta Bogdanovna: She ate nothing at dinner.

Shpigelsky: Illness isn't the only thing that spoils the appetite.

Lizaveta Bogdanovna: Did you dine at Bolshintsov's?

Shpigelsky: Yes. . . . I went to see him. And it's only on your account I came back here, upon my soul.

LIZAVETA BOGDANOVNA: Oh, nonsense. And do you know, Ignaty Ilyitch, Natalya Petrovana is cross with you. . . . She said something not very complimentary about you at dinner.

SHPIGELSKY: Really? Ladies don't like us poor fellows to have sharp eyes, it seems. You must do what they want, you must help them, and you must pretend not to know what they're up to. A pretty set! But we shall see. And Rakitin, I dare say, looked rather in the dumps, too?

LIZAVETA BOGDANOVNA: Yes, he, too, seemed, as it were, out of sorts. . . .

SHPIGELSKY: Hm. And Vera Alexandrovna? And Beliayev?

LIZAVETA BOGDANOVNA: Everyone, absolutely everyone seemed depressed. I really can't imagine what's the matter with them all to-day.

SHPIGELSKY: If you know too much, you'll grow old before your time, Lizaveta Bogdanovna. . . . But never mind them. We had better talk about our affairs. The rain hasn't left off. . . . Shall we?

LIZAVETA BOGDANOVNA (*Casting down her eyes primly*): What are you asking me, Ignaty Ilyitch?

SHPIGELSKY: Oh, Lizaveta Bogdanovna, if you'll allow me to say so, there's no need to put on airs, and to drop your eyes like that! We're not young people, you know! These performances, these sighs and soft nothings— they don't suit us. Let us talk calmly, practically, as is proper for people of our years. And so—this is the question: we like each other . . . at least, I presume that you like me.

Lizaveta Bogdanovna (*A little affectedly*): Ignaty Ilyitch, really. . . .

Shpigelsky: Oh, all right, very well. After all, perhaps, airs and graces are . . . only proper in a lady. So then, we like each other. And in other respects too we are well matched. Of course, I am bound to say about myself that I am not a man of good family: well, you're not of illustrious birth either. I'm not a rich man; if I were, I shouldn't be where I am—— (*Laughs.*) But I've a decent practice, not all my patients die; you have, as you say, fifteen thousand roubles of your own, all that's not at all bad, you see. At the same time, you're tired, I imagine, of living for ever as a governess, and then fussing round an old lady, backing her up at preference, and falling in with her whims isn't much fun, I should say. On my side, it's not so much that I'm weary of bachelor-life, but I'm growing old, and then, my cooks rob me; so you see, it all fits in nicely. But here's the difficulty, Lizaveta Bogdanovna; we don't know each other at all, that is, to be exact, you don't know me . . . I know you well enough. I understand your character. I don't say you have no faults. Being a spinster, you're a little old-maidish, but that's no harm. In the hands of a good husband, a wife is soft as wax. But I should like you to know me before marriage; or else you'll, maybe, blame me afterwards. . . . I don't want to deceive you.

Lizaveta Bogdanovna (*With dignity*): But, Ignaty Ilyitch, I believe I too have had opportunities of discovering your character.

Shpigelsky: You? Oh! nonsense. . . . That's not a woman's job. Why, I dare say you imagine I'm a man of cheerful disposition, an amusing fellow, don't you?

Lizaveta Bogdanovna: I have always thought you a very amiable man. . . .

Shpigelsky: There you are. You see how easily one may be mistaken. Because I play the fool before outsiders, tell them anecdotes and humour them, you imagine that I'm really a light-hearted man. If I didn't need these people, I shouldn't even look at them. . . . As it is, whenever I can, without much danger, you know, I turn them into ridicule. . . . I don't deceive myself, though: I'm well aware that certain gentry, who can't take a step without me and are bored when I'm not there, consider themselves entitled to look down on me; but I pay them out, you may be sure. Natalya Petrovna, for instance. . . . Do you suppose I don't see through her? (*Mimics* Natalya Petrovna.) 'Dear Doctor, I really like you so much . . . you have such a wicked tongue,' ha, ha, coo away, my dove, coo away. Ugh! these ladies! And they smile and make eyes at you, while disdain is written on their faces. . . . They despise us, do what you will! I quite understand why she is saying harsh things of me to-day. Upon my soul, these ladies are wonderful people! Because they sprinkle themselves with eau-de-Cologne every day and speak so carelessly—as though they were just dropping their words for you to pick them up—they fancy there's no catching them by the tail. Oh, isn't there, though! They're just mortals the same as all of us poor sinners!

LIZAVETA BOGDANOVNA: Ignaty Ilyitch . . . you surprise me.

SHPIGELSKY: I knew I should surprise you. So you see I'm not a light-hearted man at all, and not too good-natured even. . . . But at the same time, I don't want to make myself out what I never have been. Though I may put it on a bit before the gentry, no one's ever seen me play the fool in a low way, no one's ever dared to take insulting liberties with me. Indeed, I think they're a bit afraid of me; in fact, they know I bite. On one occasion, three years ago, a gentleman—a regular son of the soil—by way of fun at the dinner-table, stuck a radish in my hair. What do you think I did? Why, on the spot, without any show of anger, you know, in the most courteous manner, I challenged him to a duel. The son of the soil almost had a stroke, he was so terrified; our host made him apologize—it made a great sensation. As a matter of fact, I knew beforehand that he wouldn't fight. So you see, Lizaveta Bogdanovna, my vanity's immense; but my life's not been much. My talents are not great either. . . . I got through my studies somehow. I'm not much good as a doctor, it's no use my pretending to you, and if you're ever taken ill, I shan't prescribe for you myself. If I'd had talent and a good education, I should have bolted to the capital. For the aborigines here, no better doctor is wanted, to be sure. As regards my personal character, Lizaveta Bogdanovna, I ought to warn you: at home I'm ill-humoured, silent and exacting, I'm not cross as long as everything's done for me to my satisfaction; I like to be well fed and to have my habits respected; however, I'm not jealous and I'm not mean, and in my absence, you can do just as you like. Of romantic love and all that between us, you understand it's needless to speak; and yet I imagine one might live under the same roof with me . . . so long as you try to please me, and don't shed tears in my presence, that I can't endure! But I'm not given to fault-finding. There, you have my confession. Well, what do you say now?

Lizaveta Bogdanovna: What am I to say to you, Ignaty Ilyitch? . . . If you have not been blackening your character on purpose to . . .

Shpigelsky: But how have I blackened my character? Don't forget that another man in my place would, with perfect complacency, have kept quiet about his faults, as you've not noticed them, and after the wedding, it's all up then, it's too late. But I'm too proud to do that. (Lizaveta Bogdanovna *glances at him.*) Yes, yes, too proud . . . you needn't look at me like that. I don't mean to pose and lie before my future wife, not if it were for a hundred thousand instead of fifteen thousand, though to a stranger I'm ready to humble myself for a sack of flour. I'm like that. . . . I'll smirk to a stranger while inwardly I'm thinking, you're a blockhead, my friend, you'll be caught by my bait; but with you, I say what I think. That is, let me explain; I don't say everything I think, even to you; but at any rate, I'm not deceiving you. I must strike you as a very queer fish certainly, but there, wait a bit, one day I'll tell you the story of my life and you'll wonder that I've come through as well as I have. You weren't born with a silver spoon in your mouth, I expect, either, but yet, my dear, you can't conceive what real hopeless poverty is like. . . . I'll tell you all about that, though, some other time. But now you had better think over the proposition I have had the honour of laying before you. . . . Consider this little matter well, in solitude, and let me know your decision. So far as I can judge, you're a sensible woman. And by the way, how old are you?

LIZAVETA BOGDANOVNA: I . . . I . . . I'm thirty.

SHPIGELSKY (*Calmly*): And that's not true, you're quite forty.

LIZAVETA BOGDANOVNA (*Firing up*): I'm *not* forty, only thirty-six.

SHPIGELSKY: That's not thirty, anyway. Well, Lizaveta Bogdanovna, that's a habit you must get out of . . . especially as thirty-six isn't old for a married woman. And you shouldn't take snuff either. (*Getting up.*) I fancy the rain has stopped.

LIZAVETA BOGDANOVNA (*Getting up also*): Yes, it has.

SHPIGELSKY: And so you'll give me an answer in a day or two?

LIZAVETA BOGDANOVNA: I will tell you my decision to-morrow.

SHPIGELSKY: Now, I like that! That's really sensible! Bravo! Lizaveta Bogdanovna! Come, give me your arm. Let us go indoors.

LIZAVETA BOGDANOVNA (*Taking his arm*): Let us go.

SHPIGELSKY: And by the way, I haven't kissed your hand . . . and I believe it's what's done. Well, for once, here goes! (*Kisses her hand.* LIZAVETA BOGDANOVNA *blushes.*) That's right. (*Moves towards door into garden.*)

LIZAVETA BOGDANOVNA (*Stopping*): So you think, Ignaty Ilyitch, that Mihail Alexandritch is really not a dangerous man?

SHPIGELSKY: I think not.

LIZAVETA BOGDANOVNA: Do you know what, Ignaty Ilyitch? I fancy that for some time past Natalya Petrovna . . . I fancy that Mr. Beliayev. . . . She takes a good deal of notice of him . . . doesn't she? And Verotchka too, what do you think? Isn't that why to-day? . . .

Shpigelsky (*Interrupting her*): There's one other thing I've forgotten to tell you, Lizaveta Bogdanovna. I'm awfully inquisitive myself, but I can't endure inquisitive women. That is, I'll explain. To my thinking, a wife ought to be inquisitive and observant only with other people (indeed it's an advantage to her husband). . . . You understand me—with others only. However, if you really want to know my opinion concerning Natalya Petrovna, Vera Alexandrovna, Mr. Beliayev, and the folks here generally, listen and I'll sing you a little song. I've a horrible voice but you mustn't mind that.

Lizaveta Bogdanovna (*With surprise*): A song!

Shpigelsky: Listen! The first verse:

> 'Granny had a little kid,
> Granny had a little kid,
> A little grey kid!
> Yes, she did! yes, she did!'

The second verse:

> 'The kid would in the forest play,
> The kid would in the forest play,
> Yes, I say, yes, I say
> He would in the forest play.'

Lizaveta Bogdanovna: But I don't understand. . . .

Shpigelsky: Listen then! The third verse:

> 'The grey wolves ate that little kid (*Skipping about*),
> The grey wolves ate that little kid,
> They ate him up, they ate him up,
> Yes, I say, they ate him up.'

And now let us go. I must have a talk with Natalya Petrovna, by the way. Let us hope she won't bite me. If I'm not mistaken, she still has need of me. Come along.

[*They go out into the garden.*]

Katya (*Cautiously coming out from behind the column*): They've gone at last! What a spiteful man that doctor is . . . talked and talked and what didn't he say? And what a way to sing! I'm afraid Alexey Nikolaitch may have gone back indoors meanwhile. . . . Why on earth need they have come in here! (*Goes to the window.*) So Lizaveta Bogdanovna is to be the doctor's wife. . . . (*Laughs.*) So that's it! . . . Well, I don't envy her. . . . (*Keeps looking out of window.*) The grass looks as though it had been washed. . . . What a nice smell. . . it's the wild cherry. . . . Oh! here he comes! (*After waiting a moment.*) Alexey Nikolaitch! . . . Alexey Nikolaitch!

Beliayev (*Behind the scenes*): Who's calling me? Oh! is it you, Katya? (*Comes up to window.*) What do you want?

Katya: Come in here. . . . I've something to say to you.

Beliayev: Oh! very well. (*Moves away from window and a moment later comes in at door.*) Here I am.

Katya: Aren't you wet?

Beliayev: No . . . I've been sitting in the greenhouse with Potap . . . he's your uncle, isn't he?

Katya: Yes, he's my uncle.

Beliayev: How pretty you are to-day! (Katya *smiles and looks down. He takes a peach out of his pocket.*) Would you like it?

Katya: (*Refusing*): Thank you very much . . . eat it yourself.

Beliayev: I didn't refuse your raspberries when you gave me some yesterday. Take it, I picked it for you . . . really.

Katya: Oh! thank you very much. (*Takes the peach.*)

Beliayev: That's right. What did you want to tell me?

Katya: My young lady . . . Vera Alexandrovna, asked me . . . she wants to see you.

Beliayev: Ah! well, I'll go to her at once.

Katya: No . . . she'll come here. She wants to have a talk with you.

Beliayev (*With some surprise*): She wants to come here?

Katya: Yes. . . . Here, you see. . . . Nobody comes in here. You won't be interrupted here. . . . (*Sighs.*) She likes you very much, Alexey Nikolaitch. . . . She's so kind. I'll go and fetch her. And you'll wait, won't you?

Beliayev: Of course, of course.

Katya: In a minute. . . . (*Is going and stops.*) Alexey Nikolaitch, is it true what they are saying, that you are leaving us?

Beliayev: I? No. . . . Who told you so?

Katya: So you're not going away? Thank goodness! (*In confusion.*) We'll be back in a minute. (*Goes out by door leading to the house.*)

BELIAYEV (*Remains for some time without moving*): How strange it all is! Strange things are happening to me. I must say I never expected all this. . . . Vera loves me. . . . Natalya Petrovna knows it. . . . Vera has confessed it herself . . . extraordinary! Vera . . . such a sweet, dear child; but . . . what's the meaning of this note? (*Takes a scrap of paper out of his pocket.*) From Natalya Petrovna . . . in pencil. 'Don't go away, don't decide on anything till I have had a talk with you.' What does she want to talk about? (*A pause.*) Such idiotic ideas come into my head! I must say all this is very embarrassing. If anybody had told me a month ago that I . . . I . . . I simply can't get over that conversation with Natalya Petrovna. Why is my heart throbbing like this? And now Vera wants to see me. . . . What am I going to say to her? Anyway, I shall find out what's the matter. . . . Perhaps Natalya Petrovna's angry with me. . . . But whatever for? (*Looks at the note again.*) It's all queer, very queer.

> [*The door is opened softly. He quickly hides the note.* VERA *and* KATYA *appear in the doorway. He goes up to them.* VERA *is very pale, she does not raise her eyes, nor move from the spot.*]

KATYA: Don't be afraid, miss, go up to him; I'll be on the look-out. Don't be afraid. (*To* BELIAYEV.) Oh! Alexey Nikolaitch! (*She shuts the windows, goes out into the garden and closes the door behind her.*)

Beliayev: Vera Alexandrovna . . . you wanted to see me. Come here, sit down here. (*Takes her by the hand and leads her to the seat.* Vera *sits down.*) That's it. (*Looking at her with surprise.*) You've been crying?

Vera (*Without looking up*): That doesn't matter. . . . I've come to beg you to forgive me, Alexey Nikolaitch.

Beliayev: What for?

Vera: I heard . . . you have had an unpleasant interview with Natalya Petrovna . . . you are going . . . you're being sent away.

Beliayev: Who told you that?

Vera: Natalya Petrovna herself. . . . I met her just after you had been with her. . . . She told me you yourself are unwilling to stay. But I believe you are being sent away.

Beliayev: Tell me, do they know this in the house?

Vera: No . . . only Katya knows. . . . I had to tell her. . . . I wanted to see you, to beg you to forgive me. Imagine now how wretched I must be. . . . I'm the cause of it, Alexey Nikolaitch, it's all my fault.

Beliayev: Your fault, Vera Alexandrovna?

Vera: I never could have thought . . . Natalya Petrovna. . . . But I don't blame her. Don't you blame me either. . . . This morning I was a silly child, but now. . . . (*Breaks off.*)

Beliayev: Nothing's settled yet, Vera Alexandrovna. . . . I may be staying.

Vera (*Sadly*): You say nothing's settled yet, Alexey Nikolaitch. . . . No, everything's settled, everything's over. See how you are with me now, and remember only yesterday, in the garden. . . . (*A pause.*) Ah! I see Natalya Petrovna has told you everything.

BELIAYEV (*Embarrassed*): Vera Alexandrovna . . .

VERA: She has told you, I see it. . . . She tried to catch me, and I, like a silly, fell into her trap. But she betrayed herself too. . . . I'm not such a child. (*Dropping her voice.*) Oh no!

BELIAYEV: What do you mean?

VERA (*Glancing at him*): Alexey Nikolaitch, did you really want to leave us yourself?

BELIAYEV: Yes.

VERA: Why? (BELIAYEV *is silent.*) You don't answer?

BELIAYEV: Vera Alexandrovna, you are not mistaken. . . . Natalya Petrovna told me everything.

VERA (*Faintly*): What, for instance?

BELIAYEV: Vera Alexandrovna . . . I really can't. . . . You understand.

VERA: She told you perhaps that I love you?

BELIAYEV (*Hesitating*): Yes.

VERA (*Quickly*): But it's untrue. . . .

BELIAYEV (*In confusion*): What! . . .

VERA (*Hides her face in her hands and whispers in a toneless voice through her fingers*): Anyway, I didn't tell her that, I don't remember. . . (*Lifting her head.*) Oh! how cruelly she has treated me! And you . . . you meant to go away because of that?

BELIAYEV: Vera Alexandrovna, only consider. . . .

VERA (*Glancing at him*): He does not love me! (*Hides her face again.*)

BELIAYEV (*Sits down beside her and takes her hands*): Vera Alexandrovna, give me your hand. . . . Listen, there must not be misunderstandings between us. I love you as a sister; I love you because no one could help loving you. Forgive me if I . . . I've never in my life been in such a position. . . . I can't bear to wound you. . . . (*She hides her face again.*) I'm not going to pretend with you, I know that you like me, that you've grown fond of me. . . . But think, what can come of it? I'm only twenty, I haven't a farthing. Please don't be angry with me. I really don't know what to say.

VERA (*Taking her hands from her face and looking at him*): And as though I expected anything, my God! But why so cruelly, so heartlessly. . . . (*She breaks off.*)

BELIAYEV: Vera Alexandrovna, I didn't mean to hurt you.

VERA: I'm not blaming you, Alexey Nikolaitch. How are you to blame? It's all my fault. . . . And how I am punished! I don't blame her either, I know she's a kind-hearted woman but she couldn't help herself. . . . She didn't know what she was doing.

BELIAYEV (*In amazement*): Didn't know what she was doing?

Vera (*Turning to him*): Natalya Petrovna loves you, Beliayev.

Beliayev: What?

Vera: She's in love with you.

Beliayev: What are you saying?

Vera: I know what I'm saying. To-day has made me years older. . . . I'm not a child now, believe me. She was actually jealous . . . of me! (*With a bitter smile.*) What do you think of that?

Beliayev: But it's impossible!

Vera: Impossible. . . . Then why has she suddenly taken it into her head to marry me to that gentleman, what's his name, Bolshintsov? Why did she send the doctor to me, why did she try to persuade me to it herself? Oh! I know what I am saying! If you could have seen, Beliayev, how her whole face changed when I told her. . . . Oh! you can't imagine how cunningly, how treacherously she trapped me into admitting it. Yes, she's in love with you; it's only too evident. . . .

Beliayev: Vera Alexandrovna, you're mistaken, I assure you.

Vera: No, I'm not mistaken. I tell you I'm not mistaken. If she doesn't love you, why has she tortured me like this? What have I done to her? (*Bitterly.*) Jealousy is an excuse for anything. But what's the good of talking! . . . And now why is she sending you away? She imagines that you . . . that we . . . Oh! she need not worry herself! You can stay! (*Hides her face in her hands.*)

BELIAYEV: She hasn't sent me away so far, Vera Alexandrovna. . . . As I've told you already, nothing is decided yet. . . .

VERA (*Suddenly lifting her head and looking at him*): Really?

BELIAYEV: Yes . . . but why do you look at me like that?

VERA (*As though to herself*): Ah! I see. . . . Yes, yes. . . . She is still hoping. . . . (*The door into the corridor is quickly opened and* NATALYA PETROVNA *appears in the doorway. She stops short on seeing* VERA *and* BELIAYEV.)

BELIAYEV: What did you say?

VERA: Yes, now it's all clear to me. . . . She has thought better of it. She sees I'm no danger to her, and indeed what am I? A silly girl, while she!

BELIAYEV: Vera Alexandrovna, how can you imagine . . .

VERA: But who knows? Perhaps she's right . . . perhaps you love her. . . .

BELIAYEV: I?

VERA (*Standing up*): Yes, you. Why are you blushing?

BELIAYEV: Me blushing? . . .

VERA: You like her, you may come to love her? . . . You don't answer my question.

BELIAYEV: But, good Lord, what do you want me to say? Vera Alexandrovna, you're so excited. . . . Do be calm for goodness sake. . . .

VERA (*Turning away from him*): Oh! you treat me as a child. . . . You don't deign to give me a serious answer. . . . You simply want to get rid of me. You try to comfort me! (*Turns to go out but stops short at sight of* Natalya Petrovna.) Natalya Petrovna! . . . (Beliayev *looks round instantly*.)

Natalya Petrovna (*Taking a few steps forward*): Yes, I'm here. (*She speaks with some effort*.) I came for you, Verotchka.

Vera (*Coldly and deliberately*): What made you come here? So you've been looking for me?

Natalya Petrovna: Yes, I've been looking for you. You're indiscreet, Verotchka. . . . I've spoken of it more than once. . . . And you, Alexey Nikolaitch, you've forgotten your promise . . . you've deceived me.

Vera: Oh! stop that, Natalya Petrovna, leave off, do! (Natalya Petrovna *looks at her in amazement*) Give up speaking to me as though I were a child. . . . (*Dropping her voice*.) From to-day I'm a woman. . . . I'm as much a woman as you are.

Natalya Petrovna *(Embarrassed)*: Vera. . . .

Vera (*Almost in a whisper*): He hasn't deceived you. . . . Our meeting here is not his doing. He doesn't care for me, you know that, you've no need to be jealous.

Natalya Petrovna (*With rising amazement*): Vera!

Vera: It's the truth . . . don't go on pretending. These pretences are no use now. . . . I see through them now, I can assure you. To you I'm not the ward you are watching over (*Ironically*) like an elder sister. . . . (*Moves closer to her.*) I'm your rival.

Natalya Petrovna: Vera, you forget yourself. . . .

Vera: Perhaps . . . but who has driven me to it? I don't understand what has given me courage to speak to you like this. . . . Perhaps it's because I have nothing to hope for, because it has pleased you to trample upon me. . . . And you have succeeded . . . completely. But let me tell you, I don't mean to be as underhand with you as you have been with me. . . . I'll let you know I've told him everything. (*Indicating* Beliayev.)

Natalya Petrovna: What could you tell him?

Vera: What? (*With irony.*) Why, everything I have noticed. You hoped to worm everything out of me without betraying yourself. You made a mistake, Natalya Petrovna, you overrated your self-control.

Natalya Petrovna: Vera, think what you're saying. . . .

Vera (*In a whisper and coming still closer to her*): Tell me that I'm wrong. . . . Tell me that you're not in love with him. . . . He has told me that he doesn't love me! (Natalya Petrovna, *overwhelmed with confusion, is silent.* Vera *remains for some time motionless, then suddenly presses her hand to her forehead*) Natalya Petrovna . . . forgive me . . . I . . . don't know . . . what's come over me . . . forgive me, don't be hard on me. . . . (*Bursts into tears and goes out rapidly by door into corridor. A silence.*)

BELIAYEV (*Going up to* NATALYA PETROVNA): I can assure you, Natalya Petrovna. . . .

NATALYA PETROVNA (*Looking fixedly at the floor, holds out her hand in his direction*): Stop, Alexey Nikolaitch. The truth is . . . Vera is right. . . . It's time I . . . time I laid aside deceit. I have wronged her, and you— you have a right to despise me. (BELIAYEV *makes an involuntary gesture.*) I am degraded in my own eyes. The only way left me to regain your respect is openness, complete openness, whatever the consequences. Besides, I am seeing you for the last time, for the last time I am speaking with you. I love you. (*She does not look at him.*)

BELIAYEV: You, Natalya Petrovna! . . .

NATALYA PETROVNA: Yes, yes, I love you. Vera was not deceived and has not deceived you. I have loved you from the very day you arrived here, but I only recognized it yesterday. I don't mean to justify my conduct. It has been unworthy of me . . . but anyway you can understand now, you can make allowance for me. Yes, I was jealous of Vera; yes, I was planning to marry her to Bolshintsov, so as to get her away from you and from myself; yes, I took advantage of my position, of my being older, to find out her secret and—of course I didn't reckon on that—I betrayed myself. I love you, Beliayev: but let me say, it's only pride that forces me to confess it . . . the farce I have been playing revolts me at last. You cannot stay here. . . . Indeed, after what I have just told you, you will no doubt feel very awkward in my company, and you will want to get away as quickly as possible. I am certain of that. It is that certainty has given me courage. I confess I shouldn't like you to think badly of me. Now you know everything. . . . Perhaps I have spoilt things for you . . . perhaps, if all this had not happened, you might have cared for Verotchka. . . . I have only one plea to urge, Alexey Nikolaitch. . . . It has all been beyond my control. (*She pauses. She has said all this in a rather calm and measured voice, not looking at* BELIAYEV. *He is silent. She goes on with some agitation, still not looking at him.*) You don't answer me? But I understand that. There's nothing for you to say to me. The position of a man receiving a declaration of love when he feels no love is too painful. I thank you for your silence. Believe me, when I told you . . . I love you, I was not pretending . . . as before; I was not counting on anything; on the contrary, I wanted at last to throw off the mask, which I can assure you I'm not used to wearing. . . . And indeed, what's the use of affectation and duplicity, when everything's known; why pretend when there's no one to deceive? Everything is over between us now. I will not keep you. You can go away without saying another word to me, without taking leave of me. I shall not think it discourteous, I shall be grateful to you. There are circumstances in which delicacy is out of place . . . worse than rudeness. It seems we were not destined to know each other better. Good-bye! Yes, we were not destined to know each other . . . but at least I hope that now you no longer look on me as an oppressor, a furtive and deceitful creature. . . . Good-bye for ever. (BELIAYEV *in distress tries to say something, but cannot*) You are not going?

BELIAYEV (*Bows, is about to go, and after a struggle with himself turns back*): No, I can't go. . . . (NATALYA PETROVNA *for the first time looks at him.*) I can't go away like this! Natalya Petrovna, you said just now . . . you didn't want me to carry away unpleasant memories of you, and I don't want you to think of me as a man who . . . Oh dear! I don't know how to say it. . . . Natalya Petrovna, I'm sorry. . . . I don't know how to talk to women like you. . . . Up to now I've only known . . . quite ordinary women. You said that we were not destined to be friends, but, good God, how could an ordinary almost uneducated fellow like me ever dream of being anything to you? Think what you are and what I am! Think, could I dare to dream? . . . With your bringing up. . . . But why talk of that. . . . Just look at me . . . this old coat and your sweet-scented clothes. . . . My God! Oh yes, I was afraid of you and I'm afraid of you still. . . . I thought of you, without any exaggeration, as a being of a higher order, and now . . .

you, you tell me that you love me . . . you, Natalya Petrovna! Me! . . . I feel my heart beating as it never has in my life; it's not beating merely from amazement, it's not that my vanity's flattered. . . . No, indeed . . . vanity doesn't come in now. . . . But I . . . I can't go away like this, say what you like!

Natalya Petrovna (*After a pause, as though to herself*): What have I done?

Beliayev: Natalya Petrovna, for God's sake, I assure you . . .

Natalya Petrovna (*In a changed voice*): Alexey Nikolaitch. If I did not know you are an honest man, and incapable of deceit, God knows what I should think. I might regret having spoken. But I trust you. I don't want to hide my feelings from you; I am grateful for what you have just said. Now I know why we have not been friends. . . . So it was nothing in me myself that repelled you. . . . Only my position. . . . (*Breaks off.*) It's all for the best, of course . . . but now it will be easier for me to part from you. . . . Good-bye. (*Is about to go out.*)

Beliayev (*After a pause*): Natalya Petrovna, I know that it's impossible for me to stay here . . . but I can't tell you what's going on in me. You love me. . . . I'm positively terrified to utter those words . . . it's all so new to me . . . it seems as though I'm seeing you for the first time, hearing you for the first time, but I feel one thing, I must go. . . . I feel I can't answer for anything. . . .

NATALYA PETROVNA (*In a faint voice*): Yes, Beliayev, you must go. . . . Now after what you have said, you can go. . . . And can it be really, in spite of all I have done. . . . Oh, believe me, if I had had the remotest suspicion of all you have just told me—that confession would have died in me, Beliayev. . . . I only meant to put an end to all misunderstandings, I meant to expiate, to punish myself, I meant to cut the last thread. If I could have imagined. . . . (*Hides her face.*)

BELIAYEV: I do believe you, Natalya Petrovna, I do. And I, too . . . a quarter of an hour ago . . . could I have imagined. . . . It's only to-day, during our interview before dinner that I felt for the first time something extraordinary, incredible, as though a hand had squeezed my heart, and such a burning ache. . . . It is true that before then I had, more or less, avoided you and even not liked you particularly, but when you told me to-day that Vera Alexandrovna fancied . . . (*Breaks off.*)

NATALYA PETROVNA (*With an involuntary smile of happiness on her lips*): Hush, hush, Beliayev; we mustn't think of that. We must not forget that we are speaking to each other for the last time . . . that you are going to-morrow. . . .

BELIAYEV: Oh yes! I'll go to-morrow! Now I can go. . . . All this will pass. . . . You see I don't want to exaggerate. . . . I'm going . . . to take what God gives! I shall take with me a memory, I shall never forget that you cared for me. . . . But how was it I didn't know you till now? Here you are looking at me now. . . . Can I have ever tried to avoid your eyes? . . . Can I ever have felt shy with you?

Natalya Petrovna (*With a smile*): You said just now that you're afraid of me.

Beliayev: Did I? (*A pause.*) Really. . . . I wonder at myself. . . . Is it I, I talking so boldly to you? I don't know myself.

Natalya Petrovna: And you're not deceiving yourself?

Beliayev: How?

Natalya Petrovna: In thinking that you . . . (*Shuddering.*) Oh! good God, what am I doing? . . . Beliayev. . . . Help me. . . . No woman has ever been in such a position. It's more than I can bear indeed. . . . Perhaps it's for the best, everything is ended at once; but anyway, we have come to know each other. . . . Give me your hand and good-bye for ever.

Beliayev (*Takes her hand*): Natalya Petrovna . . . I don't know what to say at parting . . . my heart is so full. . . . God give you. . . . (*Breaks off and presses her hand to his lips.*) Good-bye. (*Is about to go out by door into garden.*)

Natalya Petrovna (*Looking after him*): Beliayev. . . .

Beliayev (*Turning*): Natalya Petrovna. . . .

Natalya Petrovna (*Pausing for some time, then in a weak voice*): Stay. . . .

Beliayev: What?

NATALYA PETROVNA: Stay, and may God be our judge! (*She hides her head in her hands.*)

BELIAYEV (*Goes swiftly to her and holds out his hands to her*): Natalya Petrovna. . . .

> [*At that instant the garden door opens and* RAKITIN *appears in the doorway. He gazes at them for some time, then goes suddenly up to them.*]

RAKITIN (*In a loud voice*): They are looking for you everywhere, Natalya Petrovna. . . . (NATALYA PETROVNA *and* BELIAYEV *look round.*)

NATALYA PETROVNA (*Taking her hands from her face and seeming to come to herself*): Ah, it's you. . . . Who is looking for me? (BELIAYEV *in confusion bows to* NATALYA PETROVNA *and is going out.*) Are you going, Alexey Nikolaitch? . . . Don't forget, you know what. . . . (*He bows to her a second time and goes out into the garden.*)

RAKITIN: Arkady is looking for you. . . . I must say I didn't expect to find you here . . . but as I passed by . . .

NATALYA PETROVNA (*With a smile*): You heard our voices. . . . I met Alexey Nikolaitch here and have had a complete explanation with him. . . . To-day seems a day of explanations; but now we can go into the house. . . . (*Goes towards door into corridor.*)

RAKITIN (*With some emotion*): May I ask . . . what decision?

NATALYA PETROVNA (*Affecting surprise*): Decision? . . . I don't understand you.

RAKITIN (*After a long pause, sadly*): If that's so, I understand.

NATALYA PETROVNA: Well, there it is. . . . Mysterious hints again! Oh, well, I have spoken to him and now everything is set right. . . . It was all nonsense, exaggeration. . . . All you and I talked about was childish. It must be forgotten now.

RAKITIN: I am not asking you for explanations, Natalya Petrovna.

NATALYA PETROVNA (*With forced ease*): What on earth was it I wanted to say to you. . . . I don't remember. Never mind. Let us go. It's all at an end . . . it's over.

RAKITIN (*Looking at her intently*): Yes, it's all at an end. How vexed you must be with yourself now . . . for your openness this morning. (*She turns away.*)

NATALYA PETROVNA: Rakitin. . . . (*He glances at her again; she obviously does not know what to say.*) You've not spoken to Arkady yet?

RAKITIN: No . . . I haven't thought of anything yet. . . . You see I must make up some story. . . .

NATALYA PETROVNA: How insufferable it is! What do they want of me? I'm followed about at every step I take. Rakitin, I'm really conscience-stricken you should have . . .

RAKITIN: Oh, Natalya Petrovna, pray don't distress yourself. . . . Why, it's all in the natural order of things. But how obviously this is Mr. Beliayev's first experience! Why was he so embarrassed, why did he take to flight? . . . But with time . . . (*In an under-*

tone) you will both learn to keep up appearances.... (*Aloud.*) Let us go.

> [NATALYA PETROVNA *is about to go up to him but stops short. At that instant* ISLAYEV'S *voice is heard in the garden:* 'He went in here, you say?' *and then* ISLAYEV *and* SHPIGELSKY *come in.*]

ISLAYEV: To be sure . . . here he is. Well, well, well! And Natalya Petrovna too! (*Going up to her.*) How's this? The continuation of this morning's talk? It's evidently an important matter.

RAKITIN: I met Natalya Petrovna here as I walked.

ISLAYEV: Met her? (*Looking round.*) A queer place for a walk!

NATALYA PETROVNA: Well, you've walked in, too....

ISLAYEV: I came in because . . . (*Breaks off.*)

NATALYA PETROVNA: You were looking for me?

ISLAYEV (*After a pause*): Yes—I was looking for you. Won't you come into the house? Tea's ready. It will soon be dark.

NATALYA PETROVNA (*Taking his arm*): Come along.

ISLAYEV (*Looking round*): This place might be turned into two good rooms for the gardeners—or another servants' hall—don't you think, Shpigelsky?

SHPIGELSKY: To be sure it could.

ISLAYEV: Let us go by the garden, Natasha (*Goes towards the garden door. Throughout the* scene he has not once looked at RAKITIN. *In the doorway he turns half round*.) Well, gentlemen. Let us go in to tea.

[*Goes out with* NATALYA PETROVNA.]

SHPIGELSKY (*To* RAKITIN): Well, Mihail Alexandritch, come along. . . . Give me your arm. . . . It's clear we are destined to follow in the rear. . . .

RAKITIN (*Wrathfully*): Oh, Doctor, I'm sick of you.

SHPIGELSKY (*With affected good-humour*): Ah, Mihail Alexandritch, if only you know how sick I am of myself! (RAKITIN *cannot help smiling*.) Come along, come along. (*They go out into the garden*.)

ACT V

[*The scene is the same as in the 1st and 3rd Acts. Morning.* ISLAYEV *is sitting at the table looking through papers. He suddenly jumps up.*]

ISLAYEV: No! impossible, I can't work to-day. I can't get it out of my mind. (*Walks up and down.*) I confess I didn't expect this; I didn't expect I should be so upset . . . as I am now. How is one to act? . . . that's the problem. (*Ponders and suddenly shouts.*) Matvey!

MATVEY (*Entering*): Yes, Sir?

ISLAYEV: Send the bailiff to me. . . . And tell the men digging at the dam to wait for me. . . . Run along.

MATVEY: Yes, Sir. (*Goes out.*)

ISLAYEV (*Going back to the table and turning over the papers*): Yes . . . it's a problem!

ANNA SEMYONOVNA (*Comes in and goes up to* ISLAYEV): Arkasha. . . .

ISLAYEV: Ah! it's you, Mamma. How are you this morning?

ANNA SEMYONOVNA (*Sitting down on the sofa*): I'm quite well, thank God. (*Sighs.*) I'm quite well. (*Sighs still more audibly.*)

Thank God. (*Seeing that* Islayev *is not attending to her, she sighs very emphatically, with a faint moan*.)

Islayev: You're sighing . . . what's the matter?

Anna Semyonovna (*Sighs again but less emphatically*): Oh! Arkasha, as though you don't know what makes me sigh!

Islayev: What do you want to say?

Anna Semyonovna (*After a pause*): I'm your mother, Arkasha. Of course you're a man, grown-up and sensible; but still—I'm your mother. It's a great word—mother!

Islayev: Please explain.

Anna Semyonovna: You know what I am hinting at, my dear. Your wife, Natasha . . . of course, she's an excellent woman . . . and her conduct hitherto has been most exemplary . . . but she is still so young, Arkasha! And youth. . . .

Islayev: I see what you want to say. . . . You fancy her relations with Rakitin. . . .

Anna Semyonovna: God forbid! I never thought of such a thing.

Islayev: You didn't let me finish. . . . You fancy her relations with Rakitin are not altogether . . . clear. These mysterious conversations, these tears—all strike you as strange.

Anna Semyonovna: Well, Arkasha, has he told you at last what their talks were about? . . . He has told me nothing.

ISLAYEV: I haven't asked him, Mamma, and he is apparently in no hurry to satisfy my curiosity.

ANNA SEMYONOVNA: Thai what do you intend to do now?

ISLAYEV: Do, Mamma? Why, nothing.

ANNA SEMYONOVNA: Nothing?

ISLAYEV: Why, certainly, nothing.

ANNA SEMYONOVNA (*Getting up*): I must say, I'm surprised to hear it. Of course you are master in your own house and know better than I do what is for the best. But only think of the consequences. . . .

ISLAYEV: Really, Mamma, there's no need to worry yourself.

ANNA SEMYONOVNA: My dear, I'm a mother . . . you know best. (*A pause.*) I must own I came to see whether I could do anything to help.

ISLAYEV (*Earnestly*): No, as far as that goes, I must beg you, Mamma, not to trouble yourself. . . . Pray don't!

ANNA SEMYONOVNA: As you wish, Arkasha, as you wish. I won't say another word. I have warned you, I have done my duty, and now I won't open my lips. (*A brief silence.*)

ISLAYEV: Are you going anywhere to-day?

ANNA SEMYONOVNA: Only I must warn you; you are too trustful, my dear boy; you judge everybody by yourself! Believe me, true friends are only too rare nowadays!

ISLAYEV (*With impatience*): Mamma. . . .

Anna Semyonovna: Oh, I'll say no more, I'll say no more! And what's the use, an old woman like me! I'm in my dotage, I suppose! But I was brought up on different principles, and have tried to instil them in you . . . there, there, go on with your work, I won't interrupt you. . . . I'm going. (*Goes to door and stops.*) Well, you know best. (*Goes out.*)

Islayev (*Looking after her*): Queer that people who really love you have such a passion for poking their fingers into your wounds. And of course they're convinced it's doing you good . . . that's what's so funny! I don't blame Mother, though; of course she means well, and how could she help giving advice? But that's no matter. . . . (*Sitting down.*) How am I to act? (*After a moment's thought, gets up.*) Oh! the more simply, the better! Diplomatic subtleties don't suit me. . . . I should be the first to make a muddle of them. (*Rings*, Matvey *enters.*) Is Mihail Alexandritch at home, do you know?

Matvey: Yes, Sir. I saw his honour in the billiard-room just now.

Islayev: Ah, well, ask him to come to me.

Matvey: Yes, Sir. (*Goes out.*)

Islayev (*Walking up and down*): I'm not used to these upheavals. . . . I hope they won't happen often . . . strong as I am, I can't stand them. (*Puts his hand on his heart.*) Ough! . . . (Rakitin, *embarrassed, comes in from the outer room.*)

Rakitin: You sent for me?

Islayev: Yes. . . . (*A pause.*) Michel, you know you owe me something?

Rakitin: I owe you?

Islayev: Why, yes. Have you forgotten your promise? About . . . Natasha's tears . . . and altogether . . . When my Mother and I came upon you, you remember—you told me you had a secret which you would explain.

Rakitin: I said a secret?

Islayev: You said so.

Rakitin: But what secret could we have? We had had a talk.

Islayev: What about? And why was she crying?

Rakitin: You know, Arkady . . . there are moments in the life of a woman . . . even the happiest . . .

Islayev: Rakitin, stop, we can't go on like this. I can't bear to see you in such a position. . . . Your confusion distresses me more than it does yourself. (*Takes his hand.*) We are old friends—you've known me from a child; I don't know how to pretend and you have always been open with me. Let me put one question to you. . . . I give you my word beforehand that I shall not doubt the sincerity of your answer. You love my wife, don't you? (Rakitin *looks at* Islayev.) You understand me, you love her as . . . Well, that is you love her with the sort of love that . . . it's difficult to admit to her husband?

Rakitin (*After a pause, in a toneless voice*): Yes, I love your wife . . . with that sort of love.

Islayev (*Also after a pause*): Michel, thank you for your frankness. You're an honourable man. But what's to be done now? Sit down, we'll think it over together. (Rakitin *sits down.* Islayev *walks about the room.*) I know Natasha; I know how to appreciate her. But I know how much I'm worth myself too. I'm not your equal. Michel . . . don't interrupt me, please—I'm not your equal. You're cleverer, better, more attractive, in fact. I'm an ordinary person. Natasha loves me—I think, but she has eyes, well, of course, she must find you attractive. And there's another thing I must tell you: I noticed your affection for each other long ago. . . . But I was always so sure of you both—and as long as nothing came to the surface . . . Ough! I don't know how to say things! (*Breaks off.*) But after the scene yesterday, after your second interview in the evening—what are we to do? And if only I had come upon you alone, but other people are mixed up in it; Mamma, and that sly fox, Shpigelsky. . . . Come, what do you say, Michel?

Rakitin: You are perfectly right, Arkady.

Islayev: That's not the point . . . what's to be done? I must tell you, Michel, that though I am a simple person—so much I do understand, that it's not the thing to spoil other people's lives—and that there are cases when it's wicked to insist on one's rights. That I've not picked out of books, Michel . . . it's my conscience tells me so. Leave others free. . . . Well, yes, let them be free. Only it wants some thinking over. It's too important.

RAKITIN (*Getting up*): But I have thought it over already.

ISLAYEV: How so?

RAKITIN: I must go. . . . I'm going away.

ISLAYEV (*After a pause*): You think so? . . . Right away from here altogether?

RAKITIN: Yes.

ISLAYEV (*Begins walking up and down again*): That is . . . that is a hard saying! But perhaps you are right. We shall miss you dreadfully. . . . God knows, perhaps it won't mend matters either. . . . But you can see more clearly, you know best. I expect you are right. You're a danger to me, Michel. . . . (*With a mournful smile.*) Yes . . . you are. You know what I said just now . . . about freedom. . . . And yet perhaps I couldn't survive it! For me to be without Natasha. . . . (*Waving his hand in dismissal of the idea.*) And another thing, Michel: for some time past, and especially these last few days, I've noticed a great change in her. She's all the time in a state of intense agitation and I'm alarmed about it. I'm not mistaken, am I?

RAKITIN (*Bitterly*): Oh no! you're not mistaken!

ISLAYEV: Well, you see! So you are going away?

Rakitin: Yes.

Islayev: H'm! And how suddenly this has burst on us! If only you had not been so confused when my Mother and I came upon you....

Matvey (*Coming in*): The bailiff is here.

Islayev: Ask him to wait! (Matvey *goes out*.) But, Michel, you won't be away for long? That's nonsense.

Rakitin: I don't know . . . really . . . a good time, I expect.

Islayev: But you don't take me for an Othello, do you? Upon my word, I don't believe there has been such a conversation between two friends since the world began! I can't part from you like this....

Rakitin (*Pressing his hand*): You'll let me know when I can come back....

Islayev: There's nobody who can fill your place here! Not Bolshintsov, anyway!

Rakitin: There are others....

Islayev: Who? Krinitsyn? That conceited fool? Beliayev, of course, is a good-natured lad . . . but you can't speak of him in the same breath.

Rakitin (*Ironically*): Do you think so? You don't know him, Arkady. . . . Look at him more attentively. . . . I advise you. . . . Do you hear? He's a very . . . very remarkable fellow!

Islayev: Pooh! To be sure, Natasha and you were always meaning to finish his education! (*Glancing towards the door.*) Ah! here he is, coming here, I do believe. . . .

(*Hurriedly.*) And so, dear Michel, it's settled . . . you are going away . . . for a short time . . . some days. . . . No need to hurry . . . we must prepare Natasha. . . . I'll soothe my Mother. . . . And God give you happiness! You've lifted a load off my heart. . . . Embrace me, dear boy! (*Hastily embraces him and turns to* BELIAYEV *who is coming in.*) Ah! . . . it's you! Well . . . well, how are you?

BELIAYEV: Very well, thank you, Arkady Sergeyitch.

ISLAYEV: And where's Kolya?

BELIAYEV: He's with Herr Schaaf.

ISLAYEV: Ah . . . that's right! (*Takes his hat.*) Well, I must be off, my friends. I've not been anywhere this morning, neither to the dam nor the building. . . . Here, I've not even looked through my papers. (*Gathers them up under his arm.*) Good-bye for now! Matvey! Matvey! Come with me! (*Goes out.* RAKITIN *remains in front of stage, plunged in thought.*)

BELIAYEV (*Goes up to him*): How are you feeling this morning, Mihail Alexandritch?

RAKITIN: Thank you. Just as usual. And you?

BELIAYEV: I'm quite well.

RAKITIN: That's obvious!

BELIAYEV: How so?

RAKITIN: Why . . . from your face. . . . And oh! you've put on your new coat this morning. . . . And what do I see? A flower in your buttonhole! (BELIAYEV, *blushing, snatches it out.*) Oh! why . . . why. . . . It's charming. (*A pause.*) By the way, Alexey Nikolaitch, if there's anything you want . . . I'm going to the town to-morrow.

BELIAYEV: To-morrow?

RAKITIN: Yes . . . and from there on to Moscow, perhaps.

BELIAYEV (*With surprise*): To Moscow? Why, only yesterday you said you meant to be here another month or so. . . .

RAKITIN: Yes . . . but business . . . things have turned up. . . .

BELIAYEV: And shall you be away for long?

RAKITIN: I don't know . . . a long time, perhaps.

BELIAYEV: Do you mind telling me—does Natalya Petrovna know of your intention?

RAKITIN: No. Why do you ask me about her?

BELIAYEV: Why? (*A little embarrassed.*) Oh, nothing.

RAKITIN (*Pausing and looking round*): Alexey Nikolaitch, there's nobody in the room but ourselves; isn't it queer that we should keep up a farce before each other? Don't you think so?

BELIAYEV: I don't understand you, Mihail Alexandritch.

RAKITIN: Oh, you don't? Do you really not understand why I'm going away?

BELIAYEV: No.

RAKITIN: That's strange. . . . However, I'm willing to believe you. Perhaps you really don't know the reason. . . . would you like me to tell you why I'm going?

BELIAYEV: Please do.

RAKITIN: Well, you see, Alexey Nikolaitch—but I rely on your discretion—you found me just now with Arkady Sergeyitch. . . . We have had a rather important conversation. In consequence of which I have decided to depart. And do you know why? I'm telling you all this because I think you are a really good fellow. . . . He imagined that I . . . oh! well, that I'm in love with Natalya Petrovna. What do you think of that? It's a queer notion, isn't it? But I am grateful to him for speaking to me simply, straight out, instead of being underhand, keeping watch on us and all that. Come, tell me now what would you have done in my place? Of course, there are no grounds at all for his suspicions, still he's worried by them. . . . For the peace of mind of his friends, a decent man must be ready at times to sacrifice . . . his own pleasure. So that's why I'm going away. . . . I'm sure you think I'm right, don't you? You too . . . you would certainly do the same in my place, wouldn't you? You would go away too?

BELIAYEV (*After a pause*): Perhaps.

RAKITIN: I am very glad to hear that. . . . Of course, I can't deny that my making off has its comic side. It's as though I imagine I'm dangerous; but you see, Alexey Nikolaitch, a woman's honour is such an important thing. . . . And at the same time—of course,

I don't say this of Natalya Petrovna—but I have known women pure and innocent at heart, perfect children for all their cleverness, who just through that very purity and innocence, are more apt than others to give way to sudden passion. . . . And so, who knows? One can't be too discreet in such cases, especially as . . . By the way, Alexey Nikolaitch, you may perhaps still imagine that love is the greatest bliss on earth?

BELIAYEV (*Coldly*): I have had no experience, but imagine that to be loved by a woman one loves is a great happiness.

RAKITIN: God grant you long preserve such pleasant convictions! It's my belief, Alexey Nikolaitch, that love of every kind, happy as much as unhappy, is a real calamity if you give yourself up to it completely. . . . Wait a bit! You may learn yet how those soft little hands can torture you, with what sweet solicitude they can tear your heart to rags. . . . Wait a bit! You will learn what burning hatred lies hidden under the most ardent love! You will think of me when you yearn for peace, for the dullest, most commonplace peace as a sick man yearns for health, when you will envy any man who is free and light-hearted. . . . You wait! You will know what it means to be tied to a petticoat, to be enslaved and poisoned—and how shameful and agonizing that slavery is! . . . You will learn at last how little you get for all your sufferings. . . . But why am I saying all this to you, you won't believe me now.

The fact is that I am very glad of your approval . . . yes, yes . . . in such cases one ought to be careful.

BELIAYEV (*Who has kept his eyes fixed on* RAKITIN): Thanks for the lesson, Mihail Alexandritch, though I didn't need it.

RAKITIN (*Takes his hand*): Please forgive me, I had no intention . . . it's not for me to give lessons to anyone whatever . . . I was just talking. . . .

BELIAYEV (*With slight irony*): Not apropos of anything?

RAKITIN (*A little embarrassed*): Just so, not apropos of anything in particular. . . . I only meant. . . . You haven't hitherto had occasion, Alexey Nikolaitch, to study women. Women are peculiar creatures.

BELIAYEV: But of whom are you speaking?

RAKITIN: Oh . . . no one in particular.

BELIAYEV: Of women in general?

RAKITIN (*With a constrained smile*): Yes, perhaps. I really don't know what business I have to adopt this lecturing tone, but do let me at parting give you this one piece of advice. (*Breaking off with a gesture of dismissal.*) But there! I'm not the man to give anyone advice! Please forgive my running on like this. . . .

BELIAYEV: Oh, not at all. . . .

RAKITIN: So you don't want anything in the town?

BELIAYEV: Nothing, thank you. But I'm sorry you're going away.

Rakitin: Thanks very much. . . . So am I, I can assure you. . . . (Natalya Petrovna *and* Vera *come in from the study.* Vera *is very sad and pale.*) I am very glad to have made your acquaintance. . . . (*Presses his hand again.*)

Natalya Petrovna (*Looks at them and then goes up to them*): Good morning.

Rakitin (*Turning quickly*): Good morning, Natalya Petrovna. . . . Good morning Vera Alexandrovna. . . . (Beliayev *bows to* Natalya Petrovna *and* Vera *without speaking. He is confused.*)

Natalya Petrovna (*To* Rakitin): What are you doing this morning?

Rakitin: Oh, nothing. . . .

Natalya Petrovna: Vera and I have been walking in the garden. . . . It's a lovely day. . . . The scent of the lime trees is so delicious. We've been walking under the lime trees. . . . It's delightful to listen to the humming of the bees in the shade overhead. . . . (*Timidly to* Beliayev.) We expected to meet you there. (Beliayev *is silent.*)

Rakitin (*To* Natalya Petrovna): Ah! You too can admire the beauties of nature to-day. . . . (*A pause.*) Alexey Nikolaitch couldn't go into the garden. . . . He has got his new coat on.

Beliayev (*Reddening*): Of course, it's the only one I have, and I dare say it might get torn in the garden. . . . I suppose that's what you mean?

RAKITIN (*Blushing*): Oh no . . . I didn't mean that. . . . (VERA *goes in silence to sofa on Right, sits down and takes up her work.* NATALYA PETROVNA *gives* BELIAYEV *a constrained smile. A brief, rather oppressive silence.* RAKITIN *goes on with malicious carelessness.*) Ah, I'd forgotten to tell you, Natalya Petrovna, I'm going away to-day. . . .

NATALYA PETROVNA (*With some agitation*): Going? Where?

RAKITIN: To the town. . . . On business.

NATALYA PETROVNA: Not for long, I hope.

RAKITIN: That's as my business goes.

NATALYA PETROVNA: Mind you come back as soon as you can. (*To* BELIAYEV *without looking at him.*) Alexey Nikolaitch, was it your sketches Kolya was showing me? Did you draw them?

BELIAYEV: Yes . . . they're nothing much.

NATALYA PETROVNA: Not at all, they are very charming. You have talent.

RAKITIN: I see you are discovering new talents in Mr. Beliayev every day.

NATALYA PETROVNA (*Coldly*): Perhaps . . . so much the better for him. (*To* BELIAYEV.) I expect you have some other sketches, you must show them to me. (BELIAYEV *bows.*)

RAKITIN (*Who stands all this time as though on thorns*): But I remember it's time to pack. . . . Good-bye. (*Goes to door of outer room.*)

NATALYA PETROVNA: But you'll come to say good-bye to us. . . .

RAKITIN: Of course.

BELIAYEV (*After some hesitation*): Mihail Alexandritch, wait a minute, I'm coming with you. I must have a few words with you. . . .

RAKITIN: Ah! (*They go out together.* NATALYA PETROVNA *is left in the middle of the stage; after a little while, she sits down on Left.*)

NATALYA PETROVNA (*After an interval of silence*): Vera!

VERA (*Not lifting her head*): What is it?

NATALYA PETROVNA: Vera, for goodness' sake, don't treat me like this . . . for goodness' sake, Vera . . . Verotchka. (VERA *says nothing.* NATALYA PETROVNA *gets up, walks across the stage and slowly sinks on her knees before* VERA. VERA *tries to make her get up, turns away and hides her face.* NATALYA PETROVNA *speaks on her knees.*) Vera, forgive me; don't cry, Vera. I've behaved badly to you, I'm to blame. Can't you forgive me?

VERA (*Through her tears*): Get up, get up. . . .

NATALYA PETROVNA: I won't get up, Vera, till you forgive me. It's hard for you . . . but think, is it any easier for me . . . think, Vera. . . . You know everything. . . . The only difference between us is that you have done no wrong, while I . . .

VERA (*Bitterly*): That's all the difference! No, Natalya Petrovna, there's another difference between us. . . . You're so soft, so kind, so warm this morning. . . .

NATALYA PETROVNA (*Interrupting her*): Because I feel how wrong I've been. . . .

VERA: Really? Is it only that?

NATALYA PETROVNA (*Gets up and sits beside her*): What other reason can there be?

VERA: Natalya Petrovna, don't torture me any more, don't ask me questions. . . .

NATALYA PETROVNA (*With a sigh*): Vera, I see you can't forgive me.

VERA: You're so kind and soft to-day because you feel you are loved.

NATALYA PETROVNA (*Embarrassed*): Vera?

VERA (*Turning to her*): Well, isn't it the truth?

NATALYA PETROVNA (*Sadly*): I assure you we are both equally unhappy.

VERA: He loves you!

NATALYA PETROVNA: Vera, why do we torture each other? It's time for both of us to think what we're doing. Remember the position I'm in, the position we are both in. Remember that our secret, through my fault, of course, is known to two men here already. . . . (*Breaks off.*) Vera, instead of tormenting each other with suspicions and reproaches, hadn't we better consider together how to get out of this dreadful position . . . how to save ourselves! Do you imagine I can stand these shocks and agitations? Have you forgotten who I am? But you're not listening.

VERA (*Looks dreamily at the floor*): He loves you. . . .

NATALYA PETROVNA: Vera, he's going away.

VERA (*Turning away*): Oh, leave me alone. . . . (NATALYA PETROVNA *looks at her irreso-*

lutely. *At that instant,* Islayev's *voice calls from the study:* 'Natasha, Natasha, where are you?')

NATALYA PETROVNA (*Gets up quickly and goes to study-door*): I'm here . . . what is it?

ISLAYEV (*From the study*): Come here, I've something to tell you. . . .

NATALYA PETROVNA: In a minute. (*She turns to* VERA *and holds out her hand.* VERA *does not stir.* NATALYA PETROVNA *sighs and goes out into the study.*)

VERA (*Alone; after a silence*): He loves her! . . . And I must stay in her house. . . . Oh! it's too much. . . . (*She hides her face in her hands and sits motionless.* SHPIGELSKY *puts his head in at the door leading to the outer room. He looks round cautiously and goes on tip-toe up to* VERA, *who does not notice him.*)

SHPIGELSKY (*Standing before her, his arms crossed and a malicious grin on his face*): Vera Alexandrovna! . . . Vera Alexandrovna!

VERA (*Raising her head*): Who is it? You, Doctor. . . .

SHPIGELSKY: What is it, my young lady, not well, or what?

VERA: Oh, nothing.

SHPIGELSKY: Let me feel your pulse. (*Feels her pulse.*) H'm! Why is it so quick? Ah, young lady, young lady. . . . You won't listen to me. . . . And yet it's your welfare I wish for.

VERA (*Looking at him resolutely*): Ignaty Ilyitch . . .

Shpigelsky (*Alertly*): I'm all ears, Vera Alexandrovna. . . . What a look, upon my word. . . . I'm all ears.

Vera: That gentleman . . . Bolshintsov, your friend, is he really a good man?

Shpigelsky: My friend Bolshintsov? The most excellent, the best of men . . . a pattern and paragon of all the virtues.

Vera: He's not ill-natured?

Shpigelsky: Most kind-hearted, upon my soul. He's not a man, he's made of dough, really. You've only to take him and mould him. You wouldn't find another such good-natured fellow if you searched with a candle by daylight. He's a dove, not a man.

Vera: You answer for him?

Shpigelsky (*Lays one hand on his heart and raises the other upwards*): As I would for myself!

Vera: Then, you can tell him . . . that I am willing to marry him.

Shpigelsky (*With joyful amazement*): You don't say so!

Vera: But as soon as possible—do you hear? . . . As soon as possible. . . .

Shpigelsky: To-morrow, if you like. . . . I should rather think so! Bravo, Vera Alexandrovna! You're a young lady of spirit! I'll gallop over to him at once. Won't he be overjoyed. . . . Well, this is an unexpected turn of affairs! Why, he worships the ground you tread on, Vera Alexandrovna. . . .

Vera (*With impatience*): I didn't ask you that, Ignaty Ilyitch.

Shpigelsky: As you please, Vera Alexandrovna, as you please. Only you'll be happy with him, you'll be grateful to me, you'll see. . . . (Vera *makes a gesture of impatience.*) There, I'll hold my tongue. . . . So then I can tell him? . . .

Vera: You can, you can.

Shpigelsky: Very good. So I'll set off at once. Good-bye. (*Listens,*) And here's somebody coming, by the way. (*Goes towards study and in the doorway makes a grimace expressing surprise to himself.*) Good-bye for the present. (*Goes out.*)

Vera (*Looking after him*): Anything in the world is better than staying here. (*Stands up.*) Yes, I have made up my mind. I won't stop in this house . . . not for anything. I can't endure her soft looks, her smiles, I can't bear the sight of her, basking and purring in her happiness. . . . She's happy, however she pretends to be sad and sorrowful. . . . Her caresses are unbearable. . . .

> [Beliayev *appears in the door of the outer room. He looks round and goes up to* Vera.]

Beliayev (*In a low voice*): Vera Alexandrovna, you're alone?

Vera (*Looks round, starts, and after a moment, brings out*): Yes.

Beliayev: I'm glad to find you alone. . . . I should not have come in here otherwise. Vera Alexandrovna, I've come to say good-bye to you.

Vera: Good-bye?

BELIAYEV: Yes, I'm going away.

VERA: You are going away? You too?

BELIAYEV: Yes . . . I too. *(With intense suppressed feeling.)* You see, Vera Alexandrovna, I can't stay here. I've done so much harm here already. Apart from my having—I don't know how—disturbed your peace of mind and Natalya Petrovna's, I've broken up old friendships. Thanks to me, Mr. Rakitin is leaving this house, you have quarrelled with your benefactress. . . . It's time to put a stop to it all. After I am gone, I hope everything will settle down and be right again. . . . Turning rich women's heads and breaking young girls' hearts is not in my line. . . . You will forget about me, and, in time perhaps, will wonder how all this could have happened. . . . I wonder even now. . . . I don't want to deceive you, Vera Alexandrovna; I'm frightened, I'm terrified of staying here. . . . I can't answer for anything. . . . And you know I'm not used to all this. I feel awkward. . . . I feel as though everybody's looking at me. . . . And in fact it would be impossible for me . . . now . . . with you both. . . .

VERA: Oh, don't trouble yourself on my account! I'm not staying here long.

BELIAYEV: What do you mean?

VERA: That's my secret. But I shan't be in your way, I assure you.

BELIAYEV: Well, but, you see, I must go. Think; I seem to have brought a plague into this house, everyone's running away. . . . Isn't it better for me to disappear before more harm's done? I have just had a great talk with Mr. Rakitin. . . . You can't imagine how bitterly he spoke. . . . And he might well jeer at my new coat. . . . He's right. Yes, I must go. Would you believe it, Vera Alexandrovna, I'm longing for the minute when I shall be racing along the high road in a cart. I'm stifling here, I want to get into the open air. I can't tell you how grieved and at the same time light-hearted I feel, like a man setting off on a long journey overseas; he's sad and sick at parting from his friends, yet the sound of the sea is so joyful, the wind is so fresh in his face, that it sets his blood dancing, though his heart may ache. . . . Yes, I'm certainly going. I'll go back to Moscow, to my old companions, I'll set to work. . . .

VERA: You love her, it seems, Alexey Nikolaitch; you love her, yet you are going away.

BELIAYEV: Hush, Vera Alexandrovna, why do you say that? Don't you see that it's all over? It flared up and has gone out like a spark. Let us part friends. It's time. I've come to my senses. Keep well, be happy, we shall see each other again some day. . . . I shall never forget you, Vera Alexandrovna. . . . I'm very fond of you, believe me. . . . (*Presses her hand and adds hurriedly.*) Give this note to Natalya Petrovna for me. . . .

VERA (*Glancing at him embarrassed*): A note?

BELIAYEV: Yes . . . I can't say good-bye to her.

VERA: But are you going at once?

BELIAYEV: This minute. . . . I have not said anything to anybody . . . except Mihail Alexandritch. He approves. I'm going to walk from here to Petrovskoe. There I shall wait for Mihail Alexandritch and we shall drive on to the town together. I'll write from there. My things will be sent on after me. You see it's all settled. But you can read the note. There's only a couple of words in it.

VERA (*Taking the note from him*): And you are really going?

BELIAYEV: Yes, yes. . . . Give her that note and say . . . No, there's no need to say anything. . . . What's the use? (*Listening.*) Here they come. Good-bye. (*Rushes to the door, stops an instant in the doorway, then runs away.* VERA *is left with the note in her hand.* NATALYA PETROVNA *comes in.*)

NATALYA PETROVNA (*Going up to* VERA): Verotchka. . . . (*Glances at her and breaks off.*) What's the matter? (VERA *holds out the note without a word.*) A note? From whom?

VERA (*In a toneless voice*): Read it.

NATALYA PETROVNA: You frighten me. (*Reads the note in silence and suddenly presses both hands to her face and sinks into an armchair. A long silence.*)

VERA (*Approaching her*): Natalya Petrovna.

NATALYA PETROVNA (*Not taking her hands from her face*): He is gone! . . . He wouldn't even say good-bye to me. . . . Oh, to you he said good-bye, anyway!

Vera (*Sadly*): He doesn't love me. . . .

Natalya Petrovna (*Taking her hands from her face and standing up*): But he has no right to go off like this. . . . I will . . . He can't do this. . . . Who told him he might break away so stupidly. . . . It's simply contempt. . . . I . . . how does he know I should never have the courage. . . . (*Sinks into the armchair.*) My God! my God!

Vera: Natalya Petrovna, you told me yourself just now that he must go. . . . Remember.

Natalya Petrovna: You are glad now. . . . He is gone. . . . Now we are equal. (*Her voice breaks.*)

Vera: Natalya Petrovna, you said to me just now; these were your very words; instead of tormenting each other, hadn't we better think together how to get out of this position, how to save ourselves. . . . We are saved now.

Natalya Petrovna (*Turning away from her almost with hatred*): Ah! . . .

Vera: I understand, Natalya Petrovna; don't worry yourself. . . . I shan't burden you with my company long. We can't live together.

Natalya Petrovna (*Tries to hold out her hand to* Vera *but lets it fall on her lap*): Why do you say that, Verotchka? . . . Do you too want to leave me? Yes, you are right, we are saved now. All is over . . . everything is settled again. . . .

Vera (*Coldly*): Don't disturb yourself, Natalya Petrovna. (*She looks at Natalya Petrovna without speaking. Islayev comes out of the study.*)

Islayev (*After looking for a moment at Natalya Petrovna, aside to Vera*): Does she know that he is going?

Vera (*Puzzled*): Yes . . . she knows.

Islayev (*To himself*): But why has he been in such a hurry? . . . (*Aloud.*) Natasha. . . . (*He takes her hand. She raises her head.*) It's I, Natasha. (*She tries to smile.*) You're not well, my darling? I should advise you to lie down, really. . . .

Natalya Petrovna: I'm quite well Arkady; it's nothing.

Islayev: But you're pale. . . . Come, do as I say. . . . Rest a little.

Natalya Petrovna: Oh! very well. . . . (*She tries to get up, and cannot.*)

Islayev (*Helping her*): There you see. . . . (*She leans on his arm.*) Shall I help you along?

Natalya Petrovna: Oh, I'm not so weak as all that! Come, Vera. (*Goes towards the study. Rakitin comes in from the outer room. Natalya Petrovna stops.*)

Rakitin: I have come, Natalya Petrovna, to . . .

Islayev (*Interrupting him*): Ah, Michel, come here! (*Draws him aside—in an undertone with vexation.*) What made you tell her at once like this? Didn't I beg you not to! Why be in such a hurry? . . . I found her here in such a state.

Rakitin (*Perplexed*): I don't understand.

Islayev: You've told Natasha you are going. . . .

Rakitin: So you suppose that is what has upset her?

Islayev: Sh! she is looking at us. (*Aloud*.) You're not going to he down, Natasha?

Natalya Petrovna: Yes. . . . I'm going. . . .

Rakitin: Good-bye, Natalya Petrovna! (Natalya Petrovna *takes hold of the doorhandle and makes no reply*.)

Islayev (*Laying his hand on* Rakitin's *shoulder*): Natasha, do you know this is one of the best of men. . . .

Natalya Petrovna (*With sudden vehemence*): Yes, I know he's a splendid man . . . you're all splendid men . . . all of you, all . . . and yet. . . . (*She hides her face in her hands, pushes the door open with her knee and goes out hurriedly*. Vera *goes out after her*. Islayev *in silence sits down to the table and leans on his elbows*.)

Rakitin (*Looks at him for some time and with a bitter smile shrugs his shoulders*): Nice position mine! Glorious, it certainly is! Really it's positively refreshing. And what a farewell after four years of love! Excellent, serve the talker right. And thank God, it's all for the best. It was high time to end these sickly, morbid relations. (*Aloud to* Islayev.) Well, Arkady, good-bye.

Islayev (*Raises his head. There are tears in his eyes*): Good-bye, my dear, dear boy. It's

. . . not quite easy to bear. I didn't expect it. It's like a storm on a clear day. Well, grind the corn and there'll be flour. But anyway, thank you, thank you. You're a true friend.

RAKITIN (*Aside through his teeth*): This is too much. (*Abruptly.*) Good-bye. (*Is about to go into outer room.* SHPIGELSKY *runs in, meeting him.*)

SHPIGELSKY: What is it? They tell me Natalya Petrovna is ill. . . .

ISLAYEV (*Getting up*): Who told you so?

SHPIGELSKY: The girl . . . her maid. . . .

ISLAYEV: No, it's nothing, Doctor. I think better not disturb Natasha just now. . . .

SHPIGELSKY: Ah! well, that's all right. (*To* RAKITIN.) I hear you're going to the town?

RAKITIN: Yes, on business.

SHPIGELSKY: Ah! on business! . . . (*At that instant* ANNA SEMYONOVAN, LIZAVETA BOGDANOVNA, KOLYA *and* SCHAAF *burst in from the outer room, all at once.*)

ANNA SEMYONOVNA: What is it? What's the matter? What's wrong with Natasha?

KOLYA: What's the matter with Mamma? What is it?

ISLAYEV: Nothing's the matter with her. . . . I saw her a minute ago. What's the matter with all of you?

ANNA SEMYONOVNA: Really, Arkasha, we were told Natasha's been taken ill. . . .

ISLAYEV: Well, you shouldn't have believed it.

ANNA SEMYONOVNA: But why are you so cross, Arkasha? Our sympathy's only natural.

ISLAYEV: Of course . . . of course.

RAKITIN: It's time for me to start.

ANNA SEMYONOVNA: You are going away?

RAKITIN: Yes. . . . I am going.

ANNA SEMYONOVNA (*To herself*): Ah! Well, now I understand.

KOLYA (*To* ISLAYEV): Papa . . .

ISLAYEV: What do you want?

KOLYA: Why has Alexey Nikolaitch gone out?

ISLAYEV: Where's he gone?

KOLYA: I don't know. . . . He kissed me, put on his cap and went out. . . . And it's time for my Russian lesson.

ISLAYEV: I expect he'll be back soon. . . . We can send to look for him, though.

RAKITIN (*Aside to* ISLAYEV): Don't send after him, Arkady, he won't come back. (ANNA SEMYONOVNA *tries to overhear*; SHPIGELSKY *is whispering with* LIZAVETA BOGDANOVNA.)

ISLAYEV: What's the meaning of that?

RAKITIN: He's going away, too.

ISLAYEV: Going away . . . where?

RAKITIN: To Moscow.

ISLAYEV: To Moscow? Why, is everybody going mad to-day, or what?

RAKITIN (*In a still lower voice*): Well, the fact is . . . Verotchka's fallen in love with him . . . so being an honourable man he decided to go. (ISLAYEV, *flinging up his hands, sinks into an arm–chair.*) You understand now, why. . . .

ISLAYEV (*Leaping up*): Understand? I understand nothing. My head's going round. What is one to make of it? All fluttering off in different directions like a lot of partridges, and all because they're honourable men. . . . And all at once on the same day. . . .

ANNA SEMYONOVNA (*Coming up from one side*): But what's this? Mr. Beliayev, you say . . .

ISLAYEV (*Shouts hysterically*): Never mind, Mamma, never mind! Herr Schaaf, kindly give Kolya his lesson now instead of Mr. Beliayev. Take him away.

SCHAAF: Yes, Sir. (*Takes* KOLYA'S *hand*.)

KOLYA: But, Papa . . .

ISLAYEV (*Shouting*): Go along, go along! (SCHAAF *leads* KOLYA *away*.) I'll come part of the way with you, Rakitin. . . . I'll have my horse saddled, and wait for you at the dam. . . . And you, Mamma, meanwhile, for God's sake, don't disturb Natasha, nor you either, Doctor. . . . Matvey! Matvey! (*Goes out hurriedly.* ANNA SEMYONOVNA *sits down with melancholy dignity.* LIZAVETA BOGDANOVNA *takes her stand behind her.* ANNA SEMYONOVNA *turns her eyes upwards, as though disclaiming all connexion with what is going on around her.*)

SHPIGELSKY (*Slyly and stealthily to* RAKITIN): Well, Mihail Alexandritch, may I have the honour of driving you along the high road with my three new horses?

Rakitin: Why? Have you got the horses already?

Shpigelsky (*Discreetly*): I had a little talk with Vera Alexandrovna. . . . So may I?

Rakitin: By all means! (*Bows to* Anna Semyonovna.) Anna Semyonovna, I have the honour to . . .

Anna Semyonovna (*Still as majestically, not getting up*): Good-bye, Mihail Alexandritch. . . . I wish you a successful journey. . . .

Rakitin: I thank you . . . Lizaveta Bogdanovna. . . . (*Bows to her. She curtsies in reply. He goes into outer room.*)

Shpigelsky (*Going up to kiss* Anna Semyonovna's *hand*): Good-bye, gracious lady. . . .

Anna Semyonovna (*Less majestically but still severely*): Ah! you are going too, Doctor. . . .

Shpigelsky: Yes. My patients, you know, madam. . . . Besides, you see my presence here is not needed. (*As he bows himself out, winks slyly at* Lizaveta Bogdanovna, *who replies with a smile.*) Good-bye for the present. . . . (*Runs off after* Rakitin.)

Anna Semyonovna (*Lets him disappear, then folding her arms, turns deliberately to* Lizaveta Bogdanovna): And what do you think of all this, my dear, pray?

Lizaveta Bogdanovna (*Sighing*): I really don't know what to say, Anna Semyonovna.

Anna Semyonovna: Did you hear, Beliayev too has gone? . . .

LIZAVETA BOGDANOVNA (*Sighing again*): Ah, Anna Semyonovna, perhaps I, too, may not be staying here much longer. . . . I too am going away. (ANNA SEMYONOVNA *stares at her in unutterable amazement* LIZAVETA BOGDANOVNA *stands before her, without raising her eyes.*)

CURTAIN

1850

A PROVINCIAL LADY
(*A Comedy in One Act*)

Characters in the Play

ALEXEY IVANOVITCH STUPENDYEV, a district Government clerk, aged 48.

DARYA IVANOVNA, his wife, aged 28.

MISHA, a distant cousin of Darya Ivanovna, aged 19.

VALERIYAN NIKOLAYEVITCH, COUNT LYUBIN, aged 49.

VALET OF THE COUNT, aged 30.

VASSILYEVNA, Stupendyev's cook, aged 50.

APOLLON, Stupendyev's house-boy, aged 17.

A PROVINCIAL LADY

[*The action takes place in a provincial town in the house of the* STUPENDYEVS.

The drawing-room in the house of a not well-to-do Government clerk. In Centre, door into hall; on Right, door into study; on Left, two windows and door into little garden. On Left in corner, a low screen and in foreground a sofa, two chairs, a little table, and an embroidery frame; on Right, a small piano in background, and in foreground a table and chair.

DARYA IVANOVNA *is sitting at embroidery frame. She is simply but tastefully dressed.* MISHA *is sitting quietly on the sofa, reading a book.*]

DARYA (*Going on with her work and not raising her eyes*): Misha!

MISHA (*Putting down the book*): What is it?

DARYA: Have you . . . been to Popov's?

MISHA: Yes.

DARYA: What did he say?

MISHA: He said that everything shall be sent punctually. I particularly asked him about the red wine. You can be sure of that, he said. (*A pause.*) May I ask, are you expecting somebody, Darya Ivanovna?

Darya: I am.

Misha (*Again a pause*): May I ask, whom?

Darya: You are inquisitive. However, you are not a gossip, and I can tell you whom I am expecting, Count Lyubin.

Misha: That rich gentleman who has come to his estate here lately?

Darya: Yes.

Misha: Well, he is expected to-day at Kulyeshkin's hotel. But may I ask, do you know him?

Darya: I don't now.

Misha: Ah! then you used to?

Darya: Are you cross-examining me?

Misha: I beg your pardon. (*A pause.*) It was stupid of me to ask, though. Of course he must be the son of the Countess Lyubin who was your benefactress.

Darya (*Looking at him*): Yes, my benefactress.

> [*Behind the scenes the voice of* Stupendyev *is heard*: 'Told you not to? Why did she tell you not to?']

Darya: What's the matter out there?

> [Stupendyev *and* Vassilyevna *come in from the study,* Stupendyev *in shirt-sleeves and waistcoat;* Vassilyevna *with a man's coat in her hands.*]

Stupendyev (*To* Darya): Dasha, did you really tell? . . . (Misha *stands up and bows.*) Ah, good morning, Misha, good morning. Did you really tell this woman (*Points to* Vassilyevna) not to give me my dressing-gown to-day, eh?

Darya: I did not.

Stupendyev (*Turning to* Vassilyevna *with a triumphant expression*): There! Now then?

Darya: I only told her to ask you not to put on your dressing-gown....

Stupendyev: Why, what's wrong with my dressing-gown? It's so pretty with its stripes and patterns. You gave it me yourself!

Darya: That was a very long time ago!

Vassilyevna: Come, put on your coat, Alexey Ivanovitch, put it on.... Upon my word!... A fine sight—your striped gown! It's in holes at the elbows, and looked at from behind it's simply a disgrace.

Stupendyev (*Putting on his coat*): And who told you to look at me from behind? Gently, gently! Didn't you hear? You ought to have asked me.

Vassilyevna: Oh, go on with you.... (*Goes out.*)

Stupendyev (*Calling after her*): Don't argue, woman! It's awful how it cuts me under the arms, hang it all! These miserable tailors! I feel as though I were being dragged up on a string. Really, Dasha, I can't understand what possesses you to want to rig me out in my best coat; it will soon be eleven o'clock, time to go to the office, and then I shall have to put on my uniform anyway.

Darya: We may be having visitors.

Stupendyev: Visitors? What visitors?

Darya: Count Lyubin. You know who he is, don't you?

STUPENDYEV: Lyubin? I should think so. So you're expecting him?

DARYA: Yes. (*Glancing at him.*) What is there so marvellous in that?

STUPENDYEV: There's nothing marvellous in it, I quite agree with you; but let me tell you, my love, it's absolutely out of the question.

DARYA: Why so?

STUPENDYEV: It's out of the question, absolutely out of the question. What should he come here for?

DARYA: He has to talk things over with you.

STUPENDYEV: Suppose he has, suppose he has, but that proves nothing, that proves absolutely nothing. He'll send for me to go to him. He'll just send for me.

DARYA: used to know him; he used to see me at his mother's.

STUPENDYEV: That proves nothing either. What do you think, Misha?

MISHA: Me? I don't think anything.

STUPENDYEV (*To his wife*): There you see. . . . He won't come. . . . Really how you can. . . .

DARYA: Very well, perhaps not; but don't take off your coat. . . .

STUPENDYEV (*After a pause*): I quite agree with you, though. (*Walking up and down the room.*) So that's why they've been stirring up such a dust all the morning. . . . Oh, this hateful tidying! And you're dressed up to the nines!

DARYA: No personal remarks, Alexis, please.

STUPENDYEV: No, no, no personal remarks, of course. . . . This Count has run through his fortune, it seems, and that's why he's come into these parts. Is he a young man?

DARYA: Younger than you.

STUPENDYEV: H'm. . . . Quite, I quite agree with you. . . . So that's why you kept on practising on the piano yesterday. . . . (*Flings wide his hands.*) Yes, yes. (*Hums through his teeth.*)

MISHA: I looked in at Kulyeshkin's this morning. They're expecting him there.

STUPENDYEV: They are? Well, let them expect. (*To his wife.*) How was it I never saw him at Countess Lyubin's?

DARYA: He was in the Government service in Petersburg then. . . .

STUPENDYEV: H'm. . . . He's high up in the service now, I'm told. And you imagine he'll come to see us. What an idea!

> [APOLLON *comes in from Hall He is wearing a very badly fitting, light blue livery, adorned with white buttons. His face wears an expression of vacant astonishment.*]

APOLLON (*Mysteriously to* STUPENDYEV): There's a gentleman asking for you.

STUPENDYEV (*Alarmed*): What sort of gentleman?

APOLLON: I don't know, in a hat and whiskers.

STUPENDYEV (*Agitated*): Show him in. (APOLLON *glances mysteriously at* STUPENDYEV *and goes out.*) Can it be the Count?

> [*The Count's* VALET *comes in from hall. He is stylishly dressed in travelling clothes and he does not take off his hat.* VASSILYEVNA *and* APOLLON *peep in inquisitively at hall-door.*]

VALET (*With German accent*): Does Mr. Stupendyev, a Government clerk, live here?

STUPENDYEV: Yes. What is your pleasure?

VALET: Are you Mr. Stupendyev?

STUPENDYEV: Yes. What is your pleasure?

DARYA: Alexey Ivanitch!

VALET: Count Lyubin has arrived and told me to ask you to go to him.

STUPENDYEV: Then you come from him?

DARYA: Alexey Ivanitch, come here.

STUPENDYEV (*Going up to her*): Well?

DARYA: Tell him to take off his hat.

STUPENDYEV: You think so? H'm. . . . Yes, yes. (*Going up to the* VALET.) Don't you feel it rather warm in here? . . . (*Motioning towards his hat.*)

VALET: Here it is not warm. Consequently, you will come at once?

STUPENDYEV: I'll. . . . (DARYA *makes a sign to him.*) But allow me to ask who are you exactly?

VALET: I am his Excellency's hired man . . . his valet.

STUPENDYEV (*Suddenly firing up*): Take off your hat, take off your hat, take off your hat,

I tell you! (*The* Valet *slowly and with dignity removes his hat*.) And tell his Excellency that I'll lose no time. . . .

Darya (*Standing up*): Tell the Count that my husband is very busy just now and cannot leave the house. And that if the Count wishes to see him, let him come himself. You can go. (Valet *goes out*.)

Stupendyev (*To* Darya): Really though, Dasha, I think you . . . (Darya *walks up and down without speaking*.) I quite agree with you, though. But didn't I give it him, eh? Sent him off with a flea in his ear, as the saying is. An impudent fellow! (*To* Misha.) That was well done, wasn't it?

Misha: It was, Alexey Ivanitch, very well.

Stupendyev: To be sure it was.

Darya: Apollon!

[Apollon *comes in, followed by* Vassilyevna.]

Darya (*Gazing for some time at* Apollon): No, you are too absurd in that livery. You'd better not show yourself.

Vassilyevna: What's there absurd about him, ma'am, pray? He's the same as anybody else and my nephew too. . . .

Stupendyev: Woman, don't argue!

Darya (*To* Apollon): Turn round! (Apollon *turns round*.) No, you certainly must not appear before the Count. Go along and keep in hiding somewhere. . . . And you, Vassilyevna, sit in the hall, please.

Vassilyevna: But I've my work to do in the kitchen, ma'am.

STUPENDYEV: Who tells you to do your work, you saucy woman?

VASSILYEVNA: Upon my word. . . .

STUPENDYEV: Don't argue, woman! For shame! Off now, both of you! (VASSILYEVNA *and* APOLLON *go out*.) (*To* DARYA.) And so you really imagine that the Count will come now?

DARYA: I do.

STUPENDYEV (*Walking about*): I'm upset. . . . He will come in a rage. . . . I'm upset.

DARYA: Please be as calm and cool as you can.

STUPENDYEV: I will. But I'm upset. Misha, aren't you upset?

MISHA: No, Alexey Ivanitch, I'm not.

STUPENDYEV: Well, I'm upset. . . . (*To* DARYA.) Why didn't you let me go to him?

DARYA: That's my business. Remember that he can't do without you.

STUPENDYEV: He can't do without me. . . . I'm upset. . . . What's that?

APOLLON (*Rushes in with an extraordinarily agitated face*): I hadn't time to hide. The gentleman has come. I hadn't time to hide.

STUPENDYEV (*In a whisper*): Well, make haste and go in here! (*Pushes him into the study*.)

APOLLON: I hadn't time to hide and Vassilyevna is gone into the kitchen. (*Vanishes*.)

VOICE OF COUNT LYUBIN (*Behind the scenes*): What's the meaning of it? Is there nobody here? Why did that fellow run off?

STUPENDYEV (*In despair to* DARYA): Vassilyevna is gone into the kitchen!

VOICE OF COUNT: Boy!

DARYA: Misha, go and open the door.

> [MISHA *opens the door to* COUNT LYUBIN, *who comes in. He is dressed in the fashionable and rather foppish style common to elderly dandies.*]

MISHA: Please come in.

COUNT: Is Mr. Stupendyev here?

STUPENDYEV (*Bowing in confusion*): I . . . am Stupendyev.

COUNT: Glad to meet you. I'm Count Lyubin. I sent my man to you, but it was not convenient for you to come to me.

STUPENDYEV: I'm sorry, your Excellency, I . . .

COUNT (*Turning round, bows frigidly to* DARYA IVANOVNA, *who has withdrawn a little aside*): My respects. I must own I was surprised—I suppose you have business, urgent business?

STUPENDYEV: Precisely, your Excellency, business.

COUNT: Perhaps, I don't dispute it, but I imagine that for some people, one may leave one's business, particularly when . . . one is asked . . . (VASSILYEVNA *comes in from the hall.* STUPENDYEV *makes a sign to her to go*) when . . . (*The* COUNT *looks round wondering;* VASSILYEVNA *stares him in the face and runs away. The* COUNT *turns with a smile to* STUPENDYEV.)

Stupendyev: Never mind, your Excellency. It's of no consequence, the woman came in and is gone away; unfortunately, she came in, and fortunately, she's gone away. I'd better, if you'll allow me, introduce my wife here. . . .

Count (*Scarcely looking at her, bows frigidly*): Ah, delighted.

Stupendyev: Darya Ivanovna, your Excellency, Darya Ivanovna.

Count (*Still as frigidly*): Delighted, delighted; but I have come . . .

Darya (*Modestly*): You don't recognize me, Count?

Count (*Looking round*): Oh, good heavens . . . why it's actually . . . Darya Ivanovna! What an unexpected meeting! How many years! Is it really you? Well, I declare!

Darya: Yes, Count, it is a long time since we met. . . . I'm much changed since then, it seems.

Count: Not at all, you're only handsomer. With me . . . I'm sure, it's quite another thing.

Darya (*Innocently*): You're not changed in the least, Count.

Count: Oh, come! But I'm very glad now that your husband could not come to me; it gives me the opportunity of renewing my acquaintance with you. We are old friends, you know.

Stupendyev: Well, you see, your Excellency, it was her. . . .

Darya (*Hurriedly cutting him short*): Old friends. . . . I expect you have never all this time thought of . . . your old friends?

Count: That's not so at all. I must own I didn't quite remember to whom you were married. . . . My mother did write and tell me not long before her death . . . but . . .

Darya: Why, how could you—in Petersburg, in the great world, how could you help forgetting us. We poor provincials now—we don't forget. (*With a faint sigh.*) We forget nothing.

Count: It's not so, I assure you. (*A pause.*) Believe me, I always took the keenest interest in your future, and am glad to see you now . . . (*Hesitates for words*) so securely settled.

Stupendyev (*Bowing gratefully*): Quite, quite securely, your Excellency. The only thing is poverty—insufficient means—that's the trouble!

Count: Ah, quite so, quite so. . . . (*A pause.*) But (*Addressing* Stupendyev) allow me to ask your name and your father's?

Stupendyev (*Bowing*): Alexey Ivanitch, your Excellency, Alexey Ivanitch.

Count: Well, my good Alexey Ivanitch, we must talk over our business. . . . I imagine this won't interest your wife . . . so had we not better withdraw, you know . . . be alone for a while? We will discuss things. . . .

Stupendyev: As your Excellency prefers. . . . Dasha. . . . (Darya *is about to go.*)

Count: Oh, no, don't let us disturb you, please stay. . . . Alexey Ivanitch and I can go elsewhere. Shall we go into your room, Alexey Ivanitch?

Stupendyev: Into my room . . . h'm . . . into my study, that is. . . .

Count: Yes, yes, into your study. . . .

Stupendyev: As your Excellency pleases but . . .

Count (*To* Darya): We shall see each other again, Darya Ivanovna . . . I hope. (Darya *curtsies*.) Au revoir. (*To* Stupendyev.) Where are we to go . . . here? (*Motions with his hat towards door of study*.)

Stupendyev: In there . . . but . . . your Excellency. . . .

Count (*Not hearing him*): Very good, very good. . . . (*Goes to study, followed by* Stupendyev, *who as he goes out makes vague signs to his wife*. Darya *remains musing and looks after them. A few seconds later* Apollon *shoots like an arrow out of the study and runs off into the hall*. Darya *starts, smiles and sinks again into a reverie*.)

Misha (*Going up to her*): Darya Ivanovna!

Darya (*Rouses herself*): Well?

Misha: May I ask if it is long since you saw his Excellency?

Darya: Yes, twelve years.

Misha: Twelve years! Good gracious! And have you received any news from him during that time?

Darya: I? No. He has thought no more of me than of the Emperor of China.

Misha: Goodness! How was it then that he said he took the keenest interest in your future?

Darya: You're surprised at that? How young you are still—if that really surprises you! (*A pause.*) How much older he is!

Misha: Older?

Darya: Rouged . . . powdered . . . his hair's dyed . . . and his wrinkles . . . his wrinkles. . . .

Misha: Does he really dye his hair? Oh, I say, how shameful! (*A pause.*) I expect he means to go off at once.

Darya (*Turning quickly to him*): What makes you think so?

Misha (*Modestly looking down*): Oh, nothing.

Darya: No . . . he'll stay to dinner!

Misha (*With a sigh*): Oh, what a good thing that would be!

Darya: How so?

Misha (*Discreetly*): The provisions will be wasted . . . and the wine . . . if he doesn't stay, that is. . . .

Darya (*Impressively*): Yes. Now listen, Misha, this is important. They will come back in a minute.

Misha (*Looking at her intently*): Yes.

Darya: So, leave me here alone now, do you see.

Misha: Yes.

Darya: I shall invite the Count to dinner, but Alexey Ivanitch . . .

Misha: I understand. . . .

DARYA (*With a slight frown*): What do you understand? I shall send Alexey Ivanitch out to you. . . .

MISHA: Just so.

DARYA: And you must keep him . . . it won't be for very long. . . . Tell him that I must have a little talk with the Count for his benefit. . . . Do you understand?

MISHA: Yes.

DARYA: Well then, I rely on you. You can take him for a little walk if you like.

MISHA: Of course, we may as well go for a walk.

DARYA: Very well then. You can go now, leave me alone.

MISHA: Yes. (*Stops as he is going.*) Don't forget me too, Darya Ivanovna. You know how devoted I am to you, body and soul, I may say. . . .

DARYA: What do you mean?

MISHA: Oh, Darya Ivanovna, you know I, too, am simply dying to go to Petersburg! What shall I do here without you? Do this for me, Darya Ivanovna, and I will repay you. . . .

DARYA (*After a pause*): I don't understand you, I can't tell yet. . . . Very well, though, go along.

MISHA: I go. (*Raising his eyes to heaven.*) I will repay you, Darya Ivanovna! (*Goes out into hall.*)

DARYA (*Remains for some time motionless*): He didn't take the slightest notice of me—that's clear. He has forgotten me. And it seems I was foolish to have expected anything from his coming. What hopes I've been building on his visit. . . . (*Looks round her.*) Am I to remain here for ever, here? Well, there's no help for it! (*A pause.*) It's not quite certain yet, though. He has scarcely seen me. . . . (*Glancing in the looking-glass.*) I don't dye my hair, at any rate. . . . We'll see, we'll see. (*Walks up and down the room, goes to the piano and plays a few chords.*) This suspense is a torture. (*Sits down on sofa.*) But perhaps I too have run to seed in this wretched little town. . . . How can I tell? Who is there here to say what I'm like now, who is there who can make me feel what I've become? I'm superior to all of them, unhappily. . . . I'm above their level; but in his eyes—I'm none the less a provincial, the wife of a local clerk, his mother's old protégée, married off somehow . . . while he, he is a distinguished man, high up in the service, wealthy . . . well, he's not exactly wealthy; his affairs are in a bad way in Petersburg, and I expect he'll be here for a good deal more than a month. He's good-looking, that is, he was good-looking . . . now he powders and dyes his hair. They say that to men of his age the memories of young days are particularly precious; he knew me twelve years ago, he flirted with me. . . . Yes, yes, of course he had nothing better to do, that's why he flirted with me, but still . . . (*Sighs.*) And in those days I remember I dreamed . . . the dreams one has at sixteen! (*Suddenly *draws herself up erect.*) Good heavens, I do believe I have still one of his letters . . . I'm sure I have. But where is it? How annoying that I didn't think of it before! . . . I've still time, though. . . . (*A pause.*) Well, we shall see. And how lucky the music and books came just now! It makes me laugh. . . . Like a general before a battle, I'm preparing to meet the enemy. . . . And how I have changed in these last years! Can this be me, so coolly, so calmly thinking over what I'm to do? Necessity will drive one to learn anything, and to unlearn many things. No, I'm not calm, I'm excited now, but only because I don't know whether I can succeed. . . . Come, is that so? I'm not a girl now, of course, and memories have become precious to me, too . . . such as they are. . . . I shall have no others, and half my life, more than half is over. (*Smiles.*) But they are a long time. And what do I ask? What am I struggling for? The merest nothing. For him to give us a chance to move to Petersburg, to find us a post there—is nothing. And Alexey Ivanitch will be glad of any post. . . . Can I fail to get even that? If so, it's right I should stay in a provincial town . . . I deserve nothing better. . . . (*Pressing her hands to her cheeks.*) I'm in a fever with this suspense, these thoughts; my cheeks are simply burning. (*A pause.*) Well, so much the better. (*Hearing a sound in the study.*) They are coming . . . the battle is beginning. . . . Oh cowardly, ill-timed fears, away with you! (*Takes up a book and leans back on the sofa.* STUPENDYEV *and* COUNT LYUBIN *come in.*)

COUNT: And so I can rely on you, my good Alexey Ivanitch?

STUPENDYEV: Your Excellency, I am ready for my part to do all in my power....

COUNT: Very much obliged to you. And I'll send you the deeds very shortly. . . . I am going home to-day, and to-morrow or the day after ...

STUPENDYEV: Oh yes, yes.

COUNT (*Going up to* DARYA IVANOVNA): Darya Ivanovna, excuse me, please; to-day unfortunately I cannot stay any longer, but I hope some other time.

DARYA: Won't you dine with us, Count? (*Gets up.*)

COUNT: Thank you for the invitation, but ...

DARYA: And I have been so looking forward. . . . I was hoping you would spend a little time with us! Of course we must not presume to detain you....

COUNT: You are too kind, but really . . . if you knew—I am so busy....

DARYA: Think how long it is since we've met . . . and God knows when we shall see each other again! You are such a rare bird in these parts....

STUPENDYEV: Just so, your Excellency, a phœnix, one must say....

DARYA (*Interrupting him*): Besides, you can't be back in time for dinner at home now. . . .

I can assure you that you will dine better here than anywhere in the town.

STUPENDYEV: You see we knew your Excellency was coming.

DARYA (*Interrupting him*): So you will stay, won't you?

COUNT (*With some constraint*): You ask me so charmingly that I cannot refuse. . . .

DARYA: Ah! (*Takes his hat and puts it on the piano.*)

COUNT (*To* DARYA): I confess when I set off this morning I did not expect to have the pleasure of meeting you. (*A pause.*) Your town is not bad as far as I have seen it.

STUPENDYEV: For a provincial town, your Excellency, it's not so bad.

DARYA (*Sitting down*): Sit down, Count, please. . . . (COUNT *sits down.*) You can't imagine how happy I am, how delighted to see you here. (*To* STUPENDYEV.) Oh! by the way, Alexis, Misha is asking for you.

STUPENDYEV: What does he want?

DARYA: I don't know; but he seems very anxious to see you; please go to him.

STUPENDYEV: But how can I . . . with his Excellency . . . just now it's impossible.

COUNT: Oh, don't stand on ceremony, please. You leave me in very agreeable company. (*Passes his hand over his hair with an indifferent air.*)

STUPENDYEV: But what's he in such a hurry about?

DARYA: He wants you; go along, mon ami.

STUPENDYEV (*After a pause*): Very well. . . . But I'll be back in a minute . . . to your Excellency. . . . (*Bows*; COUNT *bows to him.* STUPENDYEV *goes out into study, saying to himself*: 'What can be the matter with him all of a sudden?' *A brief silence follows.* COUNT *looks sideways at* DARYA *with a faint smile, and shakes his head*.)

DARYA (*Casting down her eyes*): Have you come into our parts for long, your Excellency?

COUNT: For two months or so; I shall go as soon as my business is settled.

DARYA: You are staying at Spasskoye?

COUNT: Yes, on my mother's estate.

DARYA: In the same house?

COUNT: Yes. I must own it's rather cheerless living there now. It's so dilapidated, it's almost in ruins; next year I mean to pull it down.

DARYA: You say it's cheerless living there now. . . . I can't tell, my memories of it are so very pleasant. Can you really think of pulling it down?

COUNT: Do you regret it?

DARYA: I should think so! I spent the happiest years of my life in it. Besides, the memory of my benefactress, your dear mother. . . . You understand . . .

COUNT (*Cutting her short*): Oh yes, yes, I understand. (*A pause.*) Well, in old days certainly it was pleasant there. . . .

DARYA: You've not forgotten?

COUNT: What?

DARYA (*Again casting down her eyes*): The old days?

COUNT (*Gradually turning round and beginning to show some interest in* DARYA IVANOVNA): I have forgotten nothing, believe me. . . . Tell me, Darya Ivanovna, please, how old were you then? . . . Wait a bit, though. . . . Do you know you can't hide your age from me?

DARYA: I'm not trying to. . . . I am just as old as you were then, Count—twenty-eight.

COUNT: Was I really as old as that then? I think you must be mistaken. . . .

DARYA: Oh, no, Count, I'm not mistaken. . . . I remember too well everything that concerns you. . . .

COUNT (*With a forced laugh*): How old I am if that's so!

DARYA: You old? Nonsense!

COUNT: Well, so be it; I won't dispute that with you. (*A pause.*) Yes, that was a good time! Do you remember our early morning walks in the lime avenue before breakfast? (DARYA *casts down her eyes.*) Come, tell me, do you remember them?

DARYA: I have told you already, Count, that we who live in the country cannot forget the past, particularly when nothing like it has happened since. For you now—it's quite another thing!

COUNT (*Still more animated*): No, Darya Ivanovna, you really mustn't think that. I'm speaking seriously. Of course in big cities, there are so many distractions, especially for a young man; of course life is so full of noise and variety. . . . But I can assure you, Darya Ivanovna, the first, you know, the first early impressions are never effaced, and at times in the midst of the giddy whirl the heart . . . the heart, weary, you understand, of frivolity . . . simply longs, you know, for . . .

DARYA: Oh, yes, Count, I agree with you; first impressions do not pass away. I know it from experience.

COUNT: Ah! (*A pause.*) Confess, Darya Ivanovna, you must be rather dull here?

DARYA (*Speaking slowly*): I don't say that. At first, certainly, it was hard for me to get used to this different style of living, but then . . . my husband is such a kind, excellent man!

COUNT: Oh, yes . . . I quite agree. . . . He is a most worthy man, most worthy, but . . .

DARYA: Then I . . . I got used to it. I need little to make me happy. Home, family life . . . (*Dropping her voice*) and a few happy memories. . . .

COUNT: You have such memories?

DARYA: Yes, like everyone else; they make it easier to put up with being bored.

COUNT: So then you are bored at times, all the same?

DARYA: Do you wonder at it, Count? You remember I had the good fortune to be brought up in your mother's house. Compare what I was accustomed to in my youth with my surroundings now. Of course neither my position nor my birth—nothing, in fact—gave me the right to expect that I should go on living as I had begun; but you said yourself: the first impressions are never effaced, and it's impossible to expel from the memory (*Bowing her head*) what good sense would urge one to forget. . . . I will be open with you, Count. Do you suppose that I don't feel how poor . . . and ridiculous . . . everything here must seem to you? That page-boy racing away from you like a hare, that cook—and . . . and perhaps I myself. . . .

Count: You, Darya Ivanovna? Why, you must be joking! I assure you . . . No, indeed I am surprised. . . .

Darya: I'll tell you what you're surprised at, Count. You're surprised that I have not quite lost the habits of my youth yet, that I've not had time to become altogether provincial. . . . Is that surprise very flattering, do you think?

Count: How wickedly you turn my words, Darya Ivanovna!

Darya: Perhaps; but let us leave that, please. There are wounds which hurt when touched, even after they have healed. Besides, I am completely reconciled to my lot, I live alone in my obscure little corner; and if your arrival had not stirred many memories, all this would not have come into my mind. I should never have spoken of it, at any rate. I feel ashamed indeed that instead of trying to entertain you, so far as possible . . .

Count: But what do you take me for, allow me to ask? Do you suppose that I don't value your confidence, that I am not able to appreciate it? But you are unfair to yourself. It can't be true, I won't believe it, that you with your intelligence, your education, can have lived here without attracting friends.

Darya: Absolutely, I assure you, Count. And I don't in the least regret it. Let me tell you: I have pride. That is all that is left me from my past. I have no desire to attract people who do not attract me. . . . Besides, we are poor, we are dependent on other people; all that hinders intimacy—such intimacy as would not be wounding to me. Such intimacy is out of the question. . . . And I prefer solitude. Besides, solitude has no terrors for me—I read, I study; I am fortunate in having a husband who is an honest man. . . .

Count: Yes, one can see that at once.

Darya: My husband, of course, has his peculiarities. . . . I say this so freely to you because with your keen insight you cannot have failed to notice them—but he is an excellent man. And I should not complain of anything, I should be quite contented, if only. . . .

Count: If what?

Darya: If . . . at times . . . unforeseen . . . circumstances . . . did not trouble my peace.

Count: I can't venture to interpret your words, Darya Ivanovna. . . . What circumstances? You spoke just now of memories. . . .

Darya (*Looking him straight in the face with an innocent expression*): I will tell you, Count; I am going to be quite open with you. Indeed, I'm not good at pretence at any time, and with you it would be simply absurd. Can you imagine that it means nothing to a woman to see a man whom she has known in her youth, known in an utterly different world, in different surroundings—and to see him as I see you now . . . (Count *stealthily straightens his hair*) . . . to talk with him, to recall the past . . .

Count (*Interrupting her*): And do you imagine that it means nothing to a man, whom destiny has, so to speak, tossed about the world —that it means nothing to him to meet a woman like you, who has kept all . . . all the charm of youth, the . . . the intelligence, the elegance—cette grâce?

Darya (*With a smile*): And yet that woman had much ado to persuade that man to stay to dinner!

Count: Ah! you are malicious! No, tell me, do you really suppose it means nothing to him?

Darya: I don't suppose it. You see how open I am with you. It is always pleasant to recall one's young days, especially when one has nothing to reproach oneself with in them.

Count: Well, tell me then what that woman will answer if that man assures her that he has never, never forgotten her, that seeing her has, so to speak, touched him to the heart. . . .

DARYA: What she answers?

COUNT: Yes, yes, what does she answer?

DARYA: She answers that she too is touched by his friendly words and (*Holding out her hand to him*) offers him her hand for the renewing of the real friendship of old days.

COUNT (*Seizing her hand*): Vous êtes charmante. (*Tries to kiss her hand but* DARYA *draws it away*.) You are charming, exceedingly charming.

DARYA (*Gets up with a light-hearted air*): Ah, how glad I am! How glad I am! I was so afraid you would not care to remember me, that you would feel uncomfortable and ill at ease with us, that you might even think us impolite.

COUNT (*Still sitting, watches her intently*): Tell me, Dayra Ivanovan . . .

DARYA (*Turning slightly towards him*): What?

COUNT: Was it you persuaded Alexey Ivanitch not to come to me? (DARYA *nods slyly*.) You did? (*Getting up*.) I vow on my honour you shall not regret it.

DARYA: I should think not! I am seeing you.

COUNT: No, no, I didn't mean that.

DARYA (*Innocently*): Not that? What then?

COUNT: Why, it's a sin that you should remain here. I can't put up with that. I can't bear to think that such a pearl should be wasted in the wilderness. . . . I will get you . . . your husband, I mean . . . a post in Petersburg.

DARYA: Nonsense!

COUNT: You will see.

DARYA: Don't talk nonsense, I tell you.

COUNT: You think, perhaps, Darya Ivanovna, that I have not enough . . . er . . . er . . . (*He tries to find the word*) *influence* to do so?

DARYA: Oh! J'en suis parfaitement persuadée!

COUNT: Tiens! (*This exclamation escapes him unconsciously.*)

DARYA (*Laughing*): I believe you said 'tiens,' Count? Did you suppose I had forgotten my French?

COUNT: No, I didn't . . . mais quelaccent!

DARYA: Oh, come!

COUNT: Well, I promise you the position, all the same.

DARYA: Really? You're not joking?

COUNT: Not joking at all, quite in earnest.

DARYA: Well, so much the better. Alexey Ivanitch will be very, very grateful to you. (*A pause.*) Only please don't imagine . . .

COUNT: What?

DARYA: No, nothing. Such an idea could not occur to you, and it ought not to me. And so we may perhaps be in Petersburg? Oh, what happiness! How glad Alexey Ivanitch will be!

Count: We shall often see each other, shan't we? I look at you, at your eyes, at your curls—and I really feel as though you were sixteen and we were walking together as in old days in the garden sous ces magnifiques tilleuls. . . . Your smile has not changed in the least, your laugh is just as musical, just as sweet, aussi jeune qu'alors. . . .

Darya: How do you know that?

Count: How? Do you suppose I don't remember?

Darya: I didn't laugh in those days. . . . I was in no laughing humour. I was melancholy, pensive, silent—have you forgotten?

Count: Sometimes, though . . .

Darya: You should be the last person to forget that, monsieur le comte. Ah, how young we were then . . . I especially! You—you were already a dashing young officer when you came to us. Do you remember how delighted your dear mother was to see you, how she couldn't make enough of you. . . . Do you remember how even your old aunt, Princess Liza, completely lost her heart to you. . . . (*A pause.*) No, I didn't laugh in those days.

Count: Vous êtes adorable . . . plus adorable que jamais.

Darya: En verité. Memory can do wonders, it seems! You didn't say that to me then.

Count: I? I who . . .

Darya: Come, that's enough. Or I may fancy you are meaning to pay me compliments; that's out of place between old friends.

Count: I? I pay you compliments?

Darya: Yes, yes. Do you imagine you have changed very much since I saw you last? But let us talk of something else. You had better tell me what you are doing, how you spend your time in Petersburg—all that's so interesting to me. . . . You keep up your music, don't you?

Count: Yes, in my spare time, you know.

Darya: Have you still the same splendid voice?

Count: A splendid voice I never had, but I do sing still.

Darya: Ah, I remember you had a delightful voice, so sympathetic. . . . I believe you used to compose, too?

Count: I do compose a little now.

Darya: In what style?

Count: In the Italian. I don't care for any other. moi—Pour moi—je fais peu; mais ce que je fais est bien. By the way, you used to be fond of music. You yourself, I remember, used to sing very charmingly, and to play the piano very well. I hope you haven't dropped all that?

Darya (*Pointing to the piano and the music lying on it*): There's my answer.

Count: Ah. (*Goes up to the piano.*)

Darya: But unhappily our piano is a very poor one; it is in tune, though. It's a little shaky, but it's not an agony to hear it.

Count (*Strikes two or three chords*): It's not a bad tone. Oh—what an idea! I believe you played at sight?

Darya: If it's not too difficult, I can.

Count: Oh, it's not at all difficult. I have a little tiny thing here, une bagatelle que j'ai composée, a little duet from my opera for tenor and soprano—as perhaps you've heard—I'm writing an opera—just to amuse myself, you know . . . sans aucune prétention.

Darya: Really?

Count: I tell you what, if you'll allow me, I'll send for that little duet, or, no, I'd better go and fetch it. We'll try it together, shall we?

Darya: Have you got it here?

Count: Yes, at my hotel.

Darya: Oh, Count, for goodness' sake, make haste and get it. Oh dear, I am grateful to you! Please go and fetch it.

Count (*Takes his hat*): At once. Vous verrez cela n'est pas mal. I hope you will like this little trifle.

Darya: Can you doubt it? Only I beg you beforehand not to be critical.

Count: Oh, how can you? On the contrary it is I . . . (*As he is going to the door.*) Ah! so you were in no mood for laughter in those days!

Darya: I believe you are laughing at me now. . . . And yet I have something I could show you. . . .

Count: What is it? What is it?

Darya: That I have treasured. . . . I should like to see if you would recognize it. . . .

Count: But what is it you are talking of?

Darya: I know what. Go now and fetch your little duet, and then we'll see.

Count: Vous êtes un ange. I'll be back in a moment. Vous êtes un ange. (*Kisses his hand to her and vanishes into hall.*)

Darya (*Looks after him and after a brief silence, exclaims*): Victory! Victory! . . . Can it really be? And so quickly, so unexpectedly! Ah! Je suis un ange! je suis adorable! So I have not quite gone to seed yet. I can still attract even men like him . . . (*Smiling*) like him. . . . Oh, my dear Count! I can't disguise the fact that you are rather funny and have certainly seen your best days. And he didn't turn a hair when I told him he was twenty-eight then instead of thirty-nine . . . how coolly I told the lie, though. Go and fetch your little duet, as you call it. You may be sure I shall think it charming. (*Stops before the mirror, looks at herself, and passes both hands down her figure.*) My poor countrified dress, good-bye to you, I shall soon part from you! It's a good thing I begged that fashion plate from our Mayor's wife. You've done me good service. I'll never throw you away; but I'm not going to put you on in Petersburg. (*Prinking before the glass.*) I fancy velvet would not look out of place on these shoulders. (*The door from hall is opened a little way and* Misha's *head appears.*

He looks for some time at DARYA *and, without coming in, says in an undertone*: 'Darya Ivanovna.')

DARYA (*Turning round quickly*): Ah, it's you, Misha! What do you want? I've no time....

MISHA: I know, I know . . . I'm not coming in; I only wanted to warn you that Alexey Ivanitch will be here in a minute.

DARYA: Why didn't you take him for a walk?

MISHA: I did go for a walk with him, Darya Ivanovna, but he said he wanted to go to his office; I couldn't prevent him.

DARYA: Well, did he go to the office?

MISHA: Yes, he certainly did go into the Department; but a little while afterwards he came out again.

DARYA: How do you know he came out?

MISHA: I was watching round the corner. (*Listens*) There, I believe he's just coming in. (*Vanishes, and a minute later reappears.*) You won't forget me, will you?

DARYA: No, no.

MISHA: All right. (*Disappears.*)

DARYA: Can Alexey Ivanitch have taken it into his head to be jealous? A happy moment for it, I must say! (*She sits down.* STUPENDYEV *comes in from hall. He is embarrassed.* DARYA *looks round.*) Oh, it's you, Alexis?

STUPENDYEV: Me, me, my love. Has the Count gone?

DARYA: I thought you were at the office.

Stupendyev: I did just look in at the Department, you know, to tell them not to expect me. How could I go to-day? We have such an honoured guest. . . . But what has become of him?

Darya (*Gets up*): Listen, Alexey Ivanitch, do you want to get a good post, with a good salary, in Petersburg?

Stupendyev: Me? I should rather think so!

Darya: You would like it?

Stupendyev: Of course . . . what a question?

Darya: Then leave me alone.

Stupendyev: Alone? How do you mean?

Darya: Alone with the Count. He'll be here in a minute. He's gone to his hotel for a little duet.

Stupendyev: A little duet?

Darya: Yes, a little duet. He has composed a duet. We want to try it over together.

Stupendyev: Then why must I go? . . . I should like to hear it too.

Darya: Oh, Alexey Ivanitch! You know all composers are frightfully shy, and a third person—seems simply awful to them.

Stupendyev: Composer? H'm. . . . A third person. . . . But I really don't know whether it's quite proper. . . . How can I go out of the house? . . . The Count may be offended, in fact.

Darya: Not a bit—I assure you. He knows you are a busy man, with official duties; s, you'll be back to dinner.

Stupendyev: To dinner? Yes.

Darya: At three o'clock.

Stupendyev: Three o'clock. H'm! Yes . . . I quite agree with you. . . . To dinner. Yes, at three o'clock. (*Fidgets*.)

Darya (*After waiting a little*): Well, what are you going to do?

Stupendyev: I don't know . . . I've got . . . a bit of a headache. Here on the left side.

Darya: Have you? On the left side?

Stupendyev: Yes, really . . . here, here, on the left side; I don't know . . . I think I'd better remain at home.

Darya: I tell you what, my dear, you are jealous of the Count, that's clear.

Stupendyev: Me jealous! What an idea! That would be too stupid. . . .

Darya: Of course, it would be very stupid, there's no doubt about that; but you are jealous.

Stupendyev: I am?

Darya: You are jealous of a man who dyes his hair.

Stupendyev: Does the Count dye his hair? What of it? I wear a wig.

Darya: That's true; and so, as your peace of mind is more precious to me than anything, stay, by all means. . . . But give up all thought of Petersburg.

Stupendyev: But why so? Can this post in Petersburg . . . can it depend on my being absent?

Darya: Precisely.

Stupendyev: H'm! Queer. Of course, I agree with you; but still you must admit, it is queer.

Darya: Perhaps.

Stupendyev: How queer it is . . . how queer it is! (*Walks about the room.*) H'm!

Darya: But make up your mind quickly, anyway. . . . The Count will be back in a minute. . . .

Stupendyev: How queer it is! (*A pause.*) Do you know what, Dasha, I will remain.

Darya: As you please.

Stupendyev: But did the Count actually say anything about this post?

Darya: I can add nothing to what I have told you already. Stay or go, as you please.

Stupendyev: And is it a good post?

Darya: It is.

Stupendyev: I quite agree with you . . . I . . . will stay. Yes, decidedly I will stay, Dasha. (*From the hall comes the voice of the* Count, *carolling a roulade.*) Here he is! (*After a brief hesitation.*) At three o'clock! Good-bye! (*Runs off into study.*)

Darya: Thank God! (*The* Count *comes in, a roll of music in his hands.*) At last! I thought you were never coming, Count.

Count: Me voilà, me voilà, ma toute belle. I was detained.

Darya: Show me, show me. . . . You can't imagine how impatient I feel! (*Takes the roll from his hands and eagerly examines it.*)

Count: Please, you mustn't expect anything too extraordinary. I told you beforehand, you know, that it's just a trifle, a mere trifle.

DARYA (*Not taking her eyes from the music*): Quite the contrary. . . . Oh, mais c'est charmant! Ah, how sweet this transition is! (*Pointing with her finger.*) Ah, I'm in love with that passage.

COUNT (*With a modest simper*): Yes, it is a little out of the ordinary.

DARYA: And this rentrée!

COUNT: Ah! you like it?

DARYA: Very, very charming! Well, come along, come along; why waste time? (*Goes to piano, sits down, puts up stand and lays music on it. The* COUNT *takes up his position behind her.*)

DARYA: It is—andante?

COUNT: Andante, andante amoroso quasi cantando. . . . (*Clearing his throat.*) H'm, h'm! I'm not in voice to-day. . . . But you must make allowances. . . . Une voix de compositeur, vous savez.

DARYA: The usual excuse. Poor me, what can I say after that? I'll begin. (*She plays the ritournelle.*) This is difficult.

COUNT: Not for you.

DARYA: The words are very nice.

COUNT: Yes. . . . I found them, I think, dans Metastase. . . . I don't know whether they are legibly written, (*pointing with his finger.*) He sings this to her:

> 'La dolce tua imagine
> O, vergine amata
> Dell'a ma inamorata.'

Well, so listen. (*Sings a song in the Italian style;* Darya Ivanovna *accompanies him*.)

Darya: Splendid, splendid. . . . Oh, que c'est joli.

Count: You think so?

Darya: Wonderful, wonderful!

Count: I didn't sing it as it should be sung. But, my goodness, how you accompanied it! I assure you no one has ever accompanied me so well . . . no one!

Darya: You flatter me.

Count: I flatter? That's not in my character, Darya Ivanovna. Believe me, c'est moi qui le dit. You are a great pianist.

Darya (*Who seems still absorbed in contemplation of the music*): I do like this passage! How original it is!

Count: It is, isn't it?

Darya: And can the whole opera be as fine?

Count: You know a composer cannot judge of that; but I fancy the rest is no worse, if not better.

Darya: Oh dear! Won't you play me something from the opera?

Count: I should be only too glad and happy to do what you ask, Darya Ivanovna, but I'm sorry to say I don't play the piano, and I have brought nothing with me.

Darya: What a pity! (*Getting up.*) Another time then. I hope, Count, you will come and see us again before you go away?

Count: If you allow me, I should be glad to come every day. As regards my promise, you need have no doubts about that.

Darya (*Innocently*): What promise?

Count: I will obtain a post for your husband in Petersburg, I give you my word of honour. You must not remain here. Why, it would be simply outrageous! Vous n'êtes pas faite pour . . . pour . . . végéter ici. You ought to be one of the brilliant ornaments of our Petersburg world, and I should like . . . I shall be proud to be the first. . . . But you seem absorbed . . . in what may I ask?

Darya (*Humming as though to herself*): La dolce tua imàginè. . . .

Count: Ah! I knew that phrase would stay in your memory, I knew it. . . . As a rule, all I write est très chantant.

Darya: That air is most charming. But I beg your pardon, Count . . . I didn't hear what you were saying . . . thanks to your music.

Count: I was saying that you really must move to Petersburg, Darya Ivanovna—for your own sake and your husband's in the first place and for my sake in the second. I venture to bring in myself because. . . . because our old friendship, I may say, gives me a certain right to do so. I have never forgotten you, Darya Ivanovna, and now more than ever I can assure you I am sincerely devoted to you . . . that this meeting with you . . .

DARYA (*Mournfully*): Count, why are you saying this?

COUNT: Why shouldn't I say what I feel?

DARYA: Because you ought not to arouse in me . . .

COUNT: Arouse what? . . . Arouse what? . . . Tell me. . . .

[STUPENDYEV *appears in study doorway*.]

DARYA: Vain expectations.

COUNT: Why vain? And what expectations?

DARYA: I will be frank with you, Valeryan Nikolaitch.

COUNT: You remember my name!

DARYA: Well, you see . . . here you have shown . . . some interest in me, but in Petersburg I shall perhaps seem so insignificant that I dare say you will regret what you are now intending to do for us.

COUNT: Oh, good heavens, how can you say such things! You don't know your own value. Is it possible you don't understand. . . . Mais vous êtes une femme charmante. . . . Regret what I'm doing for you, Darya Ivanovna!

DARYA (*Seeing* STUPENDYEV): For my husband, you mean.

COUNT: Well, yes, yes, for your husband. Regret it. . . . No, you don't yet know my real feelings. . . . I want to be open with you . . . in my turn.

DARYA (*Embarrassed*): Count. . . .

COUNT: You don't know my real feelings, I tell you, you don't know them.

Stupendyev (*Comes rapidly into the room, approaches the* Count *who is standing with his back to him and bows*): Your Excellency, your Excellency....

Count: You don't know what I am feeling, Darya Ivanovna....

Stupendyev (*Shouts*): Your Excellency, your Excellency....

Count (*Turns round quickly, looks at him for some time, and says calmly*): Oh, is it you, Alexey Ivanitch? Where have you sprung from?

Stupendyev: From the study . . . from the study, your Excellency. I've been here, in the study, your Excellency....

Count: I thought you were at your office. Here your wife and I have been making music. Mr. Stupendyev, you are the happiest of men! I tell you this so simply, so directly, because I've known your wife from a child.

Stupendyev: You are too kind, your Excellency.

Count: Yes, yes . . . you are a happy man!

Darya: My dear, you may thank the Count . . .

Count (*Quickly interrupting*): Permettez. . . . Je le lui dirai moi-même . . . plus tard. . . quand nous serons plus d'accord. (*Aloud to* Stupendyev.) You are a happy man! Are you fond of music?

Stupendyev: Oh, yes, your Excellency. . . . I . . .

Count (*Turning to* Darya Ivanovna): By the way . . . there was something you meant to show me, have you forgotten?

Darya: To show you?

Count: Yes . . . you . . . Vous avez déjà oublié?

Darya (*In a rapid aside*): Il est jaloux et il comprend le français. Oh yes, of course . . . I remember now: I meant to . . . I meant to show you our garden; there is still time before dinner.

Count: Ah! (*A pause.*) So you have a garden?

Darya: A little one, but plenty of flowers in it.

Count: Yes, yes, I remember; you were always very fond of flowers. Show me your garden, do, please do. (*Goes to piano for his hat.*)

Stupendyev (*Going up to* Darya, *in an undertone*): What's this . . . what's this . . . what does this mean, eh?

Darya (*In an undertone*): Three o'clock . . . or you won't get the post. (*Moves away from him and takes her parasol from the table.*)

Count (*Coming back to her*): Give me your arm. (*Aside.*) I understand you.

Darya (*With a scarcely perceptible smile*): You think so?

Stupendyev (*As though waking up*): Allow me, allow me . . . I'll come with you.

Darya (*Stopping and looking round*): You'd like to come too, mon ami? Come along, come with us. (*She goes with the* Count *towards the door into garden*.)

Stupendyev: Yes . . . yes, I'm coming. (*Seizes his hat and takes a few steps*.)

Darya: Come along, come along. . . . (*She goes out with the* Count.)

Stupendyev (*Takes a few steps further, crushes up his hat and flings it on the floor*): No, hang it all! I'll stay here! I'm not going! (*Walks about the room*.) I'm a man of action, I don't like half-measures. I want to see how far . . . I want to see this through to the end. I want the evidence of my own eyes. That's what I want. . . . Why, it's something unheard of! What though she did know him in childhood, what though she is a woman of culture, a woman of the highest culture—what does she want to make a fool of me for? Is it because I've not had a good education? In the first place that's not my fault. Talking of a post up in Petersburg—why, what nonsense! Am I to believe that? Is it likely? This Count's going to give me a post all at once! And after all he's nobody so high and mighty himself—his affairs are in a shocking mess. . . . Even supposing he really is going to get me a post of some sort up in Petersburg—why all this tête and tête with him the whole day? . . . It's not proper! Why, he's promised—and that's the end of it. Three o'clock. . . . Tells me, too, to wait till three o'clock (*Looks at his watch*) and now it's only a quarter past two! (*Stops short*.) I will go into the garden, so there! (*Looks out*) I say, they're not in sight. (*Picks up hat and straightens it*) I will go, dash it all, I will. She herself, she actually said (*Mimics his wife*) do come, mon ami, come along! (*A pause.*) Yes, going indeed, not likely! No, my dear, I know you . . as though you'd go! You're going this minute, are you? Ugh! (*With vexation flings his hat on floor again.* Misha *walks in.*)

Misha (*Going up to* Stupendyev): What's the matter, Alexey Ivanitch? You don't seem quite yourself. (*Picks up hat, straightens it and lays it on the table.*) What's wrong?

Stupendyev: Let me alone, please. You needn't come bothering me anyway.

Misha: Alexey Ivanitch, please don't say such things; I hope I haven't been worrying you in any way?

Stupendyev (*A pause*): It's not you who's worrying me, but (*Waves arm in direction of the garden*) that's who is!

Misha (*Glancing towards the door, in an innocent voice*): Who's that, may I ask?

Stupendyev: Who? . . . He. . . .

Misha: Who is he, Alexey Ivanitch?

Stupendyev: As though you don't know! This Count!

Misha: In what way can he be worrying you?

Stupendyev: In what way! . . . Here he's not left Darya Ivanovna's side all the morning, singing with her, going for a walk. . . . Do you suppose . . . that . . . that's pleasant? Is it pleasant—eh? for a husband, that is.

Misha: For a husband it does not matter.

Stupendyev: Doesn't matter? Don't you hear: he's walking with her, singing with her.

Misha: Is that all? . . . Really, Alexey Ivanitch, it's too bad of you to . . . be worried. You know it's all being done for your benefit, so to speak. The Count is a person of consequence, with influence, and knew Darya Ivanovna as a child—what, are we to refuse to take advantage of it? Good gracious, Alexey Ivanitch! Why, we should be ashamed to look any right-thinking man in the face if we did! I feel I'm expressing myself strongly, too strongly, but it's my devotion to you. . . .

Stupendyev: Get along with your devotion! (*Sits down and turns away.*)

Misha: Alexey Ivanitch. . . . (*A pause.*) Alexey Ivanitch!

STupendyev (*Without stirring*): Well, what do you want?

Misha: Why are you sitting like this? Let's go for a walk.

Stupendyev: I don't want to.

Misha: Come along . . . really, we'd better, Alexey Ivanitch.

Stupendyev (*Turning quickly and folding his arms*): And what are you after, eh? Why have you been following me about all the morning? Have you been told off to look after me like a nurse, or what?

Misha (*Dropping his eyes*): Well, yes, Alexey Ivanitch.

STUPENDYEV (*Getting up*): Who put you up to it, if I may ask?

MISHA: It's all for your good, Alexey Ivanitch.

STUPENDYEV: Kindly inform me who set you to look after me?

MISHA (*With a sort of moan*): Only for goodness' sake, do listen to me, Alexey Ivanitch. Two words, Alexey Ivanitch, just two words. . . . I can't explain exactly. There, I do believe it's coming on to rain . . . they'll be here in a minute. . . .

STUPENDYEV: It's coming on to rain and you ask me to come for a walk!

MISHA: But we needn't go out of doors. . . . Really, Alexey Ivanitch, don't be so upset. . . . What are you afraid of? . . . We are here, you know, we are watching. . . . Why, the whole thing seems so ordinary. . . . You'll be back, you see, at three o'clock. . . .

STUPENDYEV: But what are you fussing about? What did she tell you?

MISHA: She didn't tell me anything, Alexey Ivanitch, precisely . . . but only . . . Oh dear, you know you are both my benefactors. You are my benefactor, and Darya Ivanovna is my benefactress, and besides, she's a relation. How can I help doing my best? . . . (*Takes him by the arm.*)

STUPENDYEV: I shall stay, I tell you! My place is here! I'm master in this house. . . . I will defeat their plot! Here!

Misha: Of course you are master, Alexey Ivanitch; but since I tell you I know all about it . . .

Stupendyev: What of it? Do you suppose she can't bamboozle you? No fear, you're young and foolish, my boy. You don't know what women are. . . .

Misha: How should I? . . . Only you see . . .

Stupendyev: I found the Count here and with my own ears heard him persisting: you don't know my feelings, madam, he said; I'll reveal them, my feelings, that is, he said; . . . And you ask me to go for a walk!

Misha (*Miserably*): I do believe it's spotting with rain. . . . Alexey Ivanitch! Alexey Ivanitch!

Stupendyev: How he keeps on! (*A pause.*) It really is raining!

Misha: They are coming here, they are coming. . . . (*Again takes him by the arm.*)

Stupendyev (*Resisting*): I won't, I tell you! (*A pause.*) Well, hang it all, then, let's go!

Misha: The hat! The hat! Let me get it. . . .

Stupendyev: Never mind the hat! Leave it! (*They run out into hall* Darya *and the* Count *come in from garden.*)

Count: Charmant, charmant!

Darya: You like it?

Count: Your garden is extremely nice, like everything else here. (*A pause.*) Darya Ivanovna, I must own . . . I didn't expect all this; I'm enchanted, simply enchanted. . . .

Darya: What didn't you expect, Count?

Count: You understand me. But when will you show me that letter?

Darya: What do you want it for?

Count: What for? . . . I should like to know whether I felt the same in those days, those splendid days when we were both so young . . . .

Darya: Count, I think we had better not recall those days.

Count: But why not? Surely, Darya Ivanovna, you must see what an impression you have made on me! . . .

Darya (*Embarrassed*): Count. . . .

Count: Do, do listen to me. . . . I am telling you the truth. When I came here, when I saw you, I confess that I thought—forgive me, please—I thought that you only wanted to renew your acquaintance with me. . . .

Darya (*Raising her eyes*): And you were not mistaken.

Count: And so I . . . I . . .

Darya (*With a smile*): Go on, Count, go on.

Count: Then I suddenly realized that I have to do with an exceedingly fascinating woman, and now I must frankly acknowledge you have completely turned my head. . . .

Darya: You are laughing at me, Count.

Count: Me laughing at you?

Darya: Yes, you are. Let us sit down, Count. Allow me to say a few words. (*Sits down.*)

Count (*Sitting down*): You still won't believe me!

Darya: And would you have me believe you? Nonsense. . . . As though I don't know the sort of impression I'm making on you. To-day, goodness knows why, you find me attractive; to-morrow you will forget me. (*He tries to break in but she stops him.*) Put yourself in my position. . . . You are still young and brilliant, you live in the great world; you are only a chance visitor here! . . .

Count: But . . .

Darya (*Stopping him*): You have noticed me in passing. You know that our paths in life he so far apart . . . it costs you nothing to assure me of your . . . your friendship. . . . But I, Count, I who am doomed to spend my whole life in solitude—I must treasure my peace of mind, I must keep strict watch over my heart, if I don't want later . . .

Count (*Interrupting*): Your heart, your heart; vous dîtes heart? But do you suppose I haven't a heart too? And how do you know that it, my heart, has not . . . is not stirred, in fact? You say solitude? But why solitude?

Darya: I expressed myself badly, Count; I am not alone—I have no right to speak of solitude.

Count: I understand, I understand—your husband . . . but surely . . . surely. . . . This is only between us, you know . . . it's only

. . . de la Sympathie. (*A brief silence.*) Only something, I must own, wounds me: it wounds me that you won't be just to me, that you look on me as some sort . . . I don't know . . . sort of deceiver . . . that you won't believe in me, in fact. . . .

Darya (*After a pause, looking sideways at him*): So I am to believe you, Count?

Count: Ah, vous êtes charmante. (*Takes her hand. Darya Ivanovna seems at first about to withdraw it, then leaves it. The Count kisses it ardently.*) Yes, believe me, Darya Ivanovna, believe me, I'm not deceiving you. I will keep all my promises. You are going to live in Petersburg. You . . . you . . . will see. And not in solitude . . . I'll answer for that. You say I shall forget you! If only you don't forget me!

Darya: Valeryan Nikolaitch!

Count: Now you see yourself how unpleasant, how wounding it is to be doubted! Why, I might just as well fancy that you were playing a part, que ce n'est pas pour mes beaux yeux. . . .

Darya: Valeryan Nikolaitch!

Count (*More and more ardent and getting up from his seat*): But no matter what opinion you may have of me! . . . I . . . I must tell you that I am devoted to you, heart and soul, that I'm in love with you, in fact, passionately in love with you, passionately, and ready to swear it on my knees!

Darya (*Getting up*): On your knees, Count!

Count: Yes, on my knees, if that weren't considered—well, somewhat theatrical.

Darya: Why so? . . . No, I confess that must be very delightful—for a woman. (*Turning quickly to the* Count.) Do go down on your knees, Count, if you really are not laughing at me.

Count: With pleasure, Darya Ivanovna, if only that will make you believe me. . . . (*With some difficulty kneels down.*)

Darya (*Lets him kneel, then quickly goes up to him*): Good heavens, Count, what are you doing! Get up, I was joking.

Count (*Tries to get up but cannot*): Never mind, let me be Je vous aime, Dorothée. . . . Et vous?

Darya: Get up, I entreat you. . . . (*From hall appears* Stupendyev *whom* Misha *tries in vain to hold back.*) Get up . . . (*She makes signs while with difficulty suppressing laughter.*) Get up. . . . (*The* Count *looks at her in amazement and notices her signs.*) But get up, I tell you. . . .

Count: To whom are you signalling?

Darya: Get up, for goodness' sake, get up!

Count: Give me your hand.

> [*During this dialogue* Stupendyev *has come up to the* Count. Misha *has remained in the doorway.* Darya Ivanovna *looks at the* Count *and at her husband and sinks into a low chair with a peal of laughter. The* Count *looks round in embarrassment*

and sees STUPENDYEV. *The latter bows to him. The* COUNT *addresses him with annoyance.*]

COUNT: Kindly help me to get up, sir. . . . I have . . . somehow . . . fallen on my knees. Do help me!

[DARYA IVANOVNA *leaves off laughing.*]

STUPENDYEV (*Tries to lift him under the arm-pits*): Certainly, your Excellency. . . . Excuse me . . . if . . . er. . . .

COUNT (*Pushing him away and gallantly leaping up*): Oh, very well, very well, you needn't go on. (*Going up to* DARYA IVANOVNA.) Capital, Darya Ivanovna, I am very grateful to you.

DARYA (*Assuming an imploring tone*): How am I to blame, Valeryan Nikolaitch?

COUNT: Oh, you are not to blame, not in the least! No one can help laughing at what is ridiculous—I'm not reproaching you for it, I assure you; but as far as I could observe, this has all been arranged with your husband beforehand.

DARYA: What makes you think that, Count?

COUNT: Why do I think so? Because one does not usually make signs and laugh in such circumstances.

STUPENDYEV (*Who has been listening*): Indeed, your Excellency, nothing was arranged between us, I assure you, your Excellency. (MISHA *tugs at his coat.*)

COUNT (*To* DARYA IVANOVNA *with a bitter laugh*): Well, after that, it will be hard for you to deny it. . . . (*A pause.*) Though there's really no reason you should. I have thoroughly deserved it.

DARYA: Count. . . .

COUNT: Please don't apologize. (*A pause. To himself.*) What a disgrace! There's only one way to get out of this silly position. . . . (*Aloud to* DARYA IVANOVNA.) Darya Ivanovna. . . .

DARYA: Yes?

COUNT: You are expecting perhaps that I shan't keep my word now, that I'm going away at once, and shan't forgive you your performance. I might perhaps be justified in doing so, for after all it's not the thing to make fun of a decent man like this; but I should like you too to find out with whom you have had to do. Madame, je suis un galant homme. Besides, I always respect the fair sex even when I suffer at their hands. . . . I will stay to dinner, if Mr. Stupendyev does not object—and I repeat I will keep all my promises, now more than ever. . . .

DARYA: Valeryan Nikolaitch, you too I hope will not have such a poor opinion of me; you won't think, will you, that I don't appreciate . . . that I am not deeply touched by your generosity? . . . I have been to blame towards you, but you will come to know me better, as I have you now. . . .

COUNT: Oh dear! Why all these protestations? . . . It's not worth so much gratitude. . . . But how well you play your comedy!

Darya: Count, you know one can only play it well when one feels what one is saying....

Count: Ah, you're at it again! ... No, excuse me—I'm not going to be caught twice over. (*Turning to* Stupendyev.) I must seem very ridiculous to you at this moment, sir; but I will endeavour to prove my desire to be of use to you....

Stupendyev: Your Excellency, I assure you . . . (*Aside.*) I can't make head or tail of it.

Darya: And there's no need you should. ... Only thank his Excellency.

Stupendyev: Your Excellency, believe me ...

Count: That's enough, that's enough.

Darya: I will thank you in Petersburg, Valeryan Nikolaitch.

Count: And you'll show me the letter?

Darya: I will, and perhaps with an answer.

Count: Eh bien! il n'y a pas à dire, vous êtes charmante après tout . . . and I regret nothing.

Darya: I may perhaps not be able to say that. . . . (Count *strikes an attitude, she smiles.*)

Stupendyev (*Aside, looking at his watch*): I came in at a quarter to three instead of at three.

Misha (*Timidly approaching* Darya Ivanovna): Darya Ivanovna, what about me? . . . I think you've forgotten me. . . . And I have worked so hard!

DARYA (*Aside*): I haven't forgotten you. . . . (*Aloud.*) Count, allow me to present to you a young man. (MISHA *bows*.) I take an interest in him and if . . .

COUNT: You take an interest in him? . . . That is enough. . . . Young man, you may reckon on it, we won't forget you.

MISHA (*Obsequiously*): Your Excellency . . .

[APOLLON *comes in from entry.*]

APOLLON: Dinner. . . .

[VASSILYEVNA *follows him in.*]

VASSILYEVNA: Dinner is ready.

STUPENDYEV: Ah! your Excellency, please . . .

COUNT (*Giving his arm to* DARYA IVANOVNA, *says to* STUPENDYEV): You permit me?

STUPENDYEV: Please, your Excellency. (COUNT *and* DARYA IVANOVNA *go towards door.*) I came in though, not at three, but at a quarter to . . . no matter; I don't know what it's all about; but my wife is a great woman!

MISHA: Come along, Alexey Ivanitch.

DARYA: Count, I must beg you to make allowances for our provincial dinner.

COUNT: Yes, yes. . . . Au revoir in Petersburg, my provincial lady!

CURTAIN

1851

A POOR GENTLEMAN

(*A Comedy in Two Acts*)

Characters in the Play

Pavel Nikolayevitch Yeletsky, aged 32, a collegiate councillor, and typical Petersburg official; frigid, formal, precise and quite intelligent; simply-dressed, in good taste. A commonplace man, not ill-natured, but cold-hearted.

Olga Petrovna, his wife, aged 21. A kind, soft-hearted creature; dreams of the great world and is afraid of it; loves her husband. Well-bred and well-dressed.

Vassily Semyonitch Kuzovkin, a gentleman by birth, aged 50, who is living in the Yeletskys' house at their expense. Wears a frock-coat with a stand-up collar and brass buttons.

Flegont Alexandrovtch Tropatchov, a neighbour of the Yeletskys, aged 36. A landowner with 400 serfs, unmarried. Tall, good-looking, loud-voiced, and affected. Has served in the cavalry, and retired with the rank of lieutenant. Visits Petersburg and talks of going abroad. Coarse and even rather base in character.

Wears a dark green cut-away coat, pea-green trousers, a check waistcoat, a silk cravat with a huge pin, and patent-leather top-boots. Carries a cane with a gold knob. His hair is cropped short *à la malcontent.*

Ivan Kuzmitch Ivanov, another neighbour, aged 45. A silent and unassuming person, not without a certain pride of his own. A friend of Kuzovkin's. Is easily depressed. Wears an old cinnamon-coloured coat, a yellowish waistcoat, faded from much washing, and grey trousers. Very poor.

Karpatchov, another neighbour, about 40. A very stupid man with moustaches, and a bass voice. By way of a follower of Tropatchov's. Not well-off. Wears a braided coat and full trousers.

Nartsyss Konstantinitch Trembinsky, butler and *maître d'hôtel* of the Yeletskys. Cunning, clamorous, fussy. Fundamentally a brute. Well-dressed, as befitting the butler in a wealthy household. Speaks correctly, but with a White Russian accent.

Yegor Kartashov, the bailiff, aged 60. A fat, drowsy man. Steals where he can. Dressed in a dark blue coat with long skirts.

Praskovya Ivanovna, the housekeeper, aged 50. A callous, ill-natured and ill-humoured woman. Wears a kerchief and a dark dress.

Masha, a maid, aged 20. A fresh-looking girl.

Anpadist, the tailor, aged 70. A decrepit, worn-out serf, with legs bowed with age, sinking into dotage.

Pyotr, the footman, aged 25. A sturdy young fellow. Fond of fun and joking·

Vaska, the page, aged 14.

A POOR GENTLEMAN
(*A Comedy in Two Acts*)

ACT I

[*The large dining-room in the house of a wealthy landowner; on Right, two windows and a door into the garden; on Left, a door into the drawing-room; in Centre, door into the hall. Between the windows, a folding table with a draught-board on it. In the foreground on the Left, two arm–chairs and another table. Between the doors into drawing-room and hall there is a door into the corridor.*]

TREMBINSKY (*Behind the scenes*): What a muddle! I find everything here at sixes and sevens! There's no excuse for it! (*Enters accompanied by* PYOTR *and* VASKA.) I have express instructions from our lady! Everybody here is to obey me! (*To* PYOTR.) Do you understand me?

PYOTR: Yes, sir.

TREMBINSKY: Our lady and her spouse are arriving here to-day . . . here I've been sent on beforehand—and what are we all doing? Nothing! (*Turns to the page.*) What are you here for? You like idling about, too, do you? You like doing nothing, eh? (*Takes him by the ear and pulls it.*) Doing nothing for your bread and butter! That s what suits you all! We know you! Go along! Go to your proper place! (VASKA *goes out.* TREMBINSKY *sits down in an armchair.*) Upon my word, I'm tired out! (*Leaps up.*) And why hasn't the tailor been sent to me? Where is the tailor, pray?

PYOTR (*Glancing into the hall*): The tailor's come, sir.

TREMBINSKY: Why doesn't he come in? What's he waiting for? Come here, my good man, what's your name?

    [ANPADIST *comes in and stands in the doorway, his hands behind his back.*]

TREMBINSKY (*To* PYOTR): Is this the tailor?

PYOTR: Why, yes, sir.

TREMBINSKY (*To* ANPADIST): How old are you, my good man?

ANPADIST: In my seventieth year, good sir.

TREMBINSKY (*To* PYOTR): And have you no other tailor?

PYOTR: No, sir. There was another, but he turned out good for nothing. Owing to his stuttering.

TREMBINSKY (*Flinging up his hands*): What a state of things! (*To* ANPADIST.) Well, old man, have you done what was ordered?

ANPADIST: Yes, sir.

TREMBINSKY: Put the collars on the liveries?

ANPADIST: I have, sir. Only there wasn't yellow cloth enough . . . good sir.

TREMBINSKY: Oh! How did you manage then?

ANPADIST: Well, sir, they gave me an old yellow petticoat out of the store-room.

TREMBINSKY (*Waving his hands in honor*): What next! . . . Well, there's nothing we can do about it. We can't send to town for the cloth now. You can go! (ANPADIST *is about to go.*) But mind now! Look alive! Or really I shall have to . . . There, go along. (ANPADIST *goes out.* TREMBINSKY *again sits down and at once jumps up.*) Ah, yes! are they weeding the paths in the garden?

PYOTR: To be sure, they are. Those who haven't to work in the fields have been sent in from the village to do it.

TREMBINSKY (*Stepping up to* PYOTR): And who are you?

PYOTR (*Surprised*): What is it, sir?

TREMBINSKY (*Stepping closer still*): Who are you, I ask you, who are you?

PYOTR (*Still more surprised*): I?

TREMBINSKY (*Speaking right in* PYOTR'S *face*): Yes, you, you . . . who are you?

[PYOTR, *bewildered, stares at* TREMBINSKY *and is mute.*]

TREMBINSKY: Can't you speak—I ask you, who are you?

PYOTR: I'm Pyotr, sir.

TREMBINSKY: No, you're the footman—that's what you are. The house is your job; and cleaning the lamps, that's your job, too; but the garden's not your business. Whether it's those in the fields they've fetched or others—it's nothing to do with you. That's the bailiff's business. I didn't ask you; I didn't want an answer from you. It's your business to fetch the bailiff. That's your job.

PYOTR: Well, here he is, just coming in.

[YEGOR *comes in from the hall*.]

TREMBINSKY: Ah! Yegor Alexeyitch! You've come in the nick of time. Tell me, please, have you seen to things in the garden? . . .

YEGOR: I have, Nartsyss Konstantinitch. Don't you be uneasy. . . . Won't you take some snuff?

TREMBINSKY (*Takes snuff from* YEGOR *and sniffs it*): You wouldn't believe, Yegor Alexeyitch, what a rush I've been in all day. I tell you honestly I didn't expect to find such a state of things in a big place like this! Not in your department, of course, not on the land—but in the house!

YEGOR: The–ere now!

TREMBINSKY: Only fancy, for instance, I ask is there a band? We must give the master and mistress a proper reception, you know. I'm told there is. Well, I say, send the musicians along. And would you believe it, all these—musicians indeed!—are employed in other jobs. One's in the kitchen-garden, another's the bootmaker; the bassoon looks after the cattle. Did you ever hear anything like it! And their instruments, too, are in a wretched state. It's all I could do to manage anything. (*Takes snuff again*.)

YEGOR: You've a troublesome task here.

TREMBINSKY: Yes, I think I may say I don't eat the bread of idleness. . . . Oh, were the musicians standing at the porch?

YEGOR: To be sure, they were. It was beginning to spot with rain—so thay were all huddling into the servants' room; they said it would wet their instruments. Well, I'll own I turned them out. Suppose the messenger fails us and the gentry arrive all of a sudden? And they can hold their instruments under their skirts.

TREMBINSKY: Quite right. And I do believe everything's ready now.

YEGOR: Don't you worry, Nartsyss Konstantinitch. (*Glances at* PYOTR.) Why are you hanging about here? Go along—to your proper place, my lad. (PYOTR *goes out into the hall*. MASHA *runs in from the corridor*.) Hullo, hullo, why in such a hurry, my lady?

MASHA: Oh, Yegor Alexeyitch, let me alone! Praskovya Ivanovna is worrying me to death as it is! (*Runs into hall*.)

YEGOR (*Looks after her, then turns to* TREMBINSKY *and winks*. TREMBINSKY *smirks*): Allow me to ask, Nartsyss Konstantinitch, what time is it?

TREMBINSKY (*Looking at his watch*): A quarter to eleven. They may be here any moment now.

> [KUZOVKIN *appears in the doorway, stops, makes signs to somebody behind him in the hall, comes in cautiously, and is making his way to the table by the window*.]

YEGOR: I'll run round to the counting-house. I'll be bound, the foreman hasn't combed his beard, and he'll be shoving forward to be kissed, too, I dare say....

[*As he goes out, stumbles against* KUZOVKIN.]

KUZOVKIN: Good morning, Yegor Alexeyitch.

YEGOR (*With some annoyance*): Oh, Vassily Semyonitch! I've no time for you. (*Goes out into the hall.* KUZOVKIN *continues on his way to the window.*)

TREMBINSKY (*Looks round and notices* KUZOVKIN. *Aside*): Oh! that fellow! (KUZOVKIN *bows to* TREMBINSKY. *The latter nods casually and speaks over his shoulder to him.*) Hullo! So you're coming in here? You're getting ready to welcome our young master and mistress, too ... eh?

KUZOVKIN: To be sure.

TREMBINSKY: Well—and are you pleased? (*Without waiting for an answer.*) Changed into your best, have you?

KUZOVKIN: Yes ... that is ...

TREMBINSKY: All right ... all right.... You can sit here in the corner. (KUZOVKIN *bows*.) Oh, dear ... I was forgetting! Pyotr!.... Pyotr! ... Petrushka! ... What's the meaning of it? Is there nobody in the hall?

IVANOV (*Poking his head in from the hall*): What is it?

TREMBINSKY (*Somewhat taken aback*): But excuse me ... how did you? ...

IVANOV (*Advancing no further*): Ivanov, Ivan Kuzmitch . . . a friend of this gentleman's. . . . (*Points to* KUZOVKIN.)

KUZOVKIN (*To* TREMBINSKY): A neighbour . . . from near by . . . he has come to see me.

TREMBINSKY (*Speaking impressively and shaking his head*): Ech, it's not the right moment . . . nor the right place, gentlemen. (PYOTR *comes out of the hall, brushing past* IVANOV, *who disappears*.) Where have you been? Follow me. . . . I want to see what you've been up to in the study. . . . I expect you've not done as I told you. . . . There's no relying on you fellows!

[*Both go out into the drawing-room.* KUZOVKIN *is left alone.*]

KUZOVKIN (*After a brief silence*): Vanya! . . . Vanya!

IVANOV (*From the hall, not showing himself*): Well?

KUZOVKIN: Come in, Vanya, it's all right.

IVANOV (*Coming in slowly*): I'd better be going.

KUZOVKIN: No, do stay. What does it matter? You've come to see me. Come over here. There, sit down. This is my corner, you know.

IVANOV: We'd better go up to your room.

KUZOVKIN: We can't go to my room just now. They are sorting the linen there . . . . They've taken a lot of feather-beds in, too. . . . And what's wrong here?

IVANOV: I'd rather go home.

Kuzovkin: No, Vanya, do stay. You sit here . . . sit you down. And I'll sit down. (*He sits down.*) Our people will be here soon, you know. You must have a look at them.

Ivanov: What is there to look at?

Kuzovkin: How can you! Olga Petrovna has been married in Petersburg. What is her good husband like? Besides, we haven't seen her for ever so long. More than six years. Sit down.

Ivanov: But, dear me, Vassily Semyonitch. . . .

Kuzovkin: Sit down, sit down, I tell you. Don't you take any notice of the new butler's shouting. Bless the man! That's what he's here for.

Ivanov: Olga Petrovna has married a rich man, I suppose? (*Sits down.*)

Kuzovkin: I don't know what to say about that, Vanya, but he's something important in the government, so they say. Well, that's just how it should be. Olga Petrovna couldn't go on living with her aunt for ever.

Ivanov: But what if the new master turns us out, Vassily Semyonitch?

Kuzovkin: Why should he turn us out?

Ivanov: You, I mean.

Kuzovkin (*With a sigh*): I know, Vanya, I know. Say what you will you've a place of your own after all, old man. While even my clothes are never new. They are all second-hand. The new master won't turn me out, though. . . . Even the old master didn't do that. . . . And wasn't he violent at times!

Ivanov: But you don't know these fine Petersburg gentlemen, Vassily Semyonitch.

Kuzovkin: Why, Ivan Kuzmitch, surely they're not so . . . dreadful?

Ivanov: Simply terrible, I'm told! I don't know them either, but I've heard so.

Kuzovkin (*After a moment's pause*): Well, we shall see. I rely on Olga Petrovna. She'll take my part.

Ivanov: Take your part! I expect she has completely forgotten you! Why, she was only a child when she went away with her aunt. What was she? Not more than fourteen. You used to play with dolls with her—what does that amount to? She'll pass by without looking at you.

Kuzovkin: Oh, no, Vanya.

Ivanov: Well, you'll see.

Kuzovkin: Do stop, Vanya, please.

Ivanov: Well, you will see, Vassily Semyonitch.

Kuzovkin: Leave off, Vanya, really. . . . We'd better have a game of draughts. Shall we? (Ivanov *does not speak.*) We may as well do something. Come, old man, let us. (*Takes the draught-board and begins setting the men.*)

Ivanov (*Also setting the men*): A queer time for a game, I must say. The butler won't allow it, most likely.

Kuzovkin: We're not in anybody's way, are we?

IVANOV: Well, the young people will be arriving in a minute.

KUZOVKIN: When they come—we'll leave off. Right or left?

IVANOV: They'll chase us out, Vassily Semyonitch, you'll see. Left. You to begin.

KUZOVKIN: Well, I'm going to begin like this to-day.

IVANOV: So that's your move. And I do this.

KUZOVKIN: I'll go there.

IVANOV: And I here.

> [*Suddenly there is a loud shouting in the hall. The page, VASKA, runs in headlong, shouting*: 'They're coming! They're coming! Nartsyss Konstantinitch! They're coming! they're coming!'
>
> [KUZOVKIN *and* IVANOV *jump up.*]

KUZOVKIN (*In great excitement*): Are they coming? Are they coming?

VASKA (*Shouting*): The messenger has signalled—they're coming!

> [*From the drawing-room the voice of* TREMBINSKY *is heard:* 'What is it? Are they coming?' *He runs out of the drawing-room with* PYOTR.]

TREMBINSKY (*Shouting*): The band! Musicians to their places!

> [*Runs out into the hall followed by* PYOTR *and* VASKA. MASHA *rushes in from the corridor.*]

MASHA: Are they coming?

KUZOVKIN: Yes, yes.

[IVANOV *in acute discomfort effaces himself in the corner.* MASHA *runs into the corridor, calling*: 'They are coming!' *A moment later* PRASKOVYA IVANOVNA *bursts in from the corridor and* TREMBINSKY *from the hall.*]

PRASKOVYA IVANOVNA: Are they coming?

TREMBINSKY: Call the maids here, the maids!

PRASKOVYA IVANOVNA (*Shouting into the corridor*): Girls! Girls!

YEGOR (*Running in from the hall*): Where's the bread and salt, Nartsyss Konstantinitch?

TREMBINSKY (*Shouting at the top of his voice*): Pyotr! Pyotr! The bread and salt! Where's the bread and salt? (*Six maidservants, dressed up in their best, come out from the corridor.*) Into the hall, girls, into the hall!

[*The maids run into the hall, coming into collision with* PYOTR *in the doorway. He is carrying in both hands a dish with a huge bread ring and a salt-cellar on it.*]

PYOTR: Look out, you crazy creatures!

TREMBINSKY (*Snatches the dish from* PYOTR *and puts it into* YEGOR'S *hands*): That's for you. . . . Go out on the steps, go along! (*Pushes him off together with* PYOTR *and* PRASKOVYA IVANOVNA, *runs after them himself and shouts in the hall:* 'And where are the menservants . . . send the men here!')

VOICE OF PYOTR: Call Anpadist!

ANOTHER VOICE: The foreman has taken away his boots.

Voice of Trembinsky: The coachmen this way, the coachmen!

Voices of the Maids: They're coming, they're coming!

Voice of Trembinsky: Silence now! Silence!

> [*A complete silence reigns.* Kuzovkin, *who has throughout this excitement been in a state of great agitation, yet has scarcely stirred, listens eagerly. Suddenly the band begins playing out of tune:* 'Thunder of victory resound. . . .' *A carriage drives up to the steps, there is a sound of talk, the band stops. Kissing is heard. . . . A moment later* Olga Petrovna *walks in with her husband; in one hand he holds the bread; they are followed by* Trembinsky, Yegor *with the dish,* Praskovya Ivanovna *and the* Servants, *who, however, remain in the doorway.*]

Olga (*With a smile to her husband*): Well, here we are at home at last, Paul. (Yeletsky *presses her hand.*) How glad I am! (*Turns to the servants.*) Thank you, thank you! (Indicating Yeletsky.) Here is your new master. . . . I beg you to love him and welcome him. (*To her husband.*) Rendez cela, mon ami. (Yeletsky *hands the bread ring to* Yegor.)

Trembinsky (*Bowing with the whole upper half of his body*): Will you be pleased to order something . . . to eat . . . or tea, perhaps?

Ogla: No, thank you, not yet. (*To her husband.*) I want to show you the whole house, your study. . . . It's seven long years since I've been here . . . seven years!

Yeletsky: Do show me.

Praskovya Ivanovna (*Taking Olga's hat and cloak from her*): Our dear lady, our darling. . . .

Olga (*Smiles in response and looks round*): Our house has grown older. . . . And the rooms look smaller.

Yeletsky (*In the tone of a kind schoolmaster*): It always seems like that. You were a child when you left it.

Kuzovkin (*Who all this time has not taken his eyes off* Olga, *goes up to her*): Olga Petrovna, allow me. . . . (*His voice breaks.*)

Olga (*Does not recognize him for the first moment*): Ah—ah, Vassily. . . . Vassily Petrovitch, how are you? I hardly knew you at first.

Kuzovkin (*Kissing her hand*): Allow me . . . to congratulate you.

Olga (To her husband, indicating Kuzovkin): Our old friend, Vassily Petrovitch. . . .

Yeletsky (Bows): Pleased to meet you.

[Ivanov, too, bows in the distance, though nobody has yet noticed him.]

Kuzovkin (*Bows to* Yeletsky): . . . Congratulations. . . . We are . . . all . . . so glad. . . .

Yeletsky (*Bows again; aside to his wife*): Who's this?

Olga (*Aside*): A poor gentleman who lives in our house. (*Aloud*) Well, let us go, I want to show you the whole house. . . . I was born here, Paul, I grew up here. . . .

YELETSKY: Delighted, let us . . . (*To* TREMINSKY.) And you, please tell my valet to carry my things up.

TREMBINSKY (*In a fluster*): Yes, sir, yes, sir.

OLGA: Come along, Paul. (*They go out into the drawing-room.*)

TREMBINSKY (*In a low voice to all the servants*): Well, my friends, now go to your places. You, Yegor Alexeyitch, stay in the hall—the master may ask for you.

> [YEGOR *and the menservants go out into the hall.* PRASKOVYA IVANOVNA *and the maids into the corridor.*]

PRASKOVYA IVANOVNA (*In the doorway*): Go along, go along. . . . What are you laughing at, Masha?

> [*Goes out.*]

TREMBINSKY (*To* KUZOVKIN *and* IVANOV): And you are staying here, gentlemen?

KUZOVKIN: Yes. We will stay here.

TREMBINSKY: Oh, very well. . . . But, please, you know . . . (*Gesticulates.*) . . . Quiet, for goodness' sake, or I shall be to blame for it. (*Goes out on tip-toe into hall.*)

KUZOVKIN (*Looks after him, then turns quickly to* IVANOV): Well, Vanya, what do you think of her? Come, tell me what you think of her? Hasn't she grown? Isn't she lovely? And she hasn't forgotten me. Has she? You see, Vanya, you see: I was right.

IVANOV: Hadn't forgotten you. . . . Then why did she call you Vassily Petrovitch?

Kuzovkin: What a man you are, Vanya! Why—what does it matter, Petrovitch or Semyonitch—it's all the same . . . you can see that for yourself, you're a sensible man. She introduced me to her husband. A fine-looking man! A splendid fellow. You can see from his face. . . . Oh yes, he's a great man in the service, I expect. Don't you think so, Vanya?

Ivanov: I don't know, Vassily Semyonitch, I'd better be going.

Kuzovkin: Oh, Vanya! What's the matter with you? Why, you're not like yourself. You must go and you must go! You'd much better tell me what you thought of our young lady.

Ivanov: She's handsome, I'm not denying it.

Kuzovkin: Her smile alone is worth . . . And her voice? Sweet as a warbler, simply, a canary singing. And she loves her husband. You can see that at once. You can, Vanya, can't you?

Ivanov: Goodness only knows, Vassily Semyonitch.

Kuzovkin: It's too bad of you, Ivan Kuzmitch, it's too bad. A man's happy, and you . . . But here they are coming back.

[Olga *and* Yeletsky *come in from the drawing-room.*]

Olga: Our house is not very grand, as you see. Such as it is, it's all yours.

Yeletsky: Why, it's a very fine house; so very well designed.

OLGA: Well, now let us go into the garden

YELETSKY: I shall be delighted . . . but . . . I should like to have two or three words with your bailiff.

OLGA (*Reproachfully*): Mine?

YELETSKY (*With a smile*): Ours. (*Kisses her hand.*)

OLGA: Well, as you like. I'll take Vassily Petrovitch with me. Vassily Petrovitch, let us go into the garden. . . . Will you come with me?

KUZOVKIN (*His face beaming with pleasure*): Certainly.

YELETSKY: Put on your hat, Olga.

OLGA: I don't need it. (*Throws a scarf over her head.*) Come, Vassily Petrovitch.

KUZOVKIN: Allow me, Olga Petrovna, to introduce a neighbour . . . Ivanov. (IVANOV *bows, embarrassed.*)

OLGA: Delighted. (*To* IVANOV.) Will you care to come into the garden with us? Give me your arm, Vassily Petrovitch.

KUZOVKIN (*Hardly able to believe his ears*): How? . . .

OLGA (*Laughing*): Why, like this. (*Takes his arm and puts hers on it.*) Do you remember, Vassily Petrovitch? . . . (*They go out through the glass door.* IVANOV *follows them.*)

YELETSKY (*Goes to the glass door, looks after his wife, comes back to table on Left and sits down*): Here! Boy! Whoever's there!

PYOTR (*Coming in from the hall*): What is your pleasure?

YELETSKY: What is your name, my lad?

Pyotr: Pyotr, sir.

Yeletsky: Ah! Well, then, fetch me the bailiff—what's his name—Yegor, isn't it?

Pyotr: Yes, sir.

Yeletsky: Fetch him here.

> [Pyotr *goes out. A moment later* Yegor *comes in, stands in the doorway and folds his hands behind his back.*]

Yeletsky (*Speaking like the head of a government department*): Yegor, I intend to inspect Olga Petrovna's estate to-morrow.

Yegor: Yes, sir.

Yeletsky: How many serfs are there?

Yegor: Three hundred and eighty-four of the male sex at the last census. More by now.

Yeletsky: And how many more?

Yegor (*Coughs with his hand over his mouth*): There'll be a couple of dozen or so.

Yeletsky: H'm. . . . I beg you to ascertain exactly and report to me. Is the land all in one piece?

Yegor: The estate's in one round, sir.

Yeletsky (*Stares at* Yegor *in some perplexity*): H'm. . . . Is there much good arable land?

Yegor: A fair amount, sir. Eight hundred and twenty-five acres in a wedge.

Yeletsky (*Again stares at* Yegor *in perplexity*): And how much that is not good?

Yegor (*Hesitating*): How can I reckon, sir? . . . Under copse . . . there's the ravines, too. . . . And round the homestead . . . and the pastures too. . . . (*With more assurance.*) It's mown for hay.

YELETSKY (*Raising his eyebrows*): How much precisely?

YEGOR: Who can say, sir? The land hasn't been measured. Perhaps it may be marked on a plan. It runs up to a hundred and fifty acres, may be.

YELETSKY (*To himself*): This is all very irregular. (*Aloud.*) And is there any forest?

YEGOR: Eighty-four acres and a rood or so.

YELETSKY (*Aloud and impressively*): So then there are about fifteen hundred acres in all?

YEGOR: Fifteen hundred, sir? It's over six thousand.

YELETSKY: Why, you said yourself. . . . (*Stops short.*) Yes . . . yes . . . I meant to say that. Do you understand?

YEGOR: Yes, sir.

YELETSKY (*Very seriously*): And what about the peasants here? Are they well-conducted? Obedient?

YEGOR: They're a good set. Like being kept in order.

YELETSKY: H'm. . . . And not very poor?

YEGOR: Oh dear, no, sir. Not at all. Very well satisfied.

YELETSKY: Well, I'll go into all that myself to-morrow. You can go. Oh, tell me, please, that person living here—who is he?

YEGOR: Vassily Semyonitch Kuzovkin, a gentleman. He just lives here. He's been here since the old master's time. His honour kept him for sport and diversion, you may say.

YELETSKY: He's been living here a long time then?

Yegor: For years, sir. It's twenty years since the old master died, and it was in his lifetime Vassily Semyonitch came to live here.

Yeletsky: Oh, very good. . . . I suppose you have a counting-house?

Yegor: To be sure, we couldn't do without. . . .

Yeletsky: I'll inspect it all to-morrow. You can go. (Yegor *goes out*.) This bailiff seems stupid. However, we shall see. (*Gets up and walks to and fro*.) Here I am in the country—on my own estate. It feels strange. But it's pleasant. (*In the hall the voice of* Tropatchov, *saying*: 'They've arrived? To–day?')

Yeletsky (*To himself*): Who's that?

Pyotr (*Coming from the hall*): Flegont Alexandritch Tropatchov has arrived, sir. Wishes to see you, sir. Shall I show him in, sir?

Yeletsky (*To himself*): Who on earth is it? . . . I seem to know the name. (*Aloud*.) Ask him in.

Tropatchov (*Entering*): Good morning, Pavel Nikolaitch, bonjour. (Yeletsky *bows with obvious surprise*.) I believe you don't recognize me . . . . Don't you remember, in Petersburg, at Count Kuntsov's?

Yeletsky: Oh, yes . . . delighted to meet you. . . . (*Shakes hands*.)

Tropatchov: I'm your nearest neighbour. I live only a mile and a half from here. I pass your very door on my way to the town.

I heard you were expected. . . . I thought I'd drive round and inquire to-day. But if I've come at the wrong moment, please say so. Entre gens comme il faut, you know . . . no standing on ceremony!

YELETSKY: On the contrary—I hope you'll stay and dine with us . . . though I don't know what our country cook may be giving us.

TROPATCHOV (*Affectedly and playing with his stick*): Oh, come, I say, I know you have everything in grand style. I hope you will do me the honour of dining with me one day soon. . . . You wouldn't believe how glad I am that you have come. . . . There are so few decent people here, des gens comme il faut. Et Madame? How is she? I used to know her as a little girl. Yes, yes, I know your wife, I know her very well. I congratulate you, Pavel Nikolaitch, I do indeed. Ha! ha! But I dare say she doesn't remember me. (*Strikes an attitude and strokes his whiskers.*)

YELETSKY: She'll be very glad to see you. . . . She is in the garden with that . . . that gentleman who lives here.

TROPATCHOV (*Contemptuously*): Ah! that fellow! He's something in the way of a clown, I fancy. He's a harmless person, though. And by the way, I brought another gentleman with me. . . . He's outside in the hall. . . . May I call him?

YELETSKY: By all means. . . . The idea of leaving him.

TROPATCHOV: Oh, ne faites pas attention. That's all right . . . it's of no consequence. He lives with me because he's poor, too. He drives about with me. It's a bore going about alone, you know. Please don't trouble about him . . . je vous en prie. (*Goes towards the hall.*) Karpatchov! come in, old boy. (KARPATCHOV *appears from the hall and bows.*) Here, Pavel Nikolaitch, I commend him to you.

YELETSKY: Pleased to meet you.

TROPATCHOV (*Takes* YELETSKY *by the arm and gently draws him away from* KARPATCHOV, *who humbly retires to one side*): C'est bien, c'est bien. Are you staying long among us, Pavel Nikolaitch?

YELETSKY: I have taken three months' leave. (*They begin walking up and down the room.*)

TROPATCHOV: That's a short holiday. But I quite understand you can't be spared longer. I expect it was difficult for you to get away at all. Ha, ha! But you must have a rest. Are you fond of shooting?

YELETSKY: I have never had a gun in my hand in my life. . . . But I did buy a dog before I came away. Is there much game here?

TROPATCHOV: Yes, plenty. Only leave it to me. We'll make a sportsman of you. (*To* KARPATCHOV.) How many coveys have we in Malinnik?

KARPATCHOV (*From the corner, in a deep bass*); Two, and three more in Kamenny Gryada,

TROPATCHOV: Good.

KARPATCHOV: Fedul, the forester, was telling me, too, the other day that in Goryelye . . . (OLGA *comes in from the garden with* KUZOVKIN *and* IVANOV. KARPATCHOV *breaks off and bows*.)

OLGA: Oh, Paul, our garden is so lovely . . . (*Stops on seeing* TROPATCHOV.)

YELETSKY (*To* OLGA): Let me introduce . .

TROPATCHOV (*Interrupting*): Excuse me, excuse me, we're old friends. . . . I dare say Olga Petrovna does not recognize me. . . . And no wonder. I knew her (*Holds his hand about a yard from the floor*) comme ça. (*Strikes an attitude and goes on*.) Flegont Tropatchov, don't you remember your neighbour, Flegont Tropatchov? Do you remember I used to bring you playthings from town? You were such a charming child then, but now. . . (*Emphasizes the last word significantly, bows, takes one step back, and draws himself up, very self-satisfied*.)

OLGA: Oh, Monsieur Tropatchov . . . yes. . . . I know you now. . . . (*Holds out her hand to him*.) You wouldn't believe how happy I am ever since we arrived home.

TROPATCHOV (Sugarily): Only since then?

OLGA (*Smiles in answer*): My childhood comes back so vividly. . . . Paul, you really must come into the garden with me. I'll show you the acacia I planted myself. . . . It's much taller than I am now.

YELETSKY (*To* OLGA, *indicating* KARPATCHOV): Monsieur Karpatchov, another neighbour.

> [KARPATCHOV *bows and shrinks into the corner, into which* KUZOVKIN *and* IVANOV *have already retired*.]

OLGA: I'm glad to meet you. . . .

TROPATCHOV (*To* OLGA): Ne faites pas attention. (*Aloud, rubbing his hands*.) So here you are at home and mistress in your own house. How time does fly, doesn't it?

OLGA? I hope you will stay to dinner with us?

YELETSKY: I have already asked . . . *pardon* . . . what is your name and your father's?

TROPATCHOV: Flegont Alexandritch.

YELETSKY: I have asked Flegont Alexandritch. I'm only afraid the dinner may not . . .

TROPATCHOV: Oh! Nonsense!

OLGA (*Drawing* YELETSKY *a little aside*): Unlucky this gentleman has come just now.

YELETSKY: Yes. He seems a decent fellow, though.

TROPATCHOV (*Walks away with a careless swing, biting the knob of his stick, goes up to* KUZOVKIN *and says in his face*): Hullo! Well, how are you?

KUZOVKIN: Very well. I humbly thank you.

TROPATCHOV (*Jerking his elbow towards* KARPATCHOV): You know him, of course?

KUZOVKIN: To be sure. . . . We have met, sir.

Tropatchov: Yes, yes, yes. (*To* Ivanov.) And you, what's your name? Let me see—you here too?

Ivanov: I'm here, too.

Olga (*To* Tropatchov): Monsieur . . . Monsieur Tropatchov. . . .

Tropatchov (*Turning quickly*): Madame?

Olga: May I treat you as an old friend—without ceremony?

Tropatchov: Oh, pleas. . . .

Olga: You will excuse my leaving you. . . . We have only just arrived. . . . I have to look after things. . . .

Tropatchov: Most certainly, Olga Petrovna. . . . And you too, Pavel Nikolaitch, make yourself at home, ha! ha! ha! I'll have a little chat with these gentlemen. . . .

Olga: Besides—though you are an old friend, I feel ashamed . . . in these travelling clothes. . . .

Tropatchov (*Smirking*): I couldn't accept such a . . . such an excuse . . . if I did not know that to ladies . . . dress . . . is always . . . so to speak . . . always an agreeable . . . (*Ends in a muddle, bows and smirks.*)

Olga (*Laughing*): You are malicious. . . . I will leave you, gentlemen . . . good-bye. . . . (*Goes out into the drawing-room.*)

Tropatchov: Pavel Nikolaitch, allow me to congratulate you once again. . . . You are, one may say, a fortunate man.

Yeletsky (*Smiles and presses his hand*): You are right, Faddey . . . I mean Flegont . . . Alexandritch.

Tropatchov: But, I say, perhaps I'm keeping you?

Yeletsky: Not at all, Flegont Alexandritch. Do you know, as you are used to estate management, perhaps you wouldn't mind. . . .

Tropatchov (*Swooping upon* Yeletsky *and pressing the* latter's *hand to his stomach*): Make any use of me, Pavel Nikolaitch, I beg.

Yeletsky: What would you say to our going round to the threshing barn before lunch? It's only a few steps from here—beside the garden.

Tropatchov: Enchanté—let us go.

Yeletsky: Take your hat, then. (*Loudly.*) Boy, who's there? (Pyotr *comes in.*) Tell them to serve lunch.

Pyotr: Yes, sir. (*Goes out.*)

Tropatchov: Karpatchov shall go with us, if you've no objection.

Yeletsky: Delighted. . . . (*They go out.* Karpatchov *follows them.*)

Kuzovkin (*Turning eagerly to* Ivanov): Well, Vanya, tell me now, what do you think of our Olga?

Ivanov: Well, I'm not denying it—she's nice.

Kuzovkin: And isn't she kind, Vanya?

Ivanov: Yes, she's not like him.

Kuzovkin: Why, what's wrong with him? You must remember, Vanya, he's an important person, accustomed, you know, to keep up his dignity. He might prefer to be friendly, but you understand; it's out of the question. That's expected of them. But, Vanya, did you notice her eyes?

IVANOV: No, Vassily Semyonitch, I didn't.

KUZOVKIN: Well, I wonder at you—I really do! It's too bad of you, Vanya, it's too bad.

IVANOV: Perhaps, I'm not denying it. . . . Here is the butler coming.

KUZOVKIN (*Dropping his voice*): What if he is? We're doing no harm.

[TREMBINSKY *and* PYOTR *come in.* PYOTR *is carrying lunch on a tray.*]

TREMBINSKY (*Moving out the table into the middle of the room*): There, set it down here and mind you don't break anything. (PYOTR *puts down the tray and unfolds the cloth.* TREMBINSKY *takes it from him.*) Give it me. . . . I'll see to that, while you go and fetch the wine. (PYOTR *goes out.* TREMBINSKY *lays the cloth and looks askance at* KUZOVKIN.) Dear me, some people—come to think of it, seem born with a silver spoon in their mouth. We poor fellows have to struggle like a fish on the ice to earn a crust of bread, while they get everything for nothing. Where's the justice of it, I should like to know. It's a queer business, to be sure.

KUZOVKIN (*Cautiously touches* TREMBINSKY'S *shoulder. The latter looks at him in surprise*): You've messed it—against the wall. . . .

TREMBINSKY: Well, I never . . . it doesn't matter . . . let it be.

[PYOTR *comes in with bottles and a bowl with champagne bottles in it which he puts on the little table near the door.*]

TREMBINSKY: Come along, look sharp. (*Takes bottles and places them on table.*) And clear away the draughts. . . . An odd time those gentlemen think fit to play. . . . And what sort of a game? Is that a gentleman's game?

[PYOTR *puts away draughts.*]

IVANOV (*Softly to* KUZOVKIN): Good-bye, friend.

KUZOVKIN (*Quietly*): Where are you off to?

IVANOV (*Quietly*): Home.

KUZOVKIN (*Quietly*): Nonsense, do stay.

YEGOR (*Hurriedly looking in from hall*): Nartsyss Konstantinitch . . . Nartsyss Konstantinitch. . . .

TREMBINSKY (*Looking round*): What is it?

YEGOR: Where's the master gone?

TREMBINSKY: To the threshing floor. How is it you're not with him?

YEGOR: To the threshing floor! Good Lord! (*Is about to run off, but at once draws himself up, puts his hands behind his back, and flattens himself against the door.* YELETSKY, TROPATCHOV *and* KARPATCHOV *walk in.*)

YELETSKY: And so—vous êtes content?

TROPATCHOV: Très bien, très bien, tout est très bien. Ah, Yegor, good day! (YEGOR *bows.* TROPATCHOV *slaps him on the shoulder.*) Here you have a capital fellow, Pavel Nikolaitch. . . . You can confidently rely on him. (Yegor *bows again and goes out.*) And here is lunch. (*Goes up to the table.*) Why, but this is a regular dinner! Comme c'est bien servi! (*Takes the silver cover off a dish.*) Woodcock

... if you please.... We might be at St. George's.... What a swine that St. George is! But he does you well. I have spent many a hundred roubles on his dinners!

Yeletsky: Shall we sit down? Boy—chairs!

[Pyotr *sets the chairs.* Trembinsky *fusses round the gentlemen.* Yeletsky *and* Tropatchov *sit down.*]

Tropatchov (*To* Karpatchov): You sit down, too, Karpy. C'est comme cela que je l'appelle.... Vous permettez?

Yeletsky: Oh, pray do. (*To* Kuzovkin *and* Ivanov *who have not emerged from their corner.*) But why don't you take your seats, gentlemen?... Please come and sit down.

Kuzovkin (*Bowing*): We humbly thank you.... We'll stand....

Yeletsky: Do please sit down.

[Kuzovkin *and* Ivanov *timidly sit down to the table.* Tropatchov *sits on the left* (*from point of view of audience*) *of* Yeletsky, Karpatchov *at a distance on his right, near him* Kuzovkin *and* Ivanov. Trembinsky *with a napkin over his arm stands behind* Yeletsky, Pyotr *near the door.*]

Yeletsky (*Taking cover off a dish*): Well, gentlemen, here's pot-luck.

Tropatchov (*With his mouth full*): Parfait, parfait—you have a wonderful cook, Pavel Nikolaitch.

Yeletsky: You are too kind! And so you think the harvest will be good this year?

Tropatchov (*Still eating*): I think so. (*Drinking a glass of wine.*) To your good health! Karpy, why don't you drink to Pavel Nikolaitch's health?

Karpatchov (*Leaping up*): Long life to our worthy host . . . (*Empties his glass at one gulp*) and blessings of all sorts. . . . (*Sits down.*)

Yeletsky: Thank you.

Tropatchov (*Prodding* Yeletsky *with his elbow, to* Karpatchov): Here's the man for our Marshal! Eh? What do you say?

Karpatchov: Rather! He ought to be good enough for them!

Tropatchov: I mean it, you know, Pavel Nikolaitch, if it weren't for your official duties—what marvellous cheese!—if it weren't for your official duties, you really ought to be our Marshal of Nobility!

Yeletsky: Oh, come. . . .

Tropatchov: No, I'm not joking. (*To* Kuzovkin.) Why aren't you drinking to Pavel Nikolaitch's health, eh? (*To* Ivanov.) And you too?

Kuzovkin (*With some hesitation*): I should be glad. . . .

Tropatchov: Karpy, fill his glass . . . oh, fuller! That's right, why stand on ceremony?

Kuzovkin (*Stands up*): To the health of our honoured host . . . and hostess. (*Bows, drinks and sits down.* Ivanov, *too, bows and drinks in silence.*)

Tropatchov: Bravo! (*To* Yeletsky.) Wait a bit—nous allons rire. He's rather amusing—one only has to make him drink.

(To Kuzovkin, *playing with his knife*.) Well, how have you been getting on, Mr. What's-Your-Name? I've seen nothing of you for ever so long. Pretty middling, I'll be bound?

Kuzovkin: Pretty middling as you say, sir.

Tropatchov: Oh, that's all right, then. And is Vyetrovo coming to you at last or not?

Kuzovkin (*Looking down*): You are pleased to be joking.

Tropatchov: Dear me, what makes you think that? I take an interest in you. I'm not joking.

Kuzovkin (*With a sigh*): Nothing has been decided yet.

Tropatchov: Indeed?

Kuzovkin: Nothing at all.

Tropatchov: You must have a little patience, that's all! (*To* Yeletsky, *winking*.) Perhaps Pavel Nikolaitch, you are not aware that in the person of Mr. Kuzovkin you see before you a landowner, the real owner—or rather, the heir, the lawful heir of the estate of Vyetrovo, otherwise Ugarovo. . . . I say, how many serfs have you?

Kuzovkin: At the eighth census there were forty-two in Vyetrovo; but it isn't all my share.

Tropatchov (*Aside to* Yeletsky): He's crazy over this Vyetrovo. (*Aloud.*) And how many acres are there in your share?

Kuzovkin (*Gradually losing his timidity*): Well, after deducting a seventh part and other legal dues—two hundred and fifty acres about.

Tropatchov: And how many serfs come to you?

Kuzovkin: I don't know how many. A good many have run away.

Yeletsky: But how is it you are not in possession of your estate?

Kuzovkin: There's a lawsuit, sir.

Yeletsky: A lawsuit with whom?

Kuzovkin: Other claimants turned up. There were arrears of taxes, too, and private debts as well.

Yeletsky: And has the case been going on long?

Kuzovkin (*Gradually gaining courage*): A long time, sir. In the late master's time—the Kingdom of Heaven be his—it ought to have come to me, but I hadn't the money. I'd no time to see to it either. I ought to have gone to the town, of course, have made inquiries, and taken steps—but there, I hadn't an opportunity. The stamped paper alone costs so much. And I'm a poor man, you see.

Tropatchov: Karpy, fill his glass.

Kuzovkin (*Refusing*): No, thank you very much.

Tropatchov: Nonsense. (*Drinks himself.*) To your good health. (Kuzovkin *stands up, bows, and drinks*.) Well, then, what are you doing about it? You can't go on like this. You'll lose your case.

Kuzovkin: What's to be done? It's more than a year since I made any inquiries. (Tropatchov *shakes his head reproachfully*.) It's true I have a man there . . . . I rest my hopes on him, but who can tell?

Tropatchov (*Keeps glancing at* Yeletsky): And who is the man, may I ask?

Kuzovkin: I ought not to tell—but there! . . . It's Ivan Arhipitch Lytchkov, do you know him?

Tropatchov: No, I don't; what is he?

Kuzovkin: Well . . . a provincial attorney . . . that is, he used to be . . . not here, it's true, but in Venyovo. Now he does what he can—more in the commercial line.

Tropatchov (*Still keeps looking at* Yeletsky, *who begins to be amused by* Kuzovkin): So this gentleman Lytehkov has promised to assist you?

Kuzovkin (*After a pause*): Yes, he promised to. I was godfather to his second son, and so he promised. I'll manage the case for you, he said, just wait a bit. And Ivan Lytchkov is a master at his work.

Tropatchov: You don't say so?

Kuzovkin: He is famed for it all over the province.

Tropatchov: But you say he's retired, and more in the commercial line now?

Kuzovkin: Yes, that is true; circumstances obliged him to. But he is a man of gold. It's some time since I saw him, though.

Tropatchov: How long?

Kuzovkin: Well, it will be a year or more.

Tropatchov: Oh, I say, how can you let things go like that? That's too bad.

KUZOVKIN: What you say is quite true, sir. But what would you have me do?

YELETSKY: Tell us what's the point in dispute.

KUZOVKIN (*Clearing his throat and growing excited*): This is how it is, Pavel Nikolaitch. Excuse my presumption . . . but it's your own wish. This is how it is. The Vyetrovo . . . I confess I've never been used to speaking to a great man . . . you must pardon me if I . . .

YELETSKY: Don't be afraid to tell us.

TROPATCHOV (*Indicating* KUZOVKIN'S *glass to* KARPATCHOV): And another glass? Eh?

KUZOVKIN (*Refusing*): No, excuse me.

TROPATCHOV: To give you courage?

KUZOVKIN: Well, perhaps. (*Drinks and wipes his forehead.*) And so, I must inform you, the Vyetrovo land, which is what I'm telling you about, came in direct line of descent from my grandfather, Maxim Kuzovkin, a lieutenant-major, you may perhaps have heard of him—to the brothers, Maxim's sons, my father Semyon and my uncle Niktopolion. My father Semyon and his brother, my uncle that is, did not divide the estate in their lifetime; and my uncle died childless, I beg you to note that—only he died after the decease of my father Semyon; and they had a sister, Katerina . . . and she, Katerina, married Porfiry Yagushkin; and this Porfiry Yagushkin by his first wife, a Polish woman, had a son, Ilya, a terrible drunkard and rowdy, and to this Ilya my uncle Niktopolion, at the instance of his sister Katerina, no doubt, gave an I.O.U. for one thousand seven hundred roubles, and Katerina herself assigned to her husband, Porfiry, another I.O.U. for one thousand seven hundred, and through the mediation of the assessor Galushkin she took from my father another I.O.U. . . . but that was for two thousand, in which Galushkin's wife had a share. . . . It was just then my father— the Kingdom of Heaven be his—took and died. The I.O.U.s were presented, uncle Niktopolion was at his wits' end, he said he had never divided the land, that he held the estate in common with his nephew; Katerina said, let me have my fourteenth part; and then the arrears of taxes were claimed, too. . . . It was terrible! Galushkin's wife suddenly plops down her I.O.U. . . . Niktopolion says, my nephew must be responsible for that . . . and just think, how can a minor be responsible? . . . and Galushkin took it into court. The Polish woman's son had a hand in it too, and didn't even spare his stepmother, Katerina. . . . I won't let her off, he said . . . she poisoned my servant Akulina. . . . There was a bobbery. Petitions went rolling in. First to the district court, then to the court of the province, and from that back again to the district, with comments . . . and after uncle Niktopolion's death everything went wrong. I claim the possession of my property . . . and then an order is given for the sale of the Vyetrovo estate by auction to pay arrears of taxes. The German Hanginmester sends in his claims . . . and the peasants are flying away like partridges; the district marshal reads a reprimand to me. In chancery, he says, in chancery, and how could it be? . . . The lawful heir not allowed to take possession . . . and Katerina his stepmother took a complaint against Ilya right up to the Senate. . . . (*Pulled up by a general burst of laughter* KUZOVKIN *breaks off and is terribly confused.* TREMBINSKY, *who has been obsequiously and rather uncertainly watching his superiors and deferentially sharing their amusement, guffaws with his hand before his mouth.* PYOTR *grins stupidly near the door.* KARPATCHOV *laughs on a deep bass note, but discreetly.* TROPATCHOV *roars.* YELETSKY *laughs rather disdainfully and screws up his eyes. Only* IVANOV, *who has more than once pulled at* KUZOVKIN'S *coat while the latter was speaking, sits mute with bowed head.*)

YELETSKY (*Still laughing, to* KUZOVKIN): Go on, why have you stopped?

TROPATCHOV: Oh please do, What's-Your-Name, go on.

KUZOVKIN: I . . . I beg your pardon . . . I've troubled you.

TROPATCHOV: I see what it is . . . you're shy . . . you're shy, aren't you, now?

KUZOVKIN (*In a faint voice*): Yes, sir.

TROPATCHOV: Well, we must put that right. . . . (*Picking up an empty bottle.*) Boy! bring us some more wine. . . . (*To* YELETSKY.) Vous permettez?

YELETSKY: By all means . . . . (*To* TREMBINSKY.) Have you no champagne?

TREMBINSKY: Oh yes, sir. . . . (*Runs for the bowl with champagne in it and brings it hastily;* KUZOVKIN *is smiling and nervously fingering the button of his own coat.*)

TROPATCHOV (*To* KUZOVKIN): That's not right, my worthy friend! Shyness . . . is not the proper thing in polite society. (*To* YELETSKY _ *motioning towards the champagne.*) What—iced, too? Mais c'est magnifique! (*Pours out a glassful.*) First-rate, I've no doubt. (*To* KUZOVKIN.) Here's to you. Oh, you mustn't say no. . . . Come, if you have been a little muddled—what does it matter? Pavel Nikolaitch, tell him to drink.

YELETSKY: To the health of the future master of Vyetrovo! Drink it, Vassily . . . Alexeyitch. (KUZOVKIN *drinks.*)

TROPATCHOV: Come, I like that! (YELETSKY *and he get up; all rise and come to the front of the stage.*) What a jolly lunch! (*To* KUZOVKIN.) Well now? Where had we got to? With whom is your lawsuit now, eh?

KUZOVKIN (*Beginning to become excited by the wine*): With the heirs of Hanginmester, of course.

TROPATCHOV: But who was that gentleman?

KUZOVKIN: A German, to be sure. He bought up the I.O.U.s, or some say, simply took them. That's my own opinion, too. He just frightened the woman and took them.

TROPATCHOV: And Katerina, what was she about? And the Polish woman's son, Ilya?

Kuzovkin: Oh! they are all dead! Ilya was actually burnt to death, when he was intoxicated, in an inn on the high road which was on fire. (*To* Ivanov.) Oh, leave off tugging at my coat. I'm explaining it all properly to the gentlemen. They insist on hearing it. What's the harm?

Yeletsky: Let him alone, Mr. Ivanov, we are glad to listen to him.

Kuzovkin (*To* Ivanov): There, you see. (*To* Yeletsky *and* Tropatchov.) What am I asking for, gentlemen? I ask for nothing but justice, for my lawful right. I'm not acting from ambition. . . . What's personal ambition to me? Nothing. All I say is, judge between us. If I'm in the wrong, well, then I am; but if I'm in the right—if I'm in the right . . .

Tropatchov (*Interrupting*): Another glass?

Kuzovkin: No, thank you. You see all I demand is . . .

Tropatchov: In that case, let me embrace you.

Kuzovkin (*Somewhat astonished*): I'm greatly honoured. . . . Really, sir. . . .

Tropatchov: Yes, I like you very much. . . . (*Embraces him and holds him for some time.*) I would kiss you, my dear man, but no, better later on.

Kuzovkin: As you please.

Tropatchov (*Winking to* Karpatchov): Come, Karpy, now it's your turn. . . .

Karpatchov (*With a husky laugh*): Well, Vassily Semyonitch, let me press you to my heart. (*Embraces* Kuzovkin *and twirls round with him. Everyone laughs, each in his own way.*)

Kuzovkin (*Tearing himself out of* Karpatchov's *arms*): Leave off, do.

Karpatchov: Come, don't give yourself airs. . . . (*To* Tropatchov.) You had better bid him sing us a song, Flegont Alexandritch. . . . He's our leading singer.

Tropatchov: You sing, dear friend? . . . Oh, do oblige us, give us a taste of your talent!

Kuzovkin (*To* Karpatchov): Why do you tell stories about me? As though I could sing!

Karpatchov: You used to sing at table in the old master's days, didn't you?

Kuzovkin (*Dropping his voice*): In the old master's days. . . . I've grown old since then.

Tropatchov: You old, what next!

Karpatchov (*Pointing to* Kuzovkin): He used to sing—and he used to dance, too.

Tropatchov: You don't say so! You're a talented person, I see! You might oblige us. (*To* Yeletsky.) C'est un peu vulgaire . . . but there, in the country! (*Aloud to* Kuzovkin.) Come now . . . begin 'As down the Street. . . .' (*Begins singing it.*) Well?

Kuzovkin: Kindly excuse me.

Tropatchov: I say, what a disobliging fellow. . . . Yeletsky, do tell him to. . . .

Yeletsky (*Somewhat uncertainly*): But why don't you care to sing now, Vassily Semyonitch?

KUZOVKIN: Not at my age, Pavel Nikolaitch. Spare me.

TREMBINSKY (*Listening and looking with a smile at the gentlemen*): Only lately at the wedding of this gentleman's brother (*Motioning towards* IVANOV) he distinguished himself, I'm told.

TROPATCHOV: There, you see....

TREMBINSKY: He went hopping all over the room....

TROPATCHOV: Well, if that's so, you really can't refuse us.... Why won't you oblige Pavel Nikolaitch and us?

KUZOVKIN: I wasn't forced to, then.

TROPATCHOV: And now we ask you. You might reflect that your refusal may be set down to ingratitude. Ingratitude . . . oh! what a horrid vice!

KUZOVKIN: But I've really no voice. As to gratitude.... No one could be more grateful, and I'm ready to make any sacrifice.

TROPATCHOV: We don't ask any sacrifice of you.... Only just sing us a song. Come! (KUZOVKIN *is silent.*) Come now!

KUZOVKIN (*After a brief pause, begins singing: 'As down the Street,' but his voice breaks almost at the second word*): I can't, I really can't.

TROPATCHOV: Come, come, don't be shy.

KUZOVKIN (*Glancing at him*): No, sir . . . I won't sing.

TROPATCHOV: You won't?

KUZOVKIN: I can't.

TROPATCHOV: Do you know what then? You see this glass of champagne? I am going to empty it down your neck.

KUZOVKIN (*Agitated*): You won't do that, sir. I have not deserved that. Nobody has ever treated me. . . . How can you? It's . . . it's a shame, sir.

YELETSKY (*To* TROPATCHOV): Finissez. . . . You see he's distressed.

TROPATCHOV (*To* KUZOVKIN): You won't sing?

KUZOVKIN: I cannot sing, sir.

TROPATCHOV: You won't? (*Approaching him.*) One . . .

KUZOVKIN (*In an imploring voice to* YELETSKY): Pavel Nikolayevitch. . . .

TROPATCHOV: Two . . . (*Coming nearer to* Kuzovkin.)

KUZOVKIN (*Staggering, in a voice of despairing anguish*): How can you? . . . What do you treat me like this for? I haven't the honour of knowing you. . . . And I'm a gentleman after all . . . think of that. . . . I can't sing . . . you could see that for yourself. . . .

TROPATCHOV: For the last time. . . .

KUZOVKIN: Leave off, I tell you. . . . I'm not a clown.

TROPATCHOV: As though that were anything new for you?

KUZOVKIN (*Growing angry*): You'll kindly find somebody else to play the fool for you. . . .

YELETSKY: Do leave him alone, really.

TROPATCHOV: Why, but you know he used to play the fool for your father-in-law.

Kuzovkin: That's all in the past. (*Wipes his face.*) Besides, my head's rather bad to-day, it is, truly.

Yeletsky: Well, you can please yourself.

Kuzovkin (*Miserably*): Oh, Pavel Nikolayevitch, please don't be vexed with me.

Yeletsky: Nonsense! What an idea!

Kuzovkin: Another time, truly, I would with pleasure. (*Trying to assume a good-humoured air.*) Generously forgive me to-day, if I've been disobliging. . . . I've been too hot, gentlemen, but there. . . . I'm old, that's what it is. . . . And I've got out of the way of it, too.

Tropatchov: Well, drink up this glass, anyway.

Kuzovkin (*Relieved*): That I will, with pleasure, with the greatest pleasure. (*Takes the glass and drinks.*) To the health of our honoured guest. . . .

Tropatchov: Come, is a song still impossible?

Kuzovkin (*Has been for some time more and more affected by the wine; after the last glass with his apprehensions over, he begins to be intoxicated*): Upon my soul, I can't, sir. (*Laughing.*) As a matter of fact . . . in old days I used to sing . . . with the best of them. But things are different now. What am I now? Good for nothing . . . that's the fact. No better than he, here. (*Points to* Ivanov.) I'm no use now. You must forgive me, though. I've grown old . . . that's what it is. To-day, for instance, I fancy I've only drunk two or three glasses, and yet there's a muddle in here. (*Pointing to his head.*)

TROPATCHOV (*Who has been whispering meanwhile to* KARPATCHOV): Nonsense. . . . That's just your fancy. (KARPATCHPV *goes out laughing, leading* PYOTR *off with him.*) Why didn't you finish telling us about your lawsuit?

KUZOVKIN: To be sure, to be sure; I didn't finish my story. I don't mind, though, if you wish it. (*Laughs.*) Only be so kind . . . allow me to sit down. My legs . . . somehow . . . won't obey. . . .

TROPATCHOV (*Gives him a chair*): Oh yes, do.

KUZOVKIN (*Sits down facing the audience, and speaks slowly and languidly, rapidly becoming more and more drunk*): Where did I stop? Hanginmester. That Hanginmester was a German, of course. He doesn't care. He served in the Commissariat department—so I expect he made his fortune stealing by the sackful there—so now he says—the I. O. U.'s mine. And I'm a gentleman. What was I going to say? Oh, he says: either pay or give me your estate, either pay . . . or give . . . your estate . . . either pay . . . or give me . . . your estate. . . .

TROPATCHOV: You're asleep, my friend, wake up.

KUZOVKIN (*Starts and again sinks into drowsiness. He can hardly speak by now*): Who? I? What an idea . . . never mind. I'm not asleep. We sleep at night, and it's daytime now. It isn't night now, is it? I'm talking about Hanginmester. That Hanginmester—Han-gin-mester—Hangin-mester—he was my real enemy. They tell me this and that, but I say no, Hanginmester—Han-gin-mester he's the man that wronged me. (KARPATCHOV *comes in with a huge* fool's *cap made of sugar wrapping-paper and, winking at* TROPATCHOV, *steals up behind* KUZOVKIN. TREMBINSKY is *choking with laughter.* IVANOV, *pale and crushed, looks up from under his brows.*) And I know why he doesn't like me . . . I know he's been trying to injure me all my life . . . ever since I was a child. (KARPATCHPV *cautiously puts the* fool's *cap on* KUZOVKIN'S *head.*) But I forgive him. . . . God bless him. . . . God bless him. . . .

> [*Everyone is laughing.* KUZOVKIN *stops and looks round in bewilderment.* IVANOV *goes up to him, takes him by the arm and says through his teeth:* 'Look what they've put on your head . . . you see they're making a fool of you. . . .' KUZOVKIN *raises his hands to his head, feels the cap, slowly lowers his hands to his face, covers his eyes, and suddenly begins sobbing, muttering through his tears:* 'What for, what for, what for . . . ' *but does not remove the cap.* TROPATCHOV, TREMBINSKY *and* KARPATCHOV *go on laughing.* PYOTR *laughs too, peeping in at the door.*]

YELETSKY: Hush, Vassily Semyonitch, aren't you ashamed to cry over such a trifling matter?

KUZOVKIN (*Taking his hands from his face*): Over such a trifling matter. . . . No, it's not a trifling matter, Pavel Nikolaitch. (*Stands up and throws the cap on the floor.*) The veryday of your arrival . . . the very first day. . . . (*His voice breaks.*) This is how you treat an old man . . . an old man, Pavel Nikolaitch! Like this! What are you trampling me in the mud for? What have I done to you? And I was so looking forward, I was delighted to see you. What's it for, Pavel Nikolaitch?

TROPATCHOV: Come, shut up . . . what are you saying?

KUZOVKIN (*Growing paler and more distracted*): I'm not speaking to you . . . you've been allowed to make a mock of me . . . you're pleased. It's you I'm speaking to, Pavel Nikolaitch. Because for the gift of a crust of bread and an old cast-off pair of boots your late father-in-law thought fit to make a clown of me—must you do the same? Oh well . . . his precious gifts were paid for with my blood, with bitter tears. . . . So you must make me pay, too? Oh, Pavel Nikolaitch! for shame, for shame, sir! And you a cultured gentleman from Petersburg.

YELETSKY (*Haughtily*): Let me tell you, you are forgetting yourself. Go to your room and sleep it off. . . . You can't stand upright. . . .

KUZOVKIN (*More and more carried away*): I will sleep it off, Pavel Nikolaitch, I will . . . . Perhaps I am drunk; but who made me drunk? That's not what matters, Pavel Nikolaitch. But you had better take note! Here you've made me a laughing-stock before everybody, you've rolled me in the dirt, on the very first day you are here . . . while if I liked, if I were to say the word. . . .

Ivanov (*In a low voice*): Vassily, think what you're doing. . . .

Kuzovkin: Leave me alone! Yes, honoured sir, if I chose . . .

Yeletsky: Oh, he's hopelessly drunk! He doesn't know what he's saying!

Kuzovkin: Excuse me, sir. I am drunk, but I do know what I'm saying. Here you now are a grand gentleman, a Petersburg official, a cultured man, of course . . . while I'm a clown, a fool, without a farthing of my own; I'm a beggar, living on the bread of others. . . . But do you know who I am? Here you are married . . . and who is it you have married?

Yeletsky (*Tries to draw* Tropatchov *away*): Pray excuse it, I never expected such idiocy. . . .

Tropatchov: It's my fault, I confess. . . .

Yeletsky (*To* Trembinsky): Take him away, please. . . . (*Tries to go into the drawing-room.*)

Kuzovkin: Wait a minute, gracious sir . . . you haven't told me yet who it is you have married. . . .

> [Olga *appears at the drawing-room door and stands still in amazement Her husband makes signs to her to go away. She does not understand them.*]

YELETSKY (*To* KUZOVKIN): Go away, go away....

TREMBINSKY (*Approaches* KUZOVKIN *and takes him by the arm*): Come along.

KUZOVKIN (*Pushing him away*): Don't touch me, you! (*Following* YELETSKY.) You're a gentleman, a distinguished man, aren't you? You've married Olga Petrovna Korin. . . the Korins are an old noble family, too. . . but do you know who she is, Olga Petrovna? She's . . . she's my daughter! (*Olga disappears.*)

YELETSKY (*Stands as though thunderstruck*): You . . . you've gone out of your mind.

KUZOVKIN (*After a pause, clutching his head*): Yes, I've gone out of my mind. (*Runs off staggering . . .* IVANOV *following him.*)

YELETSKY (*Turning to* TROPATCHOV): He's mad....

TROPATCHOV: Oh.... Oh, of course!

    [*Both go quietly into the drawing-room.* TREMBINSKY *and* KARPATCHOV *stare at each other in amazement.*]

THE CURTAIN FALLS

ACT II

[*A drawing-room richly furnished in old-fashioned style. On Right (from audience) a door into the dining-room, on Left door into* Olga Petrovna's *study.*

Olga *is sitting on the sofa; near her stands* Praskovya Ivanovna.]

Praskovya Ivanovna (*After a brief silence*): So then, mistress dear, which of the maids will you please to have wait on you personally?

Olga (*With some impatience*): Whichever you like.

Praskovya Ivanovna: Akulina, the one who squints, is a good girl; so is Marfa, Martchuk's daughter; will you choose them?

Olga: Very well. But what's the name of that girl . . . who's rather nice-looking . . . in a light-blue dress?

Praskovya Ivanovna (*Puzzled*): Light-blue? . . . Oh, yes, to be sure! It's Masha you are graciously inquiring about. It's as your ladyship wishes—but she is such a saucy girl, there's no doing anything with her! Unruly altogether—and not nice in her behaviour either. But as you please, my lady.

Olga: I liked her face, but if she's badly behaved....

Praskovya Ivanovna: Very badly, very. She wouldn't do, she doesn't deserve it. (*After a brief pause.*) Oh, my lady, how pretty you have grown! How like your dear mamma you are! You're our little darling. It's a joy to look at you. . . . Let me kiss your little hand, my lady.

Olga: Very well then, Praskovya, you can go.

Praskovya Ivanovna: Yes, ma'am. Is there nothing you want?

Olga: No, nothing.

Praskovya Ivanovna: So I'll send Akulina and Marfa....

Olga: Yes, you can go now. (Praskovya *is going out.*) Oh, send word to Pavel Nikolaitch that I want to see him....

Praskovya Ivanovna: Yes, ma'am. (*Goes out.*)

Olga (*Alone*): What does it mean? What did I hear yesterday? . . . I couldn't sleep all night. That old man must have been mad. . . . (*Stands up and walks about the room.*) 'She is my . . . ' Yes, yes, those were the words. But it's madness. . . . (*Stops.*) Paul has no suspicion yet. . . . Oh, here he is.

[Yeletsky *comes in.*]

Yeletsky (*Going up to her with an anxious expression*): You wanted to see me, Olya?

Olga: Yes, I wanted to ask you. . . . In the garden . . . the paths by the pond are all overgrown with grass. . . . They've been weeded in front of the house—but those have been forgotten. . . . Tell them.

YELETSKY: I have given orders about it already.

OLGA: Ah! thanks. . . . And tell them to buy some bells in the town—to put on my cows' necks. . . .

YELETSKY: It shall be done. (*Is about to go.*) No more orders for me?

OLGA: Why . . . are you so busy?

YELETSKY: They have brought the accounts from the counting-house.

OLGA: Oh! Well then, I won't keep you. . . . We might drive to the copse before dinner. . . .

YELETSKY: Of course. (*Again is about to go.*)

OLGA (*Lets him reach the door*): Paul. . . .

YELETSKY (*Turning round*): Yes?

OLGA: Tell me, please . . . I'd no chance to ask you about it yesterday . . . what was the meaning of that scene yesterday morning . . . at lunch?

YELETSKY: Oh . . . nothing really. It's only vexing that anything so unpleasant should have happened on the very day of our arrival. However, I was a little to blame. They must needs make that old man, Kuzovkin, drunk—that is, it was really our neighbour Monsieur Tropatchov who thought of it . . . and at first he certainly was rather amusing; he babbled away telling us a long yarn, but later on he began to be noisy and say all sorts of silly things, but it didn't matter. . . . It's not worth talking about.

Olga: Ah! I fancied . . .

Yeletsky: Oh, no, no. . . . We must be more careful in future, that's all. (*After a moment's reflection.*) However . . . I have already taken measures. . . .

Olga: Oh?

Yeletsky: Yes. You see, though it was of no consequence . . . still the servants were there, they saw . . . and heard it all. It was improper . . . in a respectable house. . . . So I've already made arrangements.

Olga: What arrangements?

Yeletsky: Well . . . do you see . . . I've explained to the old man that it would be unpleasant for him to remain here, in our house, after such a scene, as you call it yourself. . . . He completely agreed with me at once — he is perfectly sober now. . . . Of course, he is a poor man, he has nothing to live on . . . well, he can be given a little room on another estate of yours, a pension, rations. . . . He will be quite contented . . . of course he shall have everything he wants.

Olga: Paul, it seems to me that for such a trifling matter . . . you are punishing him too severely. . . . He has been living here in this house for years. . . . He is used to it . . . he's known me from a child . . . really, I think he might stay here.

Yeletsky: Olya . . . no . . . there are reasons. . . . Of course, we can't be hard on the old man . . . especially as he wasn't himself at the time . . . but all the same, please let me do as I think fit about it. . . . I repeat there are reasons. . . rather important ones.

Olga: As you please.

Yeletsky: Besides, I believe he has packed up all his belongings already.

Olga: But he won't go away without saying good-bye to me?

Yeletsky: I imagine he will come to say good-bye. But if that's unpleasant for you, you know—you need not see him. . . .

Olga: On the contrary, I should like to have a few words with him. . . .

Yeletsky: As you like, Olya . . . but I wouldn't advise you to. . . . You will be distressed, for after all, he's old, and has known you from a child. . . . And I must own I shouldn't like to alter my decision. . . .

Olga: Oh, no, don't be afraid . . . . Only I really expect he'll go without saying good-bye. . . . Please send and find out about him, whether he has gone already?

Yeletsky: Certainly. (*Rings.*) Vous êtes jolie comme un ange aujourd'hui.

Pyotr (*Coming in*): What is your pleasure?

Yeletsky: Go, my lad, and find out whether Mr. Kuzovkin has gone yet. (*Glancing at* Olga.) And let him come and say good-bye.

Pyotr: Yes, sir. (*Goes out.*)

Olga: Paul . . . and I have a favour to ask you.

Yeletsky (*Caressingly*): Tell me what. . . .

Olga: Please . . . when he . . . Kuzovkin . . . comes, leave me alone with him.

YELETSKY (*After a brief pause, with a cold smile*): But I think . . . on the contrary . . . it will be awkward for you.

OLGA: No, please do; I've something to say to him . . . I must ask him. . . . Yes, I want to talk to him alone.

YELETSKY (*Looking at her intently*): Why, can you have heard something yesterday?

OLGA (*Looking at her husband with the most innocent expression*): What?

YELETSKY (*Hurriedly*): Well, as you please, as you please. . . . Here, I think he's coming.

[KUZOVKIN *comes in. He is very pale.*]

OLGA: Good morning, Vassily Petrovitch. . . . (KUZOVKIN *bows without speaking.*) Good morning. (*To* YELETSKY.) Eh bien, mon ami? Je vous en prie.

YELETSKY (*To his wife*): Oui, oui. (*To* KUZOVKIN.) You are quite ready?

KUZOVKIN (*With an effort, in a toneless voice*): I'm quite ready.

YELETSKY: Olga Petrovna wants to talk to you a little . . . to say good-bye. . . . If there's anything you want, please tell her. . . . (*To* OLGA.) Au revoir . . . you won't be with him long, of course?

OLGA: I don't know. . . . I expect not.

YELETSKY: Very good. . . . (*Goes off into the dining-room.*)

OLGA (*Sits down on the sofa and motions* KUZOVKIN *to an easy-chair*): Sit down, Vassily Petrovitch. . . . (KUZOVKIN *bows, refusing.*) I beg you to sit down. (*For some time* OLGA *does not know how to begin the conversation*.) I hear you are going away!

Kuzovkin (*Without raising his eyes*): Yes.

Olga: Pavel Nikolaitch was telling me so. . . . I am very sorry, believe me. . . .

Kuzovkin: You mustn't be troubled. . . . Very grateful. . . . It's all right.

Olga: In your . . . new home . . . you will be as well off . . . better really . . . set your mind at rest . . . I'll see to that.

Kuzovkin: I'm truly thankful. I feel that . . . I don't deserve. . . . A piece of bread . . . and shelter . . . is all I should have. (*After a brief pause, he gets up*.) Now allow me to say good-bye. . . . I have been greatly to blame, certainly . . . forgive an old man.

Olga: Why in such a hurry? . . . Stay a little.

Kuzovkin: As you wish. (*Sits down again*.)

Olga (*Again after a short pause*): Listen, Vassily Petrovitch . . . tell me frankly what happened to you yesterday morning?

Kuzovkin: I'm sorry for it, Olga Petrovna, dreadfully sorry.

Olga: But how was it you. . . .

Kuzovkin: Please do not ask me about it, Olga Petrovna. . . . It's not worth it. It was my fault entirely . . . and that's all. Pavel Nikolaitch is perfectly right. I deserved far worse punishment. . . . I shall pray for him all my days.

Olga: I must confess I can't see how you're so much to blame. . . . You're not young

. . . most likely you're not used to wine now . . . you were a little noisy. . . .

Kuzovkin: No, Olga Petrovna, please don't justify me, I humbly thank you—only I feel how wrong it was.

Olga: Or did you perhaps say something insulting to my husband or Monsieur Tropatchov. . . .

Kuzovkin (*Looking down*): I am sorry.

Olga (*With some emotion*): Tell me, Vassily Petrovitch, do you remember clearly all that you said?

Kuzovkin (*Startled, looks at* Olga, *and slowly brings out*): I don't know . . . what . . .

Olga: I'm told you said something . . . .

Kuzovkin (*Hurriedly*): I talked nonsense, Olga Petrovna, utter nonsense. I said anything that came into my head. I'm sorry. I didn't know what I was doing.

Olga: But . . . I wonder what put it into your head. . . .

Kuzovkin: Goodness knows. Simply madness. I must own I'm quite unused to drinking wine now. So . . . I drank too much. . . . So I went and God knows what I babbled. It does happen like that. Still, I am greatly to blame . . . and punished as I deserve. (*Is about to get up.*) Allow me to say good-bye, Olga Petrovna. . . . Please do not remember evil against me.

Olga: I see you won't speak openly to me. Don't be afraid of me. . . . I'm not like Pavel Nikolaitch, you know. . . . Well, him perhaps you may be afraid of. . . . You don't know him. . . . He seems severe on the surface. . . . But what are you afraid of me for? . . . Why, you knew me as a child.

Kuzovkin: Olga Petrovna, you have the heart of an angel. . . . Spare a poor old man.

Olga: Oh dear, I didn't mean to . . .

Kuzovkin: Don't remind me of your childhood . . . there's bitterness enough in my heart as it is . . . oh, it is bitter! To have to leave your house in my old age . . . and through my own fault.

Olga: Listen, Vassily Petrovitch, there is still a way to put things right. Only be open with me . . . listen . . . I . . . (*Suddenly gets up and moves a little aside.*)

Kuzovkin (*Looking after her*): Don't be distressed, Olga Petrovna—really, it's not worth it. I shall pray for you over there, too. And you will sometimes think of me—and say: there's old Vassily Kuzovkin, he was a man devoted to me. . . .

Olga (*Turning to* Kuzovkin *again*): Vassily Petrovitch, are you really a man devoted to me, do you really love me?

Kuzovkin: Olga Petrovna, darling, tell me to die for you.

Olga: No, I don't ask for your death, I want the truth, I want to know the truth.

Kuzovkin: Yes.

Olga: I . . . I overheard your last exclamation.

Kuzovkin (*hardly able to articulate the words*): What . . . exclamation?

OLGA: I heard what you said about me. (KUZOVKIN *gets up from his chair and falls on his knees*): Was it true?

KUZOVKIN (*Faltering*): Please, mercifully forgive me. . . . Madness—I've told you so already. (*His voice breaks.*)

OLGA: So, you won't tell me the truth.

KUZOVKIN: Madness, Olga Petrovna, forgive me. . . .

OLGA (*Seizing his hand*): No, no . . . for God's sake . . . I call on you in God's name . . . I beseech you, tell me, was it . . . true? (*A silence.*) Why are you torturing me?

KUZOVKIN: So you will know the truth?

OLGA: Yes. Tell me, was it true?

[KUZOVKIN *raises his head and looks at* OLGA. . . . *His face expresses an agonizing conflict. All at once he bows his head and whispers*: 'It was true.' OLGA *swiftly draws back from him and stands motionless.* KUZOVKIN *hides his face in his hands. The door from the other room opens and* YELETSKY *walks in. At first he does not notice* KUZOVKIN, *who is still on his knees. He goes up to his wife.*]

YELETSKY: Well, so that's over? (*Stops in astonishment.*) Ah voilà, je vous ai dit . . . He's been begging your forgiveness. . . .

OLGA: Paul, leave us alone. . . .

YELETSKY (*Hesitating*): Mais, ma chère. . . .

OLGA: I beg you, I entreat you, leave us. . . .

Yeletsky (*After a short silence*): Very well, only I hope you will explain this mystery . . . . (Olga *nods affirmatively*, Yeletsky *slowly goes out.*]

Olga (*Goes quickly to the door, locks it and returns to* Kuzovkin, *who is still on his knees*): Get up . . . get up, I tell you.

Kuzovkin (*Slowly getting up*): Olga Petrovna. . . . (*He evidently does not know what to say.*)

Olga (*Motioning him to the sofa*): Sit here. (Kuzovkin *sits down.* Olga *remains at some distance and stands sideways to him.*) Vassily Petrovitch . . . you understand my position.

Kuzovkin (*Faintly*): Olga Petrovna, I see . . . I'm really out of my mind. Allow me to go before I do any more harm. I don't know what I'm saying.

Olga (*Breathing hard*): No, nonsense, Vassily Petrovitch. The thing's done now. Now you can't go back on your words. . . . You must tell me everything . . . the whole . . . truth now.

Kuzovkin: But you see I . . .

Olga (*Rapidly*): Do understand my position and yours . . . I tell you. . . . Either you have slandered my mother . . . in that case, you will please go away and never let me see your face again. . . . (*She stretches her hand towards the door.* Kuzovkin *tries to get up and sinks down again.*) Ah! you remain—you see you remain. . . .

Kuzovkin (*In misery*): Oh my God!

Olga: I want to know all. . . . You must tell me everything, do you hear?

Kuzovkin (*In despair*): Very well . . . yes . . . you shall know everything . . . since this terrible thing has happened. Only, Olga Petrovna, please don't look at me like that . . . or I . . . really . . . I can't.

Olga (*Trying to smile*): Vassily Petrovitch, I . . .

Kuzovkin (*Timidly*): My name . . . is Vassily Semyonitch, Olga Petrovna. . . . (Olga *flushes and faintly shrugs her shoulders. She still stands at some distance from* Kuzovkin.) Yes . . . well, where am I to begin?. . .

Olga (*reddening, in confusion*): Vassily Semyonitch, how can you . . . expect me. . . .

Kuzovkin (*On the point of tears*): But I can't speak while you're like this. . . .

Olga (*Holding out her hand to him*): Calm yourself . . . speak. . . . You see what a state I'm in . . . control yourself.

Kuzovkin: I'll try, Olga Petrovna dear. Well, where shall I begin? Oh God! . . . Very well, then. I'll tell you a little first, if I may . . . . Yes, in a minute . . . . I was something over twenty then. I was born, I may say, in poverty—and later on was deprived of my last farthing—and quite, I may say, unjustly . . . and besides, I had no sort of education, of course. . . . Your father (Olga *shudders*) —the Kingdom of Heaven be his!— took compassion on me, or I should have been utterly lost; you live in my house, he said, till I find a post for you. So that was how I came to live with your father. Well, of course, it wasn't easy to find me a situation—so I just stayed on. At that time the master was unmarried—but about two years after he began courting your mother—and married her. Well, so he began living with your mother . . . and they had two little sons . . . but they both died very soon. And I must tell you, Olga Petrovna, he was a harsh man, terribly harsh, indeed he was—and too free with his fists, and at times when he was in a passion, he didn't know what he was doing. He drank, too. Otherwise he was a good man and my benefactor. Well, at first he lived happily with your mother. . . . Only not for long. Your mother—the Kingdom of Heaven be hers!—was, one may say, a perfect angel . . . and a beauty, too. . . . But there! It was fate! A certain lady came to live near us about that time. . . . And your father must go and become attached to her. Olga Petrovna, graciously forgive me if I . . .

OLGA: Go on.

KUZOVKIN: It's you who insist on it. (*Passes his hand over his face.*) Oh Lord my God, succour me a sinner! So he became attached to this lady—(plague take her even in the other world!)—began spending every blessed day with her, often did not even come home at night. It was a bad business. Your mother would sit all alone for whole days together, not saying a word; or sometime she'd shed tears . . . . I'd sit there, of course, my heart ready to break, and not dare to open my mouth. What good would my foolish words be to her, I thought! The other neighbouring landowners were not very fond of coming to see the old master either; he'd put them all off coming, you may say, by his haughtiness; so your mother hadn't a soul to speak to. She would sit, poor darling, at the window, she wouldn't even read, but just look out at the high-road into the fields. And meantime —goodness knows why, for nobody dared contradict him—your father's temper was worse than ever. He was so violent—it was terrible! And what was strange, too; he took it into his head to be jealous; and who was there to be jealous over, the Lord only knows! He would go out himself and lock her up, he would really. He flew into a rage over every trifle. And the more your mother gave way to him, the more ill-humoured he was to her. At last he quite gave up speaking to her, he abandoned her entirely. Ah! Olga Petrovna! Olga Petrovna! What she had to put up with in those days, your poor mother! You can't remember her, Olga Petrovna, you were too young, my dear, when she died. There's not another soul as sweet on earth now. And how she loved your father! He wouldn't look at her, and she, left without him, would keep talking with me of him, only of him, and how to make things better, how to please him. Suddenly one day he got ready for a journey. Where? To Moscow, he said, I'm going alone, on business. Alone, indeed! his lady was waiting for him at the next posting station. And so they went off together and were not heard of for six months, six months, Olga Petrovna! And he didn't write one letter home all that time! All of a sudden he arrives, but so morose, so angry. . . . His lady had cast him off, as we found out afterwards. He locked himself up in his room and didn't show himself. All the servants even were wondering. At last your poor mother could bear it no longer. . . . She crossed herself—she had come to be afraid of him, poor dear!—and went in to see him. She began trying to persuade him, but all at once he shouted at her and seizing his stick. . . . (Kuzovkin *looks at* Olga.) Forgive me, Olga Petrovna.

Olga: You are speaking the truth, Vassily Semyonitch?

Kuzovkin: May God strike me dead on the spot!

Olga: Go on.

Kuzovkin: Well. He . . . yes! Ah! Olga Petrovna, he cruelly insulted your mother in words . . . and other ways . . . she ran like one crazed to her room, while he called the servants and off into the hunting field. . . . So then . . . then . . . it happened. . . . (*His voice drops*.) I can't, Olga Petrovna, really I can't. . . .

Olga (*Not looking at him*): Go on! (*After a brief silence, impatiently*.) Go on!

Kuzovkin: I obey, Olga Petrovna. One must suppose that your poor mother's mind gave way at the time from that deadly insult, it must have made her ill . . . I can see her as though it were to-day. . . . She went into the ikon room, stood before the holy ikons, lifted her hand to make the sign of the Cross, but suddenly turned away and came out . . she actually laughed softly to herself. . . The evil one was too strong even for her, it seems. My heart ached looking at her. At dinner she would eat nothing; she would not speak, but looked intently at me . . . and in the evening. . . . In the evening, Olga Petrovna, I used to sit alone with her—here in this very room—sometimes at cards, you know, to pass the time, sometimes a little talk. . . . Well, so, that evening (*He begins to be breathless*) your poor mother, after a long, long silence, suddenly turned to me. . . Olga Petrovna, I almost worshipped your mother, and I loved her . . . and all at once she said to me: 'Vassily Semyonitch, you love me, I know, while he despises me, he has cast me off, he has insulted me. . . Well, so I too . . . ' Her mind was confused from that insult, Olga Petrovna, she was utterly beside herself. . . . While I. . . I . . . I didn't know what I was doing, my head was in a whirl . . . it's dreadful to recall it, she suddenly said to me that evening . . Olga Petrovna dear, spare an old man!—I can't—I'd rather cut my tongue out! (OLGA *turns away and does not speak*; KUZOVKIN *looks at her and goes on rapidly*.) The very next day Olga Petrovna, I was not in the house . . . I remember I ran off into the woods at daybreak . . . the very next day, the huntsman galloped into the yard. . . . What was it? The master had fallen off his horse, and was lying unconscious, fatally injured. . . . The very next day, Olga Petrovna, the very next day! . . . Your mother ordered the carriage at once . . . and off to him. He was lying in a little village in the steppe, at the priest's, thirty miles away. In spite of all her haste, poor dear, she did not find him alive. My God! we all thought she would go out of her mind. . . . She was ailing right up to the time of your birth—and never recovered afterwards. . . . As you know she was not long for this world. . . . (*His head droops.*)

OLGA: So then . . . I am your daughter. . . . But what proofs have you?

KUZOVKIN (*Eagerly*): Proofs? Good gracious, Olga Petrovna, proofs! I've no proofs whatever. As though I should dare! Why, if it hadn't been for the misfortune yesterday, I wouldn't have said a word to my dying day, I'd have cut my tongue out sooner! And why didn't I die yesterday? Good gracious! Not a soul till yesterday, Olga Petrovna, what an idea. . . . I didn't dare to think of it, even by myself alone. After the death of your . . . father . . . I wanted to run away . . . anywhere . . . I did wrong to stop. I hadn't the courage, I was afraid of want, of cruel poverty. I did wrong, I remained. . . . But in your mother's presence I could hardly breathe, let alone speak or anything, Olga Petrovna. Proofs! In those first months I didn't see your mother at all—she shut herself up in her room, and wouldn't see anyone but Praskovya Ivanovna, her maid; later on . . . later on, I did see her certainly, but in the sight of God I say it, I was afraid to look her in the face. . . . Proofs! Why indeed, Olga Petrovna, I'm not a criminal anyway, and not a fool—I know my place. And if you had not yourself commanded . . . don't be troubled, Olga Petrovna, please. . . . What are you worried about? What proofs could there be! Don't you believe an old fool like me . . . I've been lying . . . that's all. . . . As a matter of fact, I sometimes don't know what I'm saying . . . . I'm in my dotage. . . . Don't believe it, Olga Petrovna, that's all. Proofs indeed!

OLGA: No, Vassily Semyonitch, I won't have any deception with you. . . . You couldn't . . . invent such a . . . To slander the dead—no, that would be too terrible. . . . (*Turning away.*) No, I believe you.

KUZOVKIN (*In a faint voice*): You believe me. . . .

OLGA: Yes. (*Glancing at him and shuddering.*) But it's awful, awful! (*Moves quickly aside.*)

KUZOVKIN (*stretching out his hands towards her*): Olga Petrovna, don't be uneasy . . . I understand you. . . . You with your education . . . and I . . . I would tell you what I am . . . only for your sake . . . but I know very well what I am. . . . Oh dear, do you suppose I don't feel it all? . . . You know I love you like my own . . . . You see, after all, you are. . . . (*Gets up quickly.*) Don't be afraid, don't be afraid, my tongue shall never utter the word. . . . Forget all our talk, and I'll go away to-day, at once. . . . You see I can't stay here now, I can't possibly. . . . Well, there too I can pray for you . . . (*Tears come into his eyes*) and everywhere . . . for you and for your husband . . . and, of course, it's all my own fault. . . . I've robbed myself, you may say, of my last happiness. . . . (*Sheds tears.*)

OLGA (*In indescribable agitation*): Oh, what does it mean! Why, he's my father, after all. . . . (*Turns, and seeing that he is weeping.*) He's crying . . . don't cry, there, there. . . . (*She goes up to him.*)

KUZOVKIN (*Stretching out his hand to her*): Good-bye, Olga Petrovna. . . .

> [OLGA, *too, holds out her hand uncertainly _ tries to force herself to embrace him, but at once turns away with a shudder and runs off into her study.* KUZOVKIN *remains where he is.*]

KUZOVKIN (*Clutching at his heart*): My God, my God, what is happening to me?

VOICE OF YELETSKY (*Speaking through the closed door*): You've locked the door! Olya! Olya!

KUZOVKIN (*Coming to himself*): Who is it? . . . He. . . . Yes. . . . What is it?

VOICE OF YELETSKY: Monsieur Tropatchov is here. Je vous l'annonce. . . . Olya, answer. . . . Vassily Semyonitch, are you there?

KUZOVKIN: Yes, sir.

VOICE OF YELETSKY: Where is Olga Petrovna?

KUZOVKIN: She has gone, sir.

VOICE OF YELETSKY: Oh! Unlock the door
> [KUZOVKIN *unlocks it*: YELETSKY *comes in*.]

YELETSKY (*Looking about him*): This is all very strange. (*To* KUZOVKIN, *coldly and sternly*.) You are going away?

KUZOVKIN: Yes, sir.

YELETSKY: Ah! Well, how did your conversation end, then?

KUZOVKIN: Conversation . . . there was no conversation exactly, but I begged Olga Petrovna's gracious forgiveness.

YELETSKY: And she?

KUZOVKIN: She was pleased to say she would no longer be angry with me . . . and so now I am ready to go. . . .

YELETSKY: So Olga Petrovna did not alter my decision?

KUZOVKIN: Oh, no. . . .

YELETSKY: H'm . . . I'm very sorry . . . but you see for yourself, Vassily Semyonitch, that . . .

KUZOVKIN: Yes, indeed, Pavel Nikolaitch, I agree with you completely. You have treated me very kindly. I humbly thank you.

YELETSKY: I am glad to see that you feel you were to blame. And so, good-bye. . . . If you want anything, please don't hesitate.

Though I have given the village elder instructions, you may at any time apply to me directly....

Kuzovkin: I humbly thank you. (*Bows.*)

Yeletsky: Good-bye, Vassily Semyonitch. Oh, wait a little, though.... H'm! Monsieur Tropatchov has called—he'll be in here immediately.... I should like you to repeat before him ... what you said to me this morning....

Kuzovkin: Yes, sir.

Yeletsky: Good. (*To* Tropatchov, *who is coming in.*) Mais venez done, venez done! (Tropatchov *comes in, strutting affectedly as usual*) Well? Who won?

Tropatchov: I did, of course. Your billiard-table's wonderfully fine. Only fancy, Mr. Ivanov refused to play with me! Said he had a headache. Mr. Ivanov—and a headache!! Eh? Et Madame? I hope she is quite well?

Yeletsky: Yes, quite—she'll be here in a minute.

Tropatchov (*With affable familiarity*): I say, you know, your arrival is a perfect godsend for us poor rustics ... ha! ha!—une bonne fortune.... (*Looks round and notices* Kuzovkin.) Hullo ... you here, too?

[Kuzovkin *bows in silence.*]

Yeletsky (*Loudly to* Tropatchov, *motioning with his chin towards* Kuzovkin): Yes ... he's terribly upset to-day—you understand—after yesterday's performance—he's been begging everybody's pardon all day.

TROPATCHOV: Ah! wine disagrees with him, it seems. . . . What do you say, eh?

KUZOVKIN (*Not raising his eyes*): I'm sorry, I must have been quite mad.

TROPATCHOV: Aha! So that's it, master of Vyetrovo. . . . (*To* YELETSKY.) And the idea occurs to me. . . . After this there's nothing so wonderful in some madman's imagining he's the Emperor of China, or I don't know what. . . . Some, they say, fancy they've the sun and moon in their stomachs, and anything else you please. . . . Ha! Ha! So that's it, that's it, master of Vyetrovo.

YELETSKY (*Who would like to change the subject*): Yes. . . . What was I meaning to ask you, Flegont Alexandritch—when are we going shooting?

TROPATCHOV: When you like. . . . You see . . . Here, I'm not standing on ceremony with you. . . . I was here yesterday and here I am again to-day. . . . So you must do the same with me. . . . Wait a minute, I'll ask Karpatchov. He knows better about it. He'll tell us where to go. (*Goes to door of the dining-room.*) Karpatchov! come here, old man! (*To* YELETSKY.) He's a first-rate shot —but I beat him at billiards. (KARPATCHPV *comes in.*) Here, Karpy, Pavel Nikolaitch would like to go shooting to-morrow—so where should we go, eh?

KARPATCHOV: Let's go into Koloberdovo. There must be plenty of woodcock there by now.

YELETSKY: Is it far from here?

Karpatchov: By the main track about twenty-five miles, but by the by-roads it will be less.

Yeletsky: Very well, then. (Praskovya Ivanovna *comes out of the study*.) What is it?

Praskovya Ivanovna (*With a bow to* Yeletsky): My lady asks you to go to her.

Yeletsky: What for?

Praskovya Ivanovna: I can't say, sir.

Yeletsky: Say, I'll come at once. (*To* Tropatchov.) You will excuse me? (Praskovya Ivanovna *goes out*.)

Tropatchov (*Shaking his head*): Oh, Pavel Nikolaitch, aren't you ashamed to ask. . . . Please. . . .

Yeletsky: We won't keep you waiting long. (*Goes out*. Kuzovkin, *who has all the time been standing not far from the door into the dining-room, tries to seize this opportunity to go out*.)

Tropatchov (To Kuzovkin): Where are you off to, my friend? Stay and let's have a little chat.

Kuzovkin: I have to . . .

Tropatchov: Oh, nonsense . . . you needn't. You're feeling ashamed, perhaps. . . . What rubbish! It's a thing that happens to everybody. (*Takes him by the arm and leads him to front of stage*.) That is—wait a bit—I mean, drinking too much is a thing that happens to everybody . . . but I must own you gave us a surprise yesterday! You discovered a likeness, did you, eh? What a notion!

KUZOVKIN: Simply through foolishness.

TROPATCHOV: To be sure, and yet it was queer. Why your daughter? . . . Queer! . . . Own up, though, you wouldn't be sorry to have a daughter like that? (*Pokes him in the ribs.*) Come . . . tell us . . . eh? (*To* KARPATCHOV.) He hadn't bad taste, eh? What do you say? (KARPATCHOV *laughs.*)

KUZOVKIN (*Tries to draw his arm away from* TROPATCHOV): Excuse me. . . .

TROPATCHOV: Why were you so cross with us yesterday, eh? Come, tell us. . . .

KUZOVKIN (*Turning his head away, in a low voice*): I am sorry.

TROPATCHOV: To be sure. Well, God will forgive you. Your daughter then? (KUZOVKIN *does not speak.*) I say, dear friend, why don't you come and see me? I'd make you welcome.

KUZOVKIN: I humbly thank you.

TROPATCHOV: And you'd find it nice, ask him here. (*Pointing to* KARPATCHOV.) You could tell me again about Vyetrovo.

KUZOVKIN (*In a toneless voice*): Yes, sir.

TROPATCHOV: Why, I don't believe you've greeted Karpatchov to-day? (*To* KARPATCHOV.) Karpy, you haven't greeted Vassily Semyonitch as you did yesterday?

KARPATCHOV: No, I haven't.

TROPATCHOV: That's too bad.

KARPATCHOV: Oh, allow me, I will at once. . . . (*Advances with outspread arms towards* KUZOVKIN. KUZOVKIN *backs. The study door opens quickly and* Yeletsky *comes in. He is pale and agitated.*)

Yeletsky (*With annoyance*): I believe I've asked you, Flegont Alexandritch, to leave Mr. Kuzovkin alone . . . .

[Tropatchov *turns in surprise and looks at* Yeletsky. Karpatchov *stays motionless.*]

Tropatchov (*With some embarrassment*): You told . . . I don't remember.

Yeletsky (*Goes on sharply and harshly*): Yes, Flegont Alexandritch, I confess that I wonder how you . . . with your education . . . your breeding . . . can care to amuse yourself . . . with such . . . I venture to say . . . stupid jokes . . . and two days running, too. . . .

Tropatchov (*Making a sign to* Karpatchov, *who at once skips away and draws himself up erect*): But, excuse me, Pavel Nikolaitch . . . of course I . . . Though I do really agree with you . . . yet on the other hand . . . And your good lady, is she quite well?

Yeletsky: Yes . . . she will be here immediately. . . . (*Smiling and pressing Tropatchov's hand.*) Please excuse me. . . . I'm rather out of sorts to-day.

Tropatchov: Oh, don't mention it, Pavel Nikolaitch, as though it mattered. . . . And indeed you are quite right. . . it never does to be too familiar with persons of that sort. . . . (Yeletsky *winces slightly.*) What a glorious day! (*A moment's silence.*) Of course, you really are right . . . it's a mistake to go on living too long in the country! On se rouille à la compagne. . . . It's awful . . . one's bored, you know. . . . One gets into bad ways.

YELETSKY: Please, say no more about it, Flegont Alexandritch.

TROPATCHOV: Oh, no; I meant in general; it was a general observation, you know. (*Again a brief silence,*) I don't believe I told you. . . I am going abroad next winter.

YELETSKY: Ah! (*To* KUZOVKIN, *who is again trying to go.*) Stay, Vassily Semyonitch . . . I have a few words to say to you.

TROPATCHOV: I propose staying a couple of years abroad. . . . And Madame? Shall we have the pleasure of seeing her to-day?

YELETSKY: Why, of course. But meanwhile wouldn't you like a turn in the garden? It's such a lovely day—un petit tour? Only if you don't mind, I won't come with you. I have to talk things over with Vassily Semyonitch. . . . But in a few minutes. . . .

TROPATCHOV: Make yourself at home, ha! ha! my dear Pavel Alexandritch! You see to your own affairs, and don't hurry—and meanwhile in company with this individual I'll enjoy the beauties of nature. . . . I'm cracked over nature! Venez ici, Karpy. (*He goes out with* KARPATCHOV.)

YELETSKY (*Walks after them, closes the door, comes back to* KUZOVKIN, *and folds his arms*): Sir! yesterday I looked on you as a nonsensical and tipsy man; to-day I am forced to regard you as a slanderer and a blackmailer. . . .

Don't interrupt me! a slanderer and a blackmailer. Olga Petrovna has told me everything. You didn't expect that, perhaps, sir? What explanation can you give me of your conduct? This morning you acknowledged yourself that what you said yesterday was pure invention. . . . To-day in conversation with my wife. . . .

Kuzovkin: I am sorry. My hear. . . .

Yeletsky: I don't care a hang about your heart. I ask you again; you were lying? (Kuzovkin *is silent*.) Were you lying?

Kuzovkin: I have told you already I didn't know what I was saying yesterday.

Yeletsky: But to-day you know what you were saying. And after that you have the courage to look a decent man in the face? And you are not crushed with shame?

Kuzovkin: Pavel Nikolaitch, indeed you are too severe with me. Kindly consider what advantage could I gain from my talk with Olga Petrovna?

Yeletsky: I'll tell you what advantage. You hoped by this absurd tale to excite her sympathy. You reckoned on her generosity —it was money you wanted. . . . Yes, yes, money. And I must tell you you have gained your object. Listen, my wife and I have decided to pay a sufficient sum to provide for your future on condition. . . .

Kuzovkin: But I want nothing!

Yeletsky: Don't interrupt me! . . . On condition that you choose your place of residence a good way off. From myself I add: by accepting this sum from us, you thereby admit your lie. . . . That word I see makes you wince—your invention, let us say, and consequently renounce all claim. . . .

Kuzovkin: But I won't take a penny from you!

Yeletsky: What, sir? You persist, then? Am I to suppose that you spoke the truth, then? Kindly explain yourself.

Kuzovkin: I can say nothing. Think what you like of me—but I won't take anything.

Yeletsky: This is beyond everything! You mean to remain here, perhaps?

Kuzovkin: I am going to-day.

Yeletsky: Oh, you are! But what a position you leave Olga Petrovna in! You might consider that if you've a trace of feeling in you.

Kuzovkin: Let me go, Pavel Nikolaitch. My head is in a whirl, indeed. What do you want of me?

Yeletsky: I want to know, will you take this money? Perhaps you think it's not enough? We are giving you ten thousand roubles.

Kuzovkin: I cannot take anything.

Yeletsky: You cannot? Then my wife is your . . . I cannot bring myself to utter the word!

Kuzovkin: I know nothing. . . . Let me go. (*Is about to go out*)

Yeletsky: This is too much! But do you know that I can force you to . . .

Kuzovkin: And how, may I ask?

YELETSKY: Don't try my patience too far! . . . Don't compel me to remind you what you are!

KUZOVKIN: I am a gentleman born. . . . That's what I am!

YELETSKY: A fine gentleman, I must say!

KUZOVKIN: One who cannot be bought, at any rate.

YELETSKY: Listen. . . .

KUZOVKIN: You can treat your clerks in Petersburg like this, if you choose . . . .

YELETSKY: Listen, you obstinate old man. You don't want to injure your benefactress, do you? You have once admitted the falsehood of your words; what do you lose by reassuring Olga Petrovna completely—and taking the money we offer you? Are you so rich that ten thousand roubles is nothing to you?

KUZOVKIN: I am not rich, Pavel Nikolaitch; but your little present is too bitter. I have swallowed shame enough without that . . . yes, indeed. You are pleased to say I want money. I don't want money, sir. I won't take a rouble for my journey from you.

YELETSKY: Oh! I know what you're reckoning on! You pretend to be so disinterested; you're hoping to get more by it. For the last time I tell you: either you'll take this money on the conditions I've put to you, or I shall have recourse to measures . . . to measures. . . .

KUZOVKIN: But what do you want of me, my God! It's not enough for you that I'm going away: you want me to be disgraced too, you want to buy me. . . . But no, Pavel Nikolaitch, that shall not be.

Yeletsky: O damnation! . . . I tell you. (*At that instant* Tropatchov's *voice is heard under the window; he is humming*: 'I am here, beloved, below thy window here.') This is insufferable! (*Going to the window.*) I'm coming . . . I'm coming. . . . (To Kuzovkin.) I give you a quarter of an hour to think things over . . . after that you must take the consequences. (*Goes out.*)

Kuzovkin: My God, what are they doing to me? I'd rather die! . . . I've been my own ruin! My tongue's my enemy. That grand gentleman—he spoke to me as though I were a dog . . . as though I have no heart! . . . Well, he may kill me. . . . (Olga *comes out of the study; there are papers in her hand.* Kuzovkin *looks round.*) Good heavens! . . .

Olga (*Going up to* Kuzovkin *irresolutely*): I wanted to see you once more, Vassily Semyonitch.

Kuzovkin (*Not looking at her*): Olga Petrovna . . . why . . . did you . . . tell your husband?

Olga: I have never concealed anything from him, Vassily Semyonitch.

Kuzovkin: Oh. . . .

Olga (*Hurriedly*): He believed me. . . . (*Dropping her voice.*) And agreed to everything.

Kuzovkin: Agreed? What did he agree to?

Olga: Vassily Semyonitch, you are kind . . . you are generous. You will understand. Tell me, can you stay here?

Kuzovkin: I cannot.

Olga: No, listen. . . . I want to know what you really think. . . . I have learned to appreciate you, Vassily Semyonitch. . . . Tell me then, tell me frankly. . . .

Kuzovkin: I feel your kindness, Olga Petrovna, and believe me, I too can appreciate. . . . (*He pauses and goes on with a sigh.*) No, I cannot stay here . . . I can't possibly. I might be beaten, may be, in my old age. And why not own the truth?—now I've grown staid and sober—there's been no master in the house for so long . . . there's been nobody to bully me. . . . But there are the old servants still living; they've not forgotten. . . . It's quite true I was something like a clown for your papa's diversion . . . . At times I would play the fool in fear of the rod . . . and sometimes of my own accord. . . . (Olga *turns away.*) Don't let it grieve you, Olga Petrovna. . . . You see, after all . . . I'm nothing but a stranger to you . . . really. . . . I can't stay.

Olga: If so. . . take. . . this . . . . (*Holds out a note to him.*)

Kuzovkin (*Takes it, wondering*): What is it?

Olga: It's. . . we offer you. . . the money. . . to buy back your Vyetrovo. . . . I hope you won't refuse us. . . me . . . I mean.

KUZOVKIN (*Drops the note and hides his face in his hands*): Olga Petrovna, why do you, you too, insult me?

OLGA: How?

KUZOVKIN: You want to buy me off. But I've told you there are no proofs whatever. . . . How do you know that I haven't made it all up, that I hadn't designs . . . in fact. . . .

OLGA (*Interrupting him eagerly*): If I didn't believe you, should we have agreed. . . .

KUZOVKIN: You believe me—what more do I want?—what do I want with this money? I've never been used to luxury from a child— I'm not going to begin in my old age. . . . What do I need? A bit of bread . . . that's all. If you believe me —— (*Stops short.*)

OLGA: Yes. . . . Yes. . . I do believe you. No, you are not deceiving me—no. . . . I believe you, I do. (*Suddenly embraces him and presses her head to his breast*)

KUZOVKIN: Olga Petrovna darling . . . give over . . . Olya . . . . (*Staggers and sinks into chair on Left.*)

OLGA (*Supports him with one arm, while with the other hand she swiftly picks the note from the floor and presses close up to him*): You might refuse a stranger, a rich woman—you might refuse my husband—but your daughter, your own daughter, you cannot, you cannot refuse. (*Thrusts the note into his hand.*)

KUZOVKIN (*Taking the note with tears*): Very well, Olga Petrovna, it shall be as you wish, bid me what you please, I'm ready, I'm glad to do it—bid me go to the ends of the earth. Now I can die, now I want nothing more. . . . (Olga *wipes his tears with her handkerchief.*) Oh, Olya, my little Olya. . . .

Olga: Don't cry—don't cry . . . . We will see each other. . . . You shall come. . . .

Kuzovkin: Oh, Olga Petrovna, Olya . . . is it me? Isn't it a dream?

Olga: There, there. . . .

Kuzovkin (*Hastily, all at once*): Olya, get up; they are coming. (Olga *who has been almost sitting on his knee jumps up quickly.*) Only give me your hand, your hand for the last time. (*He hurriedly kisses her hand. She moves away to one side.* Kuzovkin *makes an effort to get up, but cannot.* Yeletsky *and* Tropatchov *come in from door on Right; followed by* Karpatchov. Olga *goes to meet them, passing* Kuzovkin *and stands with her back to him.*)

Tropatchov (*Bowing and striking an attitude*): Enfin—we have the happiness of beholding you, Olga Petrovna. How are you?

Olga: Very well, thank you.

Tropatchov: You look a little . . .

Yeletsky (*Cutting in*): We are neither of us quite up to the mark to-day. . . .

Tropatchov: In sympathy even in that, ha! ha! Your garden is wonderfully fine.

[Kuzovkin *with effort stands up.*]

Olga: I am very glad you like it.

Tropatchov (*As though offended*): Why, I tell you it's perfectly exquisite—mais c'est très beau, très beau—the avenues, the flowers

. . the whole thing, in fact. Yes, yes! Nature and poetry—they are my two weak points! But what do I see? Albums? Just as though it were a Petersburg drawing-room.

YELETSKY (*Looking significantly at his wife*): Have you succeeded? (OLGA *nods*, TROPATCHOV *politely turns away.*) He's taken it? H'm! Good! (*Drawing her a little aside.*) I tell you again I don't believe this tale—but I approve. Domestic peace is worth more than ten thousand.

OLGA (*Going back to* TROPATCHOV, *who is beginning to turn over an album on the table*): What are you looking at, Flegont Alexandritch?

TROPATCHOV: Oh—your album—here—— It's all very charming. Tell me, do you know the Kovrinskys?

OLGA: No, I haven't met them.

TROPATCHOV: What—didn't you know them in old days? You should make their acquaintance. Their's is almost the best house in our district, or rather it was the best till yesterday, ha! ha!

YELETSKY (*Meanwhile goes up to* KUZOVKIN): You take the money?

KUZOVKIN: Yes, sir.

YELETSKY: So then—it was a lie?

KUZOVKIN: It was a lie.

YELETSKY: Ah. (*Turning to* TROPATCHOV, *who is talking gallantly to* OLGA *and gracefully swaying his body to and fro.*) Do you know, Flegont Alexandritch, only yesterday we were making fun of Vassily Semyonitch . . . and would you believe it, he's won his case. The news has just this minute come. While we were in the garden just now.

TROPATCHOV: You don't say so!

YELETSKY: Yes, yes, Olga has just told me. Ask him yourself.

TROPATCHOV: Is it really so, Vassily Semyonitch?

KUZOVON (*Who throughout the rest of the scene is smiling like a child and speaks in a voice ringing with suppressed tears*): Yes, yes, sir. It is mine.

TROPATCHOV: I congratulate you, Vassily Semyonitch, I congratulate you. (*Aside to* YELETSKY.) I understand . . . you are sending him off in the most considerate way after yesterday. . . . (YELETSKY *tries to assure him that is not so.*) Ah . . . well . . . with what fine feeling, what generosity, what delicacy. . . . Very, very nice of you. I don't mind betting (*With a sugary glance at* OLGA) it was your wife's idea . . . though you, of course . . . (YELETSKY *smiles.* TROPATCHOV *goes on aloud.*) That's capital, capital. So now Vassily Semyonitch, you have to go over there . . . and begin looking after your estate.

KUZOVKIN: Of course.

YELETSKY: Vassily Semyonitch has just told me he is getting ready to go there this very day.

TROPATCHOV: I should think so. I quite understand his impatience. Hang it all! leading a man such a dance, keeping on and on—when at last he has got his estate . . . . Anyone would want to have a look at his property, eh, Vassily Semyonitch?

KUZOVKIN: To be sure.

TROPATCHOV: I suppose you will have to go to the town?

KUZOVKIN: No doubt; everything will have to be seen to.

TROPATCHOV: So you must lose no time. (*Winks at* YELETSKY.) A fine fellow, that retired attorney, Lytchkov! It's all his doing, I dare say? (*To* KUZOVKIN.) You're pleased, are you?

KUZOVKIN: To be sure, to be sure I am.

TROPATCHOV: You'll let me come and see you in your new residence, won't you?

KUZOVKIN: That's too great an honour, Flegont Alexandritch.

TROPATCHOV (*Turning to* YELETSKY): Pavel Nikolaitch, what do you say? We ought to celebrate the occasion.

YELETSKY (*Rather uncertainly*): Yes . . . perhaps . . . yes. (*Goes to door of dining-room.*) Send me Trembinsky.

TREMBINSKY (*Popping in at once from just outside*): What is your pleasure?

YELETSKY: Ah! you here . . . a bottle of champagne.

TREMBINSKY (*Vanishing again*): Yes, sir.

YELETSKY: Oh . . . wait! (TREMBINSKY *reappears.*) I believe I saw Mr. Ivanov in the dining-room, ask him to come in,

Trembinsky: Yes, sir. (*Goes out.*)

Tropatchov (*Going up to* Olga, *who has all this time been standing at the table with the albums, alternately dropping her eyes, and softly lifting them to* Kuzovkin): Madame Kovrinsky will be extremely glad to make your acquaintance . . . enchantée, enchantée. I do hope you will like her . . . I'm quite one of the family there. . . . Such a clever woman—and so, you know. . . . (*Waves his hand in the air.*)

Olga (*With a smile*): Ah!

Tropatchov: You will see. (Trembinsky *comes in with glasses and bottles on a tray.*) Ah! Well, Vassily Semyonitch, allow me to congratulate you most warmly. . . .

> [Ivanov *comes in, stops at the door and bows.*]

Olga (*Cordially to* Ivanov): How do you do. . . . I'm very glad to see you. . . . You have heard . . . your friend has come into his estate.

> [Ivanov *bows a second time and makes his way to* Kuzovkin. Trembinsky *takes round glasses to everyone.*]

Ivanov (*Speaking quickly aside to* Kuzovkin): What nonsense are they talking?

Kuzovkin (*Also in an undertone*): Hush, Vanya, hush; I'm happy. . . .

Tropatchov (*Glass in hand*): To the health of the new landowner!

All (*Except* Ivanov, *who does not even sip his glass*): To his health! To his health!

KARPATCHOV (*In a bass voice, alone*): Long life to him!

[TROPATCHOV *looks at him severely; he is abashed.* KUZOVKIN *thanks them, bows smiling;* YELETSKY *maintains a dignified air;* OLGA *is ill at ease, she is ready to cry;* IVANOV *is amazed and looks about him suspiciously.*]

KUZOVKIN (*In a quivering voice*): Allow me now . . . on this great day for me . . . to express my gratitude for all your kindness. . . .

YELETSKY (*Interrupting, severely*): But what is it you are thanking us for, Vassily Semyonitch?

KUZOVKIN: Well, you are my benefactors anyway. . . . And as for my—what shall I say—behaviour yesterday, generously forgive an old man. . . . God knows why I took offence yesterday and said such things.

YELETSKY (*Again interrupting*): There, very good, very good.

KUZOVKIN: And what was there to take offence at? What did it matter? . . . The gentlemen were joking. . . . (*Glances at* OLGA.) No, I don't mean that, though. Good-bye, my benefactors, may you be well, happy, fortunate. . . .

TROPATCHOV: But why are you saying good-bye like this, Vassily Semyonitch— you're not going to Astrachan, you know. . . .

KUZOVKIN (*Moved, goes on*): God give you every blessing. . . . And I . . . I have nothing left to Pray for . . . I am so happy, so. . . . (*Breaks off and struggles to keep from tears.*)

Yeletsky (*Aside, to himself*): What a scene. . . . When will he go?

Olga (*To* Kuzovkin): Good-bye, Vassily Semyonitch. . . . When you are in your own home, don't forget us. . . . I shall be glad to see you (*dropping her voice*) to talk to you alone. . . .

Kuzovkin (*Kissing her hand*): Olga Petrovna. . . . The Lord will reward you.

Yeletsky: Come, that's all right, good-bye. . . .

Kuzovkin: Good-bye. . . . (*Bows and goes with* Ivanov *towards the door of the dining-room. They all accompany him. On the threshold* Tropatchov *again exclaims*: 'Long live the new landowner!' Olga *goes out quickly into the study.*)

Tropatchov (*Turns to* Yeletsky *and pats him on the shoulder*): I say, you know—you are a most generous man.

Yeletsky: Oh, come! You are too kind. . . .

Curtain

1841